Exercises for Psychological Skills

Joseph M. Strayhorn, Jr., M.D.

Psychological Skills Press

Wexford, Pennsylvania

Second printing August, 2002

Published by Psychological Skills Press
P.O. Box 607, Wexford, PA 15090
www.psyskills.com

Author's email: joestrayhorn@juno.com

Thanks to Rob Kyff for editing this book.

ISBN: 1-931773-03-3

Contents

Introduction

You can develop and maintain psychological fitness in much the same way as physical fitness. You can improve your psychological health by working at it–by "working out."

You can do exercises, for instance, that will increase your ability to be more productive, happy, kind, wise and courageous, to be less depressed or anxious, to have better relations with people, to make better decisions, to make a better mark on the world.

But at the time of this writing, most people don't know how to work on improving psychological health. One of my goals for the last twenty years has been to develop mental fitness exercises that improve people's psychological skills. I hope that this volume makes these exercises accessible both to mental health professionals and to all other readers who wish to improve their mental health or those of children with whom they work.

Most sports competitors know that they reach maximum performance not just by competing. They drill repetitively, in practice sessions. Practice affords them the chance to go slowly at first, and to pick up speed as they gain proficiency. It allows them to isolate a certain skill and practice it until mastery is reached. It allows them to rehearse a desired sequence much more often than they could in games. It allows them to

focus on their particular weaknesses and gradually turn them into strengths.

The same principles apply to mental health or psychological fitness. Mental health comprises a variety of skills, and if we want to acquire them and stay proficient at them, most of us will do well to practice them.

What are those skills? I've divided mental health into sixty-two different skills; those in turn are subdivided into sixteen groups. The sixteen groups are easier to remember, but the more fine-grained analysis of sixty-two skills is better for many purposes. The short list is as follows.

1. Productivity
2. Joyousness
3. Kindness
4. Honesty
5. Fortitude
6. Good decisions
7. Nonviolence
8. Respectful talk (Not being rude)
9. Friendship-building
10. Self-discipline
11. Loyalty
12. Conservation
13. Self-care
14. Compliance
15. Positive fantasy rehearsal
16. Courage

How do you practice these skills? Real life presents us with plenty of practice opportunities. But real-life practice opportunities often come along when we're not ready for them, or when we don't have time to think about them enough, or when the stakes are too high for the degree of skill that we have. We need ways of practicing that don't have all these disadvantages.

This book presents answers to the question, "How can we practice mental health skills other than in real life itself?" Most of these exercises involve some sort of fantasy, role-playing or other simulation.

Many people have based successful psychotherapy on just one or two of these exercises. For example, the "STEB and STEB revision" has helped many people to relieve depression through cognitive therapy. Some therapists have used the "Reflections Exercise" to resolve relationship difficulties among family members. In this compilation of exercises, there is the wherewithal to remedy and prevent a wide panoply of mental health problems. I believe that people who gain and maintain proficiency in all the exercises presented here will be inoculated against a very broad range of mental health difficulties.

Getting and maintaining such proficiency takes time. Such a large goal is indeed possible if we view preventive mental health as an essential goal of education. People take years to learn mathematics; they should devote equal time to developing a broad range of psychological skills.

There's another way to use these exercises. If you are seeking a quicker solution to a specific problem, you can select and practice just those exercises that help you meet your specific goal.

This is exactly analogous to physical fitness exercises. The person who is recovering from an injury of his right leg might do lots of right leg exercises. But if he wants to increase his general level of fitness, he will ideally engage in "cross training" by performing many different exercises.

I believe that people of all ages can benefit from almost all of these exercises. I have used versions of them with preschool children through adults. Age is no barrier to acquiring and developing these skills.

I have found it useful to record the work done on these exercises and to celebrate milestones of accomplishment. To do this, I have defined various amounts of work in each of these skills as a "unit" or a "challenge." It's useful to keep a running record of how many challenges have been completed. I like to celebrate a new "rank" each time twelve challenges have been completed. The more ranks one attains, the more proficient one is likely to be in the skills being exercised.

Whenever an "exercise" has certain criteria for proficient performance, those criteria can be changed into a "test" or "measure" of proficiency. Running two miles is an endurance exercise; timing oneself in running two miles is an endurance test. Lifting weight overhead is a strength exercise; seeing how much weight you can lift overhead is a strength test. Likewise: role-playing both parts of a conflict-resolution conversation, trying to meet certain criteria, is an exercise in conflict resolution skill; role-playing both parts as well as possible is a test of conflict resolution skill.

Almost all the exercises in this volume lend themselves to performance tests that measure how well you can execute a certain maneuver. I believe this opens up exciting possibilities for measurement in psychological science, beyond the rating scales and self-reports that form the backbone of today's measurements. IQ testing directly observes a person's performance in tasks requiring intellectual skills; the tasks described in this volume require psychological skills. As with intelligence testing, it is possible to measure those skills by seeing how well someone performs these tasks.

The most useful tests and measures are those which educators can "teach to." Students try the exercise to see how well they can do it initially. Then they work at it and do the exercise repeatedly. They gradually get better and better at it, and they plot their performance in a real or imaginary graph of their learning curve. If that curve steadily ascends toward greater proficiency, they know they are making progress on that exercise.

In well organized psychological skills training, people should be ascending learning curves. They should be getting better and better at various proficiencies. If the proficiencies are chosen correctly, and if they are indeed relevant to living life well, then the person should be able to live a fuller and happier life as a result.

In another volume, entitled Tests of Psychological Skills, I have given rudimentary directions for administering some of these exercises in test format. These all await research to determine their properties as tests.

In this volume, I do not describe the exercises in the order of the psychological skills they foster. Instead, I start with the easiest and most widely applicable ones and then present the harder and more specialized ones. A cross reference chart lists exercises according to which skills they are meant to develop or strengthen.

What if the "trainee" does not feel like doing these exercises regularly? First of all, no one should be surprised. These exercises are work. They present the classical self-discipline dilemma: they do good in the long term, but in the short term, it is often more pleasant to do something else.

This is one of the problems that "behavior mod," or applied behavior analysis, was invented to solve. Providing contingent reinforcement for greater and greater achievement in these exercises can greatly increase motivation; it can make the endeavor more fun. So I recommend rigging up a system of rewards for achievement. Contingent reinforcement can be a very potent anti-depressant.

These exercises are also easier to do if you have a personal trainer. Just as with physical workouts, it is beneficial to have a person who can help you decide how much work is enough and what level of difficulty to attempt at any given time, and to applaud your successful efforts. Since most of the exercises in this book can be done without visual aids, I have been gratified to find that the personal trainer can guide the trainee by telephone. This allows sessions to be more frequent and more convenient.

Many of these exercises can be done in written format. Here's a way of keeping track of progress that will be very rewarding. The trainer helps the trainee gradually compile a book consisting of the record of exercises the trainee has done. The trainer might, for example, set up a word processing file with the following chapter titles:

1. Celebrations
2. Revisions
3. Stories that model skills
4. Problems and options
5. Actions and consequences
6. Social conversation dialogues
7. Individual decisions
8. Joint decision dialogues
9. Twelve Thought Exercises
10. Internal sales pitches
11. Fantasy rehearsals
12. Pleasant dreams

The chapter titles can be tailored to represent the exercises of highest priority for the trainee in question.

The trainee can do one or more exercises orally in each training session. Meanwhile, the trainer, who has opened the file and has moved to the appropriate chapter, transcribes the trainee's thoughts. Perhaps the trainee does his own writing for certain exercises; in this case the trainer pastes these into the appropriate chapter. As trainees grow in maturity and self-discipline, they do writing in their own notebooks or word processing files.

The book gradually grows. At any time the trainee can read it and see examples of celebrations, Twelve Thought Exercises, decisions, and so forth, with examples from his own life experience.

Creating a book has several benefits. It gives the trainee a sense of progress. It allows review of exercises and discourages forgetting. It provides a template that the trainee can refer to in doing more exercises independently. It gives the trainee a visible, tangible product that memorializes the work done, of which the trainee can be justly proud. It can create models helpful for other trainees.

I have a vision that we will one day be able to prescribe exercise programs for a variety of mental health problems, and develop data that predict how much exercise people need to solve a certain problem. Here's an even loftier vision: by doing lots of exercises from an early age, we may effectively prevent many mental health problems. I believe that the exercises in this book, combined with people's courageous and persistent efforts of people to get them done, can accomplish wonderful results for mental health.

Exercise 1: Reading or Hearing Examples of Psychological Skills

What is it?

This exercise involves reading stories or vignettes that model positive examples of psychological functioning. It's based on the idea that the more models of positive psychological skills you encounter, the more access you have to positive patterns you can use in real life decisions.

I have written some materials that are specifically designed to provide models of psychological skills. *Illustrated Stories That Model Psychological Skills* are written for preschoolers and early elementary-school children. *Stories that Model Psychological Skills* are written for people elementary school age and up. I believe that adults can benefit a great deal from reading stories modeling psychological skills, even if these stories were written primarily for children.

In addition to the stories that I have written myself, many other stories and biographies also of course model psychological skills. A very useful variation of this exercise for adults, adolescents, or older children is to search through available literature for models of the psychological skills one most wants to develop.

What's it for?

It is crucial to stock your memory bank with positive models of psychological functioning. If you are having trouble with anxiety, for example, then it's helpful to store many examples of courage in your memory bank. Or, if you are having trouble with low frustration tolerance, then it's useful to load your memory bank with many models of fortitude. The general strategy is to figure out what psychological skill you would like to develop and to store positive examples of that skill very prominently in your consciousness.

How do you do this exercise well?

Imagine the scenes in the narratives very vividly. Try to form clear, detailed mental pictures of whatever is going on.

Here's another tip on doing this exercise well: Don't view the stories as entertainment. Instead, focus on the pattern of thought, feeling or behavior being modeled. It is often fun and entertaining to read about people making very bad decisions and acting very impulsively. It is sometimes much duller to read about people being very patient and careful and making good decisions that resolve issues and conflicts. Part of your job in performing this exercise well is to redefine your role from one who is being entertained to one who is learning.

Variations

Very young children can have someone read them stories that model psychological skills. As children get older, they can use such stories to practice reading. Older children can practice reading the stories to younger children. Acting out or role-playing the stories makes the experience more vivid for people of all ages. By reading *Stories that Model Psychological Skills* to children, adults can accomplish two goals at once: they can help the child and simultaneously encounter positive models themselves.

Example:

The following story, written for young children, is meant to model loyalty. The models of adult behavior in this story are perhaps even more difficult for people to enact widely!

Robert Sticks By His Friend

Robert had a friend named Paul who lived next door. Robert and Paul had known each other for a long time. They enjoyed playing with each other very often. Paul was always there with a smile when Robert wanted a friend.

In the fall, they started school. One day they were on the playground. Robert was happy because he was making new friends. He was just getting to know a boy who was a very fast runner and who seemed to be a leader.

After a while the new friend ran up to Robert with a big smile on his face and said, "Come on, let's see the playground pig." Robert liked animals, so he followed the new friend with great anticipation.

But the new friend ran over to a group of children who were dancing around Paul, and chanting, "Playground pig! Playground pig!" The boys and girls seemed to be having lots of fun. But Paul wasn't. Robert could see that by his face. Paul looked confused and upset.

The other kids said, "Come on Robert, join in! Do it too!" Five or six kids were joining in this game, but it felt like it was everybody.

Seeing the cruelty and meanness of the other children, Robert felt a swell of anger rise inside him. But he knew that it was good anger, an anger that came from his loyalty to Paul. And he also felt compassion for his friend.

Robert went over and stood beside Paul and put his arm around him. He shouted at the other kids, "He's my friend! Don't you know not to be cruel to people?"

At this, the other kids just laughed. But Robert's loud shouts attracted the attention of the teacher. She came closer and watched what was happening.

That school did not allow children to be cruel to others. So the teacher called all the children in from the playground. The ones who were taunting Paul went to the principal's office for a talk with the principal and the teacher.

The principal spoke on the telephone with each of their parents. The principal explained to these children that, if they kept being cruel, they could no longer go to that school.

The principal and the teacher called in Paul and Robert. "We're very sorry this happened to you, Paul," said the principal. "But it's our job to make sure this doesn't happen any more. We have strong rules against bullying in this school, and we enforce them."

"I didn't like it," Paul said. "But it wasn't so bad once Robert stuck up for me."

In the days after that, all the adults at the school spoke with the children a lot about being kind to each other. They watched very closely what went on among the children. No one taunted Paul, and Robert and Paul both made new friends.

Robert felt good that he had been loyal to his friend.

Exercise 2: Guess the Skill or Principle

What is it?

There are sixty-two psychological skills in the comprehensive list. These are divided into sixteen groups, as follows:

Productivity
Joyousness
Kindness
Honesty
Fortitude
Good decision
Nonviolence
Respectful talk (not being rude)
Friendship building
Self-discipline
Loyalty
Conservation
Self-care
Compliance
Positive fantasy Rehearsal
Courage

In doing the Guess the Skill or Principle exercise, you hear an example of a vignette that models proficiency in one of these areas. Most of the vignettes provide positive examples; sometimes they furnish negative examples. You guess which skill or principle the vignette is about.

For example, in one vignette someone has her house damaged by a flood and works very hard to get the damage repaired. Then the question to the trainee might be, "Was that an example of productivity or non-violence?"

Many vignettes offer examples of several skills. The one I just mentioned could also serve an example of fortitude. If the person decided to clean up her house rather than go bowling, that would also be an example of a good decision. This is why this exercise is done with multiple-choice questions rather than open-ended questions. Part of the challenge in constructing the choices is to pick skills that don't apply to the vignette in question!

You can take almost any story and use the plot as an exercise in Guess the Skill or Principle. Whenever the characters make a choice, they are almost always providing a good or bad example of one of these principles. To identify a principle more clearly, it's sometimes useful to retell the story with a few key words added. Usually, though, you can just read a story and use it as an exercise in classifying psychological skills and ethical principles.

What's it for?

It's essential that people encounter, explore and master these psychological skills concepts. When you learn these principles very well, you've accomplished several goals. First, you've learned what constitutes ethical and good behavior. When you are very familiar with the essence of kindness, productivity, honesty, and so forth, you grasp a set of principles that will be very useful guides to living. Second, frequent exposure to these principles tends to increase a desire to achieve proficiency in them.

At various times I've had occasion to ask a teenager or adult, "Would you like to get better at self-discipline?" Sometimes the response is, "I never really thought about self-discipline before." When you are very familiar with psychological skills and ethical principles, these concepts become part of your way of seeing the world and it becomes clearer to you that you want to become better at them.

Another benefit of the Guess the Skill or Principle exercise is that you learn to classify situations according to what skills they call for. Thus, you're able to cue yourself early about what you're going to need to do. You start to think automatically along the lines of, "Hmm. Here's a situation that calls for fortitude." Or, "Hmm. Here's where my loyalty skills are tested."

If people can think in these terms, they are readying themselves to respond in the most skillful manner possible to a variety of situations. In contrast, if they just think in terms of, "Oh what bad luck that I had this situation," or "I'm such a bad person for bringing this on myself," they are not identifying the skills that are most adaptive and useful.

How do you perform this exercise well?

Some people have the misguided notion that an exercise must be difficult in order to be useful. Accepting the use-fulness of easy tasks is sometimes the most "difficult" part of this exercise. It can be very easy to connect the concrete example in the vignette to the more abstract principle it exemplifies, and yet this relatively easy exercise can still provide very useful practice in mastering the skill concepts and very useful exposure to examples.

Variation:

A variation for children is one in which the trainee and/or the trainer do not simply verbally tell or read the stories, but act them out with puppets or toy people by techniques of improvisational drama. Some adults and adolescents will also find it acceptable to role-play positive examples. This can make the vignettes more vivid, fun and interesting.

When children are learning to read, you can accomplish two things at once: you can choose stories that while providing reading practice, also model psychological skills and give practice in identifying skill concepts. This is part of the purpose of *Programmed Readings for Psychological Skills*.

Example:

This example is from *Programmed Readings*, and is based on a play by Henrick Ibsen called *An Enemy of the People*.

In a town there were warm springs. People liked to take baths in them. Lots of people came to bathe in the springs. People in the town made money from renting rooms. People in the town made money from selling food. And they made money when the people paid to use the baths. The people in the town thought that the baths were very good for people's health.

A doctor lived in the town. He found that some people got sick after being in the baths. He studied the water. He found that the water was bad for people. The water had bad things in it. It would cost a lot of money to clean up the water.

The doctor told the leaders of the town. They didn't thank him for finding the truth. They got mad at him. They told him to keep quiet. They thought, "We will just not tell people. We can keep making money."

Did these people provide bad examples of

honesty or joyousness?

The doctor told more people. They acted the same way. They didn't want to lose their money. They didn't care very much if people got sick.

He wrote about what he had found. A science journal printed what he wrote. Then newspapers wrote about it. The people in the town got madder at him. But he knew he was right. He knew it was wrong not to tell people that the baths were unhealthy.

It was scary for him to have so many people mad at him. But he kept telling the truth about the baths.

Did the doctor show

friendship-building or courage?

Exercise 3. Composing Stories That Model Psychological Skills

What is it?

In this exercise the trainee makes up stories that model any of the sixteen major psychological skills groups or any of the sixty-two psychological skills. The trainer can simply listen or the trainer can guess the skill or principle that is being modeled. The trainer can act as a secretary, taking down the story. The trainer can write the story or can type the story and include it in a growing bank of positive modeling stories. Or the trainee can write the story herself.

What's it for?

When you compose stories that model positive psychological skills, you are simulating real-life responses that model psychological skills. This exercise involves you in producing models of psychological skills rather than simply receiving them and storing them away. Thus, in thinking up models of psychological skills, you are "auto-modeling" for yourself. You are also practicing and reinforcing these positive patterns by running them through the neuronal circuitry of your brain.

How do you do it well?

In composing stories that model psychological skills, you should think about describing vividly and thoroughly the protagonist's situation. You want to describe not only what the protagonist does but also what she thinks and feels as she is doing it. If the main character makes some decisions, you want to present what the main character says to herself. You want to make it apparent which of the twelve thoughts (listed later in the Twelve Thought Exercise) the character uses.

Here are some other guidelines for writing effective stories:

Create stories that avoid violence as much as possible.

Pose situations that produce challenges, but avoid having those challenges produced by evil or demonic villains.

Avoid any elements that would make you laugh at someone's misfortunes.

Do not use violent means to solve problems.

Make sure the problems are resolved by the choices people make, not by luck or happenstance.

Don't always have the external world reward the person for her best choice; sometimes the person's good choice goes unnoticed or chance blocks the desired outcome. Often the character has to reward herself for having made a good choice.

In addition to these guidelines, you want to include the elements of good story telling: interesting situations, likable characters, fast-moving plots without any extraneous information, and plenty of specific detail and dialog. You want to help the reader cultivate love for humanity rather than hatred.

Variations:

In one variation for use with young children, you buy or construct a deck of cards that have story elements on them: characters, settings, activities and objects. (Cards with pictures and words of this sort are available from Storytime Creations, Inc., P.O. Box 19544, Boulder, CO 80308, 303-546-6570). You pick one card of each type from the deck and make up a story that incorporates the elements. While doing so, you try to have the characters model a psychological skill.

In another variation, which I've called the "picture-story exercise," you cut out pictures from magazines and put them into a box. Without looking, you draw out a random picture from the box. Then you make up a story about it. In one variation on this, the trainer and trainee take turns drawing pictures and making up stories that model a certain psychological skill. In another variation, they take turns making up a story about any psychological skill and letting the other person guess which of two skills was modeled.

A variation for people of any age is for the trainer and the trainee to take turns thinking of a vignette that models one of the skills on the priority list for the trainee. If the trainee wants to work on all the skills, the trainer and trainee can take turns thinking of vignettes that model one of the sixteen skills and principles, and they then give a two-choice question to one another about which skill the vignette models. (In other words, they think of more vignettes that could be added to the data bank at the beginning of *Programmed Readings for Psychological Skills*.)

In another variation for older people, or skilled younger students, the student simply writes a story. One form this assignment can take is as follows. "Think of the skills that are of highest priority for you. Imagine that you are very proficient in one of your high-priority skills. Compose a story that would exemplify this proficiency." This exercise involves the creation of specific and concrete images of performing the high-priority skills, an extremely useful activity.

Example:

A trainee is asked to devise a modeling story, and composes the following. There is a two-choice question about the skill or principle being exemplified, the same pattern used in *Programmed Readings.*

A person was bored. She decided to make a to-do list. She listed some chores that should be done. She listed some practice in math and writing. Then she started doing the things on her list. She worked hard. She felt proud that

she was getting so much done. She
didn't feel bored any more.
Did she show

productivity or compliance?

Exercise 4: Conceptual Sharpening

What is it?

These are vignettes that give the trainee practice in categorizing life according to certain key concepts. For example, one set of examples gives practice in deciding which expectations of other people represent overly great entitlement and which are realistic. Other examples teach the skills of distinguishing kindness from selfishness, realistic fears from unrealistic fears, and so forth. All of these concepts can be extremely useful in categorizing and resolving situations that come up in life. *Programmed Readings for Psychological Skills* is largely devoted to such conceptual sharpening exercises.

What's it for?

How we respond to the world depends very much on how we categorize and classify the events and situations we encounter. A very important method of behavior change is to refine and improve our ways of classifying what we are experiencing and responding to.

How do you do this exercise well?

A key to proficiency in this exercise is vivid imagining of the vignettes. Trying hard to remember the names of the concepts in question and using them to think about real life examples are also important.

Variations:

For all of the concepts in the conceptual sharpening exercises, the trainee can help both herself and other people by composing further examples for other people to practice.

Another variation on conceptual sharpening exercises is to use the Glossary of Terms Useful for Psychological Skills in this book. Each term has a definition and a sentence with a blank where that term fits. The trainer can read either the definition or the sentence to the trainee and ask the trainee to pick the correct term from two choices, one correct one and one incorrect.

Examples:

Here's an example with "temptations" and "long term goals," concepts useful for the skill of self-discipline:

A person went in to work. He had lots of reports to write. He had lots of forms to fill out. When he went in, he thought, "This will be a great day. I will have lots of time to do this paper work. I need to do these things if my business is to succeed."

But he decided to go on the Internet. He found something that was very much fun to read about. This led him to other sites that taught him all sorts of good things. But he did not get his work done.

For his business to succeed, did he choose

temptation, or the long-term goal?

The fun things on the Internet were the

temptation, or the long-term goal?

Exercise 5: Celebrations

What is it?

In this exercise the trainee searches through her memory for things she's glad she did. In the simplest version of this exercise, the trainee simply recounts these celebration-worthy actions in response to the question, "What have you done lately that you're glad you've done?" or "What have you done lately that you can celebrate?"

What is it for?

It's interesting how difficult it is for many children, and adults too, for that matter, to answer the question, "What have you done lately that you're glad you've done?" Very often people will respond to this question by saying, "Nothing," or "Not much of anything."

To change from a person who can't think of anything she's glad she has done to a person who can think readily and easily of many such things constitutes a major transformation of the self. The same people who usually can't think of things they're glad they've done also find it hard to think of things they're sorry they've done. Such people are usually prone to answer the question, "What have you been doing lately?" by saying, "Nothing." Perhaps some of these people aren't in the habit of loading into memory their recent experience or at least not in such a way as they can readily retrieve it to reflect on it.

But when you can reflect upon your recent experience, you have a major advantage: You're able to learn from it. When you can remember the things that have worked out well and you feel good about having done them, you can run those patterns through the neuronal circuitry one more time so as to practice them in your imagination. You can also try to feel good about them. The combination of the practice and the association of those positive patterns with positive feelings upon recalling them makes them more likely to occur again.

Thus the rationale for the Celebrations Exercise is to comb through your recent choices and actions and pick the ones you most wish to happen again. By celebrating them, you make them more likely to occur again.

So, part of the rationale for the Celebrations Exercise is a selective practice and reinforcement of the best behaviors in your recent repertoire. But an even more basic goal of this exercise is to get into the habit of storing, retrieving, narrating and reflecting upon your recent choices. When you can do this, you are much more able to participate in a self-improvement program. It is much easier to learn the skill of recalling recent experience when you're remembering celebration-worthy actions rather than mistakes and failures. Although much psychotherapy starts out with a recounting of mistakes and failures, it makes much more sense to start out with the far less painful retrieval of positive choices. When you begin by recounting your mistakes and failures, you must immediately jump to the difficult task of not only recalling and narrating such shortcomings but also admitting them to another person. Although some people are ready for this at the beginning of therapy, many are not.

How do you do it well?

The person who is proficient at the Celebrations Exercise realizes that choices do not have to be big and important to be celebration-worthy. Life is an endless succession of choices. We should be making choices we're glad to have made a high fraction of the time, and thus celebration-worthy events should be entering our experience at a rapid rate.

For example, while working on this book, fifteen seconds ago, I had my legs crossed while propped up on a table, and I uncrossed them so that my legs wouldn't go to sleep. I'm glad I decided to do that. This is certainly one of the least momentous events of the century, but it's celebration-worthy nonetheless.

To give another example, when I was driving my car to the office and I came to a red light, I stopped my car and waited until it turned green. I'm glad I was paying enough attention to what I was doing to obey the traffic laws. When you get down to this level of micro-events, the number of possible celebrations in life becomes huge.

Another element of the Celebrations Exercise is to try to actually feel good again about the celebration-worthy events, so that you are not just cognitively reporting them but you are actually celebrating them. By celebrating I mean thinking to yourself, "Hooray!" or some synonym for this important word.

Variations:

In one variation of this exercise, the trainee simply tries to report to the trainer celebrations from recent experience.

In a little more advanced variation, the trainee reports the celebration in STEB format. This means that the trainee reports the situation, the thoughts, the emotions and the behaviors involved in the event.

In another variation, the trainee reports not only the event, but also classifies it according to the sixteen groups of psychological skills. Thus, for example, un-crossing my legs in order not to compress a nerve so my legs don't go to sleep might be an example of self-care or good decision-making; stopping at the traffic light might be an example of compliance or self care. As the trainee becomes more advanced, the trainee cannot only rapidly retrieve celebrations but put them in STEB format and classify them.

In another variation, the trainer and the trainee take turns recounting celebrations and combine this with the

"Guess the Skill or Principle" exercise. They give one another a couple of choices, and the listener gets to guess the skill or principle the teller used.

In another important variation of this exercise, the trainee writes down on paper or in a computer file the celebrations. This is a very valuable technique because the positive actions get preserved for memory and this can be used for fantasy rehearsal many times in the future. And, because the celebrations are now modeling stories, other people can use them.

Example:

The following is an example of a student's verbal report of a celebration.

I was in a class at school, and we were doing a cooperative science activity in a group. We were hooking up some wires in an electronics experiment. I said, "Let's see. I think this one should go here." A kid I was working with said, in a very argumentative tone, "No, it doesn't." I had the urge to say, "Yes, it does!" I realized he would probably go back and forth with me, with our saying, "does not" and "does too." But instead, I thought to myself, "I'll just avoid this 'does too' and 'does not' stuff altogether. I'll try listening to him. It's not an emergency that I prove that I'm right." I felt more relaxed when I thought this way. So I said to him, "Oh? Tell me your thoughts about it. Where do you think it should go?" He told me. I calmly explained why I thought it should go in the other place. He agreed to give it a try, and it worked. I didn't rub it in that I was right and he had been wrong. I just said, "Hooray, we got it."

I think this was an example of good joint decisions.

Exercise 6: The Celebrations Interview

What is it?

The celebrations interview is an exercise you do when the celebrations exercise is too hard. When the trainee can't think of any celebration-worthy things he has done, you find out what he has done. You cross-examine the trainee to try to land on the good choices, the kind acts, the acts of productivity, the times of joyousness, the uses of fortitude, and so forth, that are lurking in the trainee's recent experience but can't be recalled.

What is it for?

Through lots of experience I've come to realize how hard the celebrations exercise is. It's interesting how many people will draw a blank when asked to comb through their recent (or not-so-recent) experience to come up with examples of positive things they've done.

One of the major principles to use when doing exercises with people is the hierarchy of difficulty. If you're a trainer, you want to pick challenges on which the trainee can be successful at least 80 percent of the time. If a task proves too hard for a learner, you want to lower the hierarchy of difficulty to the point where the learner can do it successfully. Then you work your way up, with gradual steps.

How do you do it well?

Let's think about how the trainer, as interviewer, does this well. Rather than asking for the trainee to come up with something he's glad he has done, the interviewer simply tries to find out what the trainee has done, period. The key task is to get the trainee simply to recount what he did on a certain day, say yesterday, because it may be fresh in memory. The trainer might ask the person simply to begin at the beginning of the day and tell where he was at various times and what he did at each of those places.

Did any of the things the person did constitute work? Then they are examples of productivity. Were any of them play or recreation that the person enjoyed? Then they are examples of joyousness. Did he choose to do any of the actions, rather than being compelled to do them? And if he had them to do over, would he make the same choices? If so, they sound like good decisions. Did anything go wrong? If so, did the person handle it without getting too upset? Then that's fortitude.

When you hear what the person did, you form guesses in your mind about behaviors that might be celebration-worthy, and you check out those guesses. If you land on any that are positive, you have hit pay dirt.

Then you can let the trainee know that this is a celebration, this is a positive example. You can leave it at this and go on. Or you can tell the trainee which of the skills it exemplifies. Or you can let the trainee guess which one it exemplifies, just as in the Guess the Skill or Principle exercise.

Sometimes the trainer can loosen up the trainee and make it easier for him to talk about celebrations by sharing some examples from his own life. The trainer should look for small and mundane examples, the type of behaviors that most people take for granted. Mention that time that you put the milk back in the refrigerator without griping at someone for leaving it out, not that time that you won the Nobel Prize.

It's good to explain to the trainee why recalling celebrations and running them through the neural circuitry is good. Describe the concept of fantasy rehearsal and the importance of rehearsing the positive things we've done so we will do them more often. In addition, mention that celebrating our positive behaviors has a good effect on our moods—it is an antidepressant activity.

Example:

Trainer: Can you think of any things you've done that you can celebrate?

Trainee: No.

Trainer: Not ever?

Trainee: No.

Trainer: When you were coming here, just before you walked into the building, did you cross the street?

Trainee: Yes.

Trainer: Did you happen to look before you crossed to see whether cars were coming, so that you wouldn't get killed?

Trainee: I suppose I did, yes.

Trainer: Then that's an example of self-care. I know it sounds like a small example, but it's still worth celebrating.

Trainee: I see.

Trainer: What were you doing just before you came here?

Trainee: I was doing some reading.

Trainer: Were you enjoying it?

Trainee: Not really. I was doing it for school.

Trainer: If you were making yourself do it, even though it wasn't particularly pleasant, then that's an example of self-discipline.

Trainee: And if I had said I was enjoying it, you would have said it was an example of joyousness, right?

Trainer: Now you're getting the idea! And your making that connection, just now, is another thing to celebrate.

Exercise 7: Guess the Feelings

What is it?

In this exercise, one person narrates an event from his life, and also tells what he thought about the situation. The other person guesses, from choices that the teller provides, what emotion the teller felt.

Here's an example. I am driving along and a big piece of wood falls off a truck in front of me. I think to myself, "Oh my! I may hit that wood and have a wreck. I could get killed!" How do you think I feel: angry, scared or happy?

It would be obvious to most people that the correct answer is scared. On the other hand, suppose my thought was, "How could he be so stupid as to leave that wood on his truck where it wasn't tied down right. That idiot!" Then my emotion would be anger. On the other hand, if I thought to myself, "Hey, I needed a piece of wood like that, and here it is! All I have to do is pull over and pick it up. It looks as if the person on the truck is going to drive away and not even stop to get it. I just got a niece piece of wood that I can use." Then the correct guess is happy.

As these examples illustrate, when doing the Guess the Feelings exercise, it's useful to present the same or almost the same situation with several different thoughts.

Here is a list of "feeling words" for use in this exercise:

Positive: accepted, appreciative, amused, awed, attracted, calm, cheerful, compassionate, curious, close, confident, contented, elated, excited, free, friendly, fun, glad, glowing, grateful, happy, hopeful, interested, jolly, joyful, lighthearted, liking, love, moved, playful, pleasant, pleased, proud, relaxed, relieved, satisfied, self-assured, serene, silly, slaphappy, sympathetic, tenderness, thankful, tickled, wonder

Negative: afraid, angry, annoyed, ashamed, bitter, bored, bothered, burdened, disdainful, drained, brokenhearted, confused, impatient, disappointed, disgusted, displeased, disturbed, embarrassed, envious, startled, fearful, frazzled, frightened, frustrated, guilty, harried, hate, hopeless, horrified, hurt, impatient, irritated, jealous, lonely, low, mad, mortified, pain, rage, regret, resentment, sad, scared, self-critical, shocked, terrified, threatened, tormented, troubled, uncomfortable, uneasy, unfriendly, unpleasant, upset, worried

Neutral: amazed, astonished, bewildered, concerned, flabbergasted, indifferent, excited, pity, worn out, suspicious, stirred, wonder

What's it for?

One of the purposes of the Guess The Feelings exercise is simply to build up a vocabulary of feeling words such as angry, scared, sad, relieved, compassionate, grateful, and to be able to use these words to get more in touch with one's own inner experience and to be more closely attuned to the inner experience of other people. It's difficult to recognize one's one feelings or the feelings of others if you're not in the habit of using feeling words.

There are other purposes as well. One is to illustrate repeatedly the basic principle of cognitive therapy, which is that our emotions are not determined simply by the situations we encounter, but also by our appraisals and interpretations of those situations. In other words, our thoughts greatly influence our emotions. In doing this exercise, the trainee repeatedly experiences the fact that you can have different feelings about the same situation, depending upon the thoughts.

An even more basic purpose of the Guess the Feelings exercise is a goal we talked about with the celebrations exercise: practicing the ability to store, retrieve and narrate one's recent experience. When the trainee hears the trainer recounting vignettes and her thoughts and feelings about the situations, the trainee is acquiring a model of how to talk about experience. Then when the trainee is the teller in the exercise, the trainee is practicing this skill.

How Do You Do It Well?

One way to begin this activity is to cover the chapter on the Guess the Feel-ings Exercise in *Programmed Readings on Psychological Skills*. Doing this will provide a model for how to recall or compose more vignettes for the exercise.

As with all the guessing games in the psychological skills exercises, one aspect of doing it well is to realize that you are not trying to stump the other person. You are trying to make the answer so obvious that the other person will get it right every time. Some trainees don't realize that this is a cooperative game rather than a competitive game, and they will delight in baffling the other person. Such trainees should have it gently explained to them that their skill as a teller is measured by how easily the other person can guess the right answer.

Other elements of being a good teller are remembering to tell the thoughts about the situation, and telling them in a way that makes it clear what emotion is being felt. Another element of being a good teller is simply being able to search through recent experience rapidly and identify a situation worth describing.

In order to make it easiest for the guesser, the teller should pick one emotion that's very compatible with the thought being narrated and one or two others that are not.

In being a good guesser, if the teller gives you insufficient information with which to make a good choice, it's good to give the teller feedback so the teller can elaborate. For example: "Can you tell me what you said to yourself when that happened?"

Another element of proficiency for both players is to celebrate when the two of you have arrived at a correct answer.

Variation:

In the simplest variations, appropriate for very young children, you have a very short list of feeling words, sometimes as short as "happy" and "sad." As the trainee becomes more and more advanced, you move toward longer and longer lists of feeling words. Another level of advancement occurs when the trainee can take on the role of teller of the vignettes rather than that of just guesser. Finally, it's helpful for the trainee to learn to do this exercise in written fashion. Here the trainee narrates the situation, tells the thoughts and gives two choices for the emotion.

Another variation on the Guess the Feelings exercise is to use fantasy events and reactions rather than real-life ones. This is often useful if the trainee cannot think of real-life situations or if the trainee does not want to disclose personal information.

Example:

A bird hit the window of our house and knocked himself out cold. I didn't know whether he would live or die. I thought to myself, "This is my fault! I should have put some stickers or paper or something on the window so the birds would be able to see it and know not to try to fly through it."

guilty or jealous?

Then I looked at the bird, and saw that he was still alive. I thought to myself, "Poor thing. I want to help him in some way."

indifferent or compassionate?

I kept a lookout so that the neighbor's cat wouldn't get him. After a while, he revived, and he flew away! I thought to myself, "Hooray! He made it!"

curious or pleased?

Exercise 8: Identifying The STEB

What is it?

STEB stands for situation, thought, emotion and behavior. In this exercise the trainee talks about what is going on in his or her life. But the trainee completes the STEBs by telling the situations he has encountered, his thoughts about them, his feelings about them, and his behavior in response to them. Often the trainer can function in the role of transcriber during this narration.

What's it for?

Again, we are trying to achieve storage, retrieval and narration of recent experience. This also constitutes a practice exercise in noting the connection between thoughts and the emotions and behaviors they influence.

Collecting STEBs also allows one to examine the pattern in one's reactions to situations. What types of situations does one have the most trouble responding to? The answer comes from making generalizations from a list of STEBs. What are the types of thoughts most conducive to bad feelings? This answer also comes from generalizations based on a list of STEBs. Thus, a list of STEBs is the basic data base one uses to learn to be more proficient in living.

In this exercise the events are not necessarily celebrations, but they can be. To the extent that the trainee can talk about mistakes and failures, she can

progress into these more difficult reports.

How do you do it well?

The key element of this exercise is a free flow of information. If the trainee can learn to just start talking about recent experience and talk about it in terms of the STEBs, he will increase his proficiency in this exercise.

Another aspect of performing this exercise well is intuitively picking which STEBs are worth thinking about and reporting. Some trainees find it difficult to discriminate between the STEBs that really make a difference and the details of life that yield little when recounted or examined.

Variation:

We've already mentioned the variation of doing the celebration exercise in STEB format.

The written variation on this exercise is that the trainee simply writes down the recent STEBs in his or her life.

Another variation on this exercise is taking some time to look at generalizations that can be easily made from the collection of STEBs. Examples of these might be, "I need to improve in fortitude skills," or, "Situations in which my performance will be evaluated tend to cause me anxiety." If the trainee has written the STEBs down in a computer word processing file, the trainee can group them together to support various generalizations.

Example:

Situation: A friend is visiting. He becomes fascinated by a game that is a puzzle for one person to solve. He works on it without stopping.

Thought: I think to myself, "I'm bored with this. I wish he would quit. Doesn't he see that he's being rude?"

Emotions: Angry, disappointed.

Behavior: I keep watching him play the game, without saying anything about what he's doing.

In this example, as with many other STEBs that people generate, there is room for revision—for picking another pattern of response that might work better. (The trainee might try some polite assertive behavior.) But the first step is just getting the STEB spoken, written or remembered, so that it can be considered.

Exercise 9: Songs That Model Psychological Skills

What is it?

I've written and recorded several songs that model psychological skills in a collection entitled *Spirit of Nonviolence*. Of course, there are many other songs that model positivity, joyousness, fortitude, kind and loving thoughts, and the rest of the psychological skills. This exercise consists of listening to these songs, dancing to these songs or singing them.

What's it for?

Music accesses emotions in ways that non-musical language cannot. Many people find it much easier to remember words, concepts or experiences when they are set to music. And often it is much more pleasurable to repeatedly experience various ideas if they are set to enjoyable melodies. Thus, this exercise seeks to harness the power of music to foster psychological skill growth or maintenance.

How do you do it well?

The key to this exercise is enjoying the music. When experiencing the modeling songs, one wants to free up the emotional and exuberant part of oneself.

One key to doing this exercise well is not to be self-conscious about singing and dancing. So many people allow their natural pleasure from these actions to be destroyed by the fear of disapproval from other people. Undoing this self-consciousness can be a great achievement.

Variations:

The modeling songs can be listened to as background music. You can listen to them and concentrate on them, trying to remember the words. You can sing them along with a trainer. You can sing them in a group.

The "dance and freeze" exercise is one that younger children are more adept at enjoying than older people. It consists in dancing or holding still as the music is turned on or off.

In another variation, the trainee learns to play the songs on a musical instrument or to sing them while being accompanied by a musical instrument. In another variation, the trainee searches through the vast storehouse of songs for those that constitute modeling songs. In a final variation, the trainee composes his own modeling songs.

Examples:

Here are some examples of "old" songs I consider psychological skill modeling songs:

The following can be found in the *Ultimate Fake Book*, Volume I, Hal Leonard Publishing Corp, 8112 West Bluemond Road, P.O. Box 13819, Milwaukee, Wisconsin 52313, 1985.

Climb Every Mountain, by Oscar Hammerstein II, Richard Rodgers
(Sustaining Attention to Tasks, Sense of Direction and Purpose)

Edelweiss, by Oscar Hammerstein II, Richard Rodgers
(Pleasure from Blessings)

Getting to Know You, by Oscar Hammerstein II, Richard Rodgers
(Social Initiations)

The Happy Wanderer, by Antonia Ridge, Freidrich W. Moller
(Pleasure from Blessings, Social Initiations)

If I Had a Hammer, by Lee Hays and Pete Seeger
(Kindness, Sense of Direction and Purpose)

Last Night I Had the Strangest Dream, by Ed McCurdy
(Conflict Resolution)

May You Always, by Larry Markes, Dick Charles
(Kindness)

Mockingbird Hill, by Vaughn Horton
(Pleasure from Blessings)

My Favorite Things, by Oscar Hammerstein II, Richard Rodgers
(Pleasure from Blessings)

Oh, What a Beautiful Morning, by Oscar Hammerstein II, Richard Rodgers
(Pleasure from Blessings)

On the Sunny Side of the Street, by Dorothy Fields, Jimmy McHugh
(Pleasure from Blessings)

September Song, by Maxwell Anderson, Kurt Weill
(Loyalty, Intimacy, Separation-Tolerance)

The Sound of Music, by Oscar Hammerstein II, Richard Rodgers
(Pleasure from Blessings)

This Land Is Your Land, by Woody Guthrie
(Pleasure from Blessings)

Try to Remember, by Tom Jones, Harvey Schmidt
(Loyalty, Painful Emotion Tolerance, Intimacy)

Twilight Time, by Buck Ram; Morty Nevins, Al Nevins
(Pleasure from Affection)

We Shall Overcome, Traditional, Modified by Zilphia Horton, Frank Hamilton, Guy Carawan, Pete Seeger
(Purposefulness, Justice in Choosing Options)

The Way You Look Tonight, by Dorothy Fields, Jerome Kern
(Pleasure from Affection)

When the Red, Red Robin Comes Bob, Bob, Bobbin Along, by Harry Woods
(Pleasure from Blessings)

When Irish Eyes Are Smiling, by Chauncey Olcott, George Graff, Jr.; Ernest R. Ball
(Positive Aim)

Who Will Buy? by Lionel Bart
(Pleasure from Blessings)

Whistle While You Work, by Larry Morey, Frank Churchill
(Sustaining Attention to Tasks)

The World Is Waiting for the Sunrise, by Eugene Lockhart, Ernest Seitz

(Pleasure from Affection, Loyalty, Intimacy)

You'll Never Walk Alone, by Oscar Hammerstein II, Richard Rodgers
(Self-Nurturing)

The Following Are In the *Ultimate Fake Book*, Volume II

A Bushel and a Peck, by Frank Loesser
(Pleasure from Affection)

I Gave My Love a Cherry, Traditional
(Trusting, Intimacy, Pleasure from Affection)

I Will Be In Love With You, by Livingston Taylor
(Kindness)

Jambalaya, by Hank Williams
(Gleefulness)

People Got To Be Free, by Felix Cavliere, Edward Brigati, Jr.
(Kindness, Toleration)

Sunrise, Sunset, by Sheldon Harnick, Jerry Bock
(Loyalty, sustained attachment)

What a Wonderful World, by George David Weiss, Bob Thiele
(Pleasure from Blessings, Kindness)

The Following Are In *Rise Up Singing*, Edited by Peter Blood-Patterson, Sing Out Corporation, PO Box 5253, Bethlehem, PA 18015, 215-865-5366.

Somewhere, by Stephen Sondheim, Leonard Bernstein

(Kindness, Forgiving, Positive Aim)

John Riley, Traditional
(Loyalty)

Jock O'Hazeldean, Traditional
(Independent thinking)

Up On the Roof, by Gerry Goffin, Carole King
(Relaxation)

Lavender's Blue, Traditional
(Kindness, Intimacy)

Oh Had I a Golden Thread, by Pete Seeger
(Kindness, Purposefulness, Courage)

Over the Rainbow, by E.Y. Harburg, Harold Arlen
(Imagination)

What Have They Done to the Rain? by Malvina Reynolds
(Purposefulness)

Garden Song, by Dave Mallet
(Delay of Gratification, Nurturing)

This Little Light, Traditional
(Kindness, conflict resolution)

Lean on Me, by Bill Withers
(Depending, Kindness)

My Rambling Boy, by Tom Paxton
(Loyalty, Separation Tolerance)

You've Got a Friend, by Carole King
(Nurturing, Loyalty)

Believe Me, If All Those Endearing Young Charms, by Thomas Moore
(Loyalty)

I'm Looking Over a Four Leaf Clover, by Mort Dixon, Harry Woods
(Joyousness, Pleasure from Affection)

All I Really Need, by Raffi
(Joyousness, Kindness, Loyalty)
For Baby, by John Denver
(Nurturing)
Isn't She Lovely, by Stevie Wonder
(Nurturing)
Blowing in the Wind, by Bob Dylan
(Conflict Resolution, Purposefulness)
What the World Needs Now, by Hal David, Burt Bacharach
(Kindness)
Danny Boy, by Fred E. Weatherly, Traditional Melody
(Loyalty, Separation Tolerance)
Juanita, Traditional
(Pleasure from Affection)
All Through the Night, by Harold Boulton, Traditional melody
(Nurturing)
Day Is Done, by Peter Yarrow
(Nurturing)
Morningtown Ride, by Malvina Reynolds
(Nurturing)
Sweet and Low, by Alfred Tennyson, Joseph Barnaby
(Nurturing)
He Ain't Heavy, He's My Brother, by Bob Russell, Bobby Scott
(Kindness)
Morning Has Broken, by Eleanor Farjean, traditional melody
(Pleasure from Blessings)
Wild Mountain Thyme, Traditional
(Pleasure from Blessings)
Song of Peace, by Lloyd Stone, Jean Sibelius

(Tolerance, Conflict Resolution)
Down by the Riverside, Traditional
(Conflict Resolution)
Baby Beluga, by Raffi
(Nurturing)
If I Only Had a Brain, by E.Y. Harburg, Harold Arlen
(Humor)
There But For Fortune, by Phil Ochs
(Empathy)
You Can Get It If You Really Want, by Jimmy Cliff
(Sustaining Attention, Delaying Gratification)
Let's Get Together, by Chet Powers
(Kindness)
The More We Get Together, Traditional
(Social Initiations)
Four Strong Winds, by Ian Tyson
(Separation Tolerance)
I Love the Mountains, Traditional
(Pleasure from blessings)

The following are not in any of the above-mentioned collections; they are where you find them.
Ja Da, Anonymous
(Gleefulness)
When You and I Were Young, Maggie, by George W. Johnson, J.A. Butterfield
(Loyalty, sustaining attachment)
Peace Train, by Cat Stevens
(Nonviolence)
Flow Gently, Sweet Afton, by Robert Burns

Exercise 9: Songs That Model Psychological Skills

(Kindness)
I Would Be True, Traditional
(Honesty, courage, fortitude, kind-
ness)

Exercise 10: Social Conversation Role-Play

What is it?

Social conversations are those chats wherein people get to know each other better. Social conversation is an essential part of relationship-building or friendship-building skills. The Social Conversation Exercise in one form or another asks the trainee to rehearse a social conversation, usually through role-playing. After enacting the social conversation, the trainee and trainer re-examine the conversation, either its content or process or both. (This part of the exercise would not be appropriate for a young trainee in the beginning stages.)

Regarding content, the trainer and trainee can ask which of five areas the conversation touched on. There's no rule that it has to cover all these areas; these topics are regarded as a menu of options. The mnemonic "PAPER" is helpful in recalling the five content areas: Places, activities, people, events, and reactions (ideas).

PLACES:

Where do you live?
Where did you live before you came here?
How long have you been living here?
Whose class are you in?
What school are you in?
Where do you go after school?

Where do you like to go the most?
What are your favorite places?

ACTIVITIES:

What do you like to do for fun?
What are your favorite things to do?
What are your least favorite things to do?
Do you have any hobbies?
What are your favorite foods to eat?
What are your favorite games to play?
What are your favorite books that you've read?
What sports do you like to play?
What games do you like to play?
Do you play a musical instrument?
Do you like acting?
Do you like art?

PEOPLE:

Do you have any brothers or sisters?
How old are they?
What are your parent's names?
What do they like?
Who are some of your friends?
Tell me about your friends?
Do you have cousins and aunts and uncles?
Do you have grandparents?

Tell me about your other family members?

Do you have any animals?

What are your animals like?

EVENTS:

What have you been up to lately?

What has been happening to you?

Are you going on vacation anytime soon?

What are you going to do over the summer?

Do you have any fun things planned?

What is the scariest thing that has ever happened to you?

What is the funniest thing that has ever happened to you?

What event are you looking forward to the most?

What are you dreading the most?

REACTIONS/IDEAS: (Includes the person's responses to any of the above named things.)

How was your day today?

How did you feel when that happened?

Do you like that place?

What was your reaction to moving from one place to another?

Do you still like doing that activity or have you begun to tire of it?

What is your reaction to this particular person?

What are your ideas/reactions about events happening in the news?

What are your ideas about current issues (how to reduce violence, the problem of poverty, the problem of pollution of the environment, etc.)?

What are some of your religious ideas?

What are some of your philosophical ideas?

What do you think are the most important ideas to live by?

These are some of the topics people talk about as they are getting to know each other (or even long after they have gotten to know each other.

***

With respect to process, the trainer and trainee can examine the following questionnaire in looking at how the conversation was conducted.

Checklist for Conversations

How much success in each of the following?

0=None

2=Very little

4=Some but not much

6=Moderate amount, pretty much

8=High amount

10=Very high amount

1. Enough to say. Were you able to chat without being overly shy or inhibited and to think of things to say to each other?

2. Stopping talking enough. Did you stop talking often enough that the other person had plenty of chances to

influence the direction of the conversation?

3. Monitoring of other's interest. Did you tune in to, and respond to, the signals from the other person about whether the topic of conversation was interesting to the other person, and try to find a topic of mutual interest?

4. Personal vs. not personal. Was the content of the conversation not so personal so as to be threatening to the other person, but personal enough to be interesting?

5. Responsive utterances. When the other person talked, did you respond in a way that showed you had listened, with, for example, follow-up questions, follow-up statements, reflections, tracking and describing, positive reinforcement, and silence with an interested facial expression? Were your reflections accurate and in your own words?

6. Reinforcement and positivity. Did your responses to what the other person said reinforce that person for talking to you? Did you give messages of approval and enthusiasm about what the other person had said, with your tone of voice and with your words? Was a good portion of what you said of a positive, upbeat nature?

7. Questions, open ended versus closed ended. If you asked questions, did you choose well between open-ended questions (to allow the other person to land on a topic of her own choosing) and closed-ended questions (to show interest in a particular topic)?

8. Eye contact. Did you give eye contact to the other person a reasonable portion of the time (especially when the other person was talking) but avoid staring steadily the other person?

9. Humor. Did you use non-hurtful humor when you could and when it was appropriate?

Thinking back on the conversation can take the form of informally thinking and talking about these items. It can also take a more evaluative format, in which the trainer rates the trainee's conversation and determines whether the criteria have been sufficiently met.

For many trainees, the main issue in social conversation will be in doing responsive utterances. The list of seven responsive utterances is as follows:

Responsive Utterances

1. Reflection
2. Follow-up question
3. Follow-up statement
4. Facilitation
5. Tracking and describing
6. Silence
7. Positive reinforcement

One way of keeping track of this is to actually tally up the responsive utterances that were used in the conversation.

The use of responsive utterances is so important that this skill has its own exercise. But let's quickly define and give an example of each of these utterances here.

Suppose the first person says: "When I read about how many genes we share with every other living thing, it makes me worry about all the pesticides that are all over our environment. Who can really make something that kills bugs but has no effect at all on people? And what if there are just a few people who are more vulnerable than others because of some gene they have or don't have?"

Reflection: You say back to the other person in your own words what you understood him or her to be saying. "So you've got concerns about whether anybody can really prove that a pesticide is safe for all people, is that right?"

Follow-up question: You ask a question for more information on the same topic the person is already discussing. "Tell me more about what you've been reading, please."

Follow-up statement: You make a statement sharing some of your information on the same topic the person is already discussing. "I read an article the other day that was talking about how poisons in the environment might be causing learning problems."

Facilitation: You say something like "Oh?" or "Humh," or "Is that right?" or "Yes," that communicates to the other person, "I'm hearing you, keep going." "Umh humh!"

Tracking and describing: You put into words something the person is doing. You are reflecting the person's behavior rather than the words. "I see you are organizing several articles on this topic. Looks as if you've done a lot of reading on it."

Silence: You refrain from speaking so that the other person can speak more and look at the person with an interested facial expression.

Positive reinforcement: You celebrate in words some aspect of what the person said or did. "I'm so glad you're thinking about this issue. So many people just deny it."

In addition to the dimensions of evaluation we've mentioned, another very crucial one involves tones of approval and disapproval. Most very positive social conversation depends not simply on the words that are used but on the tones that are used. Many social conversations founder because there's either too much disapproval or bland neutrality and not enough enthusiasm and positive approval. Another exercise described later on gives concentrated practice in recognizing and producing these various tones of voice.

> Large approval
> Small to moderate approval
> No approval
> Small disapproval
> Large disapproval

In the social conversation exercise, the trainer and trainee can examine what percentage of each person's utterances fell into each of these categories.

What's it for?

Some people tend to think of these social conversation skills as trivial pleasantries used only at parties or other social gatherings. This point of view overlooks the fact that these social conversation skills are vital to the maintenance of a social support system, both within one's family and among close friends. The inability to have pleasant social conversations among family members is probably the root of a great deal of serious psychopathology. Conversely, the ability to take pleasure and derive excitement from social conversation with family members and friends is an antidote to the need for pleasure-seeking and thrill-seeking from drugs and other harmful pleasures. Pleasant social conversation is the bedrock upon which successful marriages are built and upon which positive parent-child interactions are built.

How do you do it well?

The various checklists specify the criteria for good social conversation.

The art of performing this exercise well, as contrasted with conducting social conversation well, depends upon an ability to act and to use the imagination to project oneself into a make-believe situation. The ability to role-play is one that comes naturally to many little children; this ability is sometimes squelched during the school years and is very inhibited in some adults.

Variations:

With very small children, the exercise can simply be that each person is given a puppet and the puppets have a conversation with one another. The trainer models the social conversation techniques she wants the children to master. Often there is no need for monitoring and reflection on the conversation afterward, except perhaps to celebrate that the characters were nice to each other, if they were, and to celebrate that there was no violence, if there was not.

For older children or adults, another way of conducting this exercise is to imagine some setting in which the two characters find themselves. As in the example above, they may be seated next to each other on a plane and don't know each other. Or they may be neighbors who see each other at a neighborhood picnic and know each other somewhat but want to know each other better. The trainer and trainee then role-play the conversation. After role-playing, they perhaps listen to an audiotape of the conversation to consider items listed on the questionnaire or on the list of responsive utterances. Or perhaps they think about tones of approval or disapproval. Or they may simply rely on their memories rather than a tape.

Another variation is the silly conversation. This one is often a really good way to get the creative juices flowing. Instead of worrying about the various checklists, you just let your imagination flow as wildly as you want. You have fun making up things to tell about your imaginary character.

In another variation on this, the trainer can specify a certain level that is necessary for the trainee to attain before the conversation qualifies as a "challenge" for the ranks and challenges program.

In another variation, the conversation to be conducted and examined is not a role-played one but a real life conversation between the trainer and the trainee.

In another variation, the trainee has a real-life conversation with someone else in his social network and reflects upon that conversation. The point of this variation, of course, is to try to generalize the skills worked on in role-playing to real-life situations.

Example:

The two people sit beside each other on an airplane. The first is a man in his seventies and the second is a woman in her early twenties.

First: How are you today?

Second: Fine, thanks. How are you?

First: Good. I'm looking forward to some more pleasant weather in Georgia than in New York.

Second: You're not a snow lover, huh?

First: Not any more. I used to be into skiing, but now I'd rather be where it's warm. I guess that's what getting old does for you.

Second: I think I skipped the stage of liking snow and went straight to where you are. I never was much of a skiing fan, even though I grew up in ski country, in Vermont.

First: And do you live in Georgia now?

Second: That's right. In Atlanta. I've been in New York on a business trip.

First: What sort of business are you in?

Second: I work for a publishing company. We publish manuals on overcoming various psychological problems and behavioral problems.

First: Sounds like a very useful business. I was just reading the other day about how many visits to family doctors really have to do with a problem that's somehow psychologically related.

Second: That's right. We publish manuals on stopping smoking and drinking alcohol and weight control and using relaxation to help with headaches. Right there you cover a really high fraction of medical visits.

First: I'll bet it feels good to be in a business that is trying to do something about these problems rather than in something that just wastes resources.

Second: I went to business school, and when I finished, I got a job offer from a company that, among other things, markets cigarettes. I'm glad to be working on the other side.

First: Let me guess. Was the salary you were offered by the cigarette maker twice as much as the company you are working for now?

Second: That's close! It was almost three times as much!

First: Congratulations to you, for making the choice you did.

Second: Thanks. What sort of business have you been in?

First: I work for an organization that tries to promote world government.

Second: Oh? Tell me more.

******

Exercise 11: The Shaping Game

What is it?

The word "shaping" means helping someone reach a target behavior by reinforcing successive approximations of it. In other words, shaping means trying to reward or feel good about each little baby step on the way toward a larger accomplishment. Suppose, for example, someone starts writing an article, and he says to himself, "Good, I've gotten started." Later he says, "Hooray, I've made some progress." Still later he thinks, "Good, I've gotten a first draft done!" This person is reinforcing himself for getting closer and closer to his goal. Or, for example, when someone is teaching a young child to play the piano, the teacher might start by simply reinforcing the child for clapping in a steady rhythm along with a song. You don't wait for accomplishment of the final goal before celebrating; you celebrate any step that gets you a little bit closer to that goal.

That's what shaping is. The Shaping Game is a teaching tool that gives practice in the shaping process. Here are the rules of the Shaping Game.

1. There are two people. The shaper thinks of some behavior for the shapee to do and writes it down without showing the shapee.

2. The object of the game for the shaper is to give clues so the shapee can perform that behavior. The object of the game for the shapee is to perform that behavior. (Thus they both share the same goal and the game is a cooperative one.)

The shapee begins the game by walking around, touching things, saying things, and so forth.

3. The Shaper can give clues only by approving actions that the shapee has already done. For example the shaper can say things like, "I liked it that you turned that direction" or "It's good that you are touching that thing." Or, "Thank you for lifting your arm like that."

4. Criticism, suggestions or commands are against the rules. Positive reinforcement is the only way that the shaper can give a clue.

Let's say that the shaper writes down the goal behavior of "turn the lights off and then back on." As the shapee is wandering around, the shaper might be saying things like, "I'm glad you walked in that direction"; "I'm glad you moved your hand closer to the wall"; "I'm glad you touched the wall"; "That's great that you moved your hand in that direction"; "Thanks for touching the light switch"; "I'm so glad you turned the lights off"; "Hurray! You did it!"

What's it for?

The Shaping Game is meant to be an analog of how both interpersonal relationships and intra-personal dialogs should be conducted more often in an ideal world.

When interpersonal relations positively reinforce successive approximations of mutually acceptable goals, then such relationships provide a great deal of positivity and a great deal of support for people working to attain their goals. Family systems in which extensive mutual shaping occurs are likely to be happier and more immune to a broad range of psychopathology.

Similarly, people whose internal dialogs provide a lot of positive reinforcement for steps toward goals tend to be happier and tend to attain those goals more often. The person who reinforces himself while writing an article would be much more likely to be both successful at writing and free of depression than one whose internal dialogs sounded more like "Oh no, I've got to write that article. I've waited too long already. What if I can't come up with a good idea? I'll be so embarrassed. I've written the first paragraph, but it's lousy. What would people think if they read that—they'd laugh at me."

Yet there are millions of us in the world who are laboring away under conditions of frequent self-punishment very similar to that of this hypothetical internal dialog. One of the mainstays of cognitive therapy for depression involves trying to replace such self-punitive talk with more self-reinforcing talk.

Another skill exercised by this game is picking up on social cues. Some people seem to have a skill deficiency in being the shapee, and seem to be baffled in spite of rather obvious social cues about what to do next. For example, when most people hear something like, "I'm so glad your hand is very near the light switch. I'm glad it's so close that you could touch it easily," they would infer that touching the light switch is desirable. But for others those messages don't compute. The shaping game allows people to practice detecting subtle embedded in social utterances.

Another skill exercised by the shaping game is reflexively seeking approval rather than disapproval. This is a very major issue for lots of children, as well as for lots of adults. Many children seem to have become hooked on the reinforcement that comes from getting excitement and attention in a negative way, for example by getting someone to shout, "Hey, stop doing that!" By playing the shaping game often, people can acquire the habit of working to produce pleasure and approval in the other person, rather than reinforcing negative emotional reactions.

The trainee will benefit from playing both parts in this game. The role of the shapee is easier, if the shaper is an expert at the game.

How do you do it well?

The first challenge for the trainee who is playing the shaping game is to realize that it is a cooperative game and not a competitive game. Some trainees are accustomed to the competitive mode that they take pleasure in stumping the shaper. They don't realize that it is always possible to stump the shaper by picking an impossible goal behavior or by giving bad clues. If a shaper who has been stuck in the competitive mode can come to realize that the shapee's success is her own success too, something major has been accomplished.

Another challenge in playing this game well is avoiding criticism and directive utterances. Some players are so habitually inclined to these methods of influence that holding their tongues and using nothing but positive reinforcement is very difficult.

Another challenge in playing the game well is to find the optimum balance between too much and too little reinforcement. If you wait for the behavior to be nearly perfect before uttering reinforcement, the shaper is frustrated by lack of clues. On the other hand, if you reinforce too indiscriminately, the shapee receives false signals about what is desirable; he's likely to think certain directions are positive, when in fact they are not. This art of withholding reinforcement and delivering it at just the proper moment is, of course, analogous to using this skill in real life.

Another related skill is figuring out the precise behavior you want to reinforce. It's possible to identify several different pathways to a goal behavior. For example, if you want someone to jump into the air, you might start reinforcing the lifting of feet off the ground while walking, and then gradually reinforce more vigorous lifting of feet off the ground. Alternatively, you can reinforce her for touching higher and higher places on the wall, until finally she tries to touch a place she can reach only by jumping.

It a complex job to figure out when significant movement in the direction of the goal behavior has occurred along any of the identified hierarchies. The shaper needs to be mentally flexible. Let's say the shaper has one pathway in mind, but the other person takes a big step along another pathway. Instantly, the shaper must detect this change in direction, reinforce that big step, and switch to the new pathway.

Another skill in playing this game well is using tones of voice to communicate degrees of approval. This gives the shapee more information than words alone provide.

Another element of good playing includes remembering it's OK to say what you like about the other person's behavior. For example, rather than saying, "That was good," you can say things such as, "I like it that you lifted your right leg quickly." Or you can say, "I like it that you moved your hand closer to the light switch." And if all else fails, you can make statements such as, "I'm glad you made a move that got you one step closer to lying on the floor and moving your legs as if you were riding a bicycle." This of course gives away the answer and detracts from the fun, but if there is too much frustration, the shaper can always resort to some variation of this tactic.

Variations:

With very young children, you can play a variation of the shaping game in which the object of the game is simply to touch an object in the room, usually something big. This makes the game simpler.

For more advanced players and for adults, an important variation is the use of fantasy behaviors as targets. In this variation, instead of physically getting up and doing things, the shapee verbalizes imaginary behaviors. Playing the shaping game with fantasy behaviors opens up a whole new realm. It allows vastly more different behaviors to be the goals. It also allows the shaping game to be played over the telephone, for those trainer/trainee relationships that are conducted over the phone.

To make this version easier, you can limit the possible choices. For example, you can specify that the goal behavior is something that people usually do in their house.

Example:

Here's an example a shaping game played with fantasy behavior.

The goal behavior is "Eat or drink something." Here's how a dialogue might go.

Shapee: I'm in my house. I'm in my bedroom. I'm walking around.

Shaper: I'm glad you're in your house, and I'm glad you're moving around.

Shapee: I'm walking down the stairs and into the family room.

Shaper: I'm glad you're trying out different rooms.

Shapee: I'm walking into the living room.

Shaper: (Silence.)

Shapee: I'm going into the kitchen.

Shaper: Oh, I especially like that room!

Shapee: I'm opening the refrigerator and getting some orange juice.

Shaper: It's wonderful that you're getting something you can drink!

Shapee: I'm drinking the orange juice.

Shaper: You did it! It was "Eat or drink something!"

Exercise 12: Reflections

What is it?

First of all, what are reflections? These are utterances where you say back what you understood the other person was communicating, to make sure you got it right. Reflections also let the other person know that you understand.

The easiest way I know to teach someone how to use reflections is with a set of prompts. If you start a sentence in one of these ways and fill in the blank, you will almost surely generate a reflection. Here are prompts:

Prompts for Yourself to Do Reflections

So you're saying _____?
What I hear you saying is _____.
In other words, _____?
So if I understand you right, _____?
It sounds like _____.
Are you saying that _____?
You're saying that _____?

In the Reflections Exercise the trainer furnishes, either verbally or in writing, some sentences about some topic. The trainee's job is to reflect every utterance the trainee makes. When doing the exercise, you can simply let the trainee practice generating reflections. Or, you can let the trainer give feedback upon every reflection, rating how accurate it was on a scale of

10. The following is a rating scale for the accuracy of reflections.

Rating Scale for Reflections

0=No resemblance at all to what I said
2=Not what I said
4=Sort of like what I said
6=Fairly close to what I said
8=Very close to what I said
10=Exactly what I said, or you said it even better

What's it for?

These exercises serve two very distinct and different purposes. The one that most therapists are familiar with is cultivating empathic listening skills for the purpose of better relationships.

When each person is trying to make his point but not taking the time to listen to the other person, the result is usually conflict and anger. Such angry conversations also tend to be very rapid. Introducing the requirement into such conversations that each utterance be reflected before it is responded to slows down the conversation greatly. By forcing the participants to listen to one another and formulate responses to one another it pulls in more of the higher-order thinking parts of the brain. Reflections improve communication by preventing misunderstandings. Often people generate reflections that indicate

49

faulty understandings of the other person's utterances; when these misunderstandings can be put into words and the other person has a chance to correct them and try again, the misunderstandings get nipped in the bud.

I have also used the Reflections Exercise for a quite a different purpose: the development of concentration skills. In order to produce accurate reflections, you need to concentrate fully on the words you are hearing. I have often performed the reflections exercise with children who have attention problems. When these children are asked to reflect each utterance, they often realize that for some utterances they have not received or stored any of the information whatsoever.

The Reflections Exercise thus monitors and reinforces a person for paying great attention to verbal information. The Reflections Exercise, when used as a concentration builder, can use not only conversation, but also sentences or paragraphs from books. The learner can even perform the reflections exercise with paragraphs from his science or social studies textbook, or from novels.

How do you do it well?

In order to execute the Reflections Exercise well, you must concentrate on the words you are hearing. Thus, one of the first challenges is to follow the rules and simply reflect or paraphrase rather than attempt to communicate any new content in the reflection. Many people

in family therapy have great difficulty with this challenge.

Another element of good reflections is using your own words, rather than parroting the other person's words. For example, if the speaker says, "I get so angry at my little brother; he's such a pig." A reflection that says, "So you get so angry at your brother; he's such a pig," would be experienced as very unusual and would usually lead to a response of "Why are you repeating what I'm saying back to me?" A better reflection would be something like, "So, if I understand you right, his being greedy irritates you."

Another challenge in this exercise is being succinct in summarizing. Reflections don't have to repeat the whole utterance. At the same time, especially when in the concentration-building exercise, it's good not to leave out very significant portions of the utterance you heard.

Another challenge is letting the reflection match the emotional intensity of the original utterance. So, for example, if the person says, "I'm just elated over meeting this wonderful man! My life is going to be different every day from now on until the day I die!" Suppose the listener says, "So, do I understand you right that you feel good about meeting him?" This fails to capture the emotional intensity. A reflection such as "You sound so excited you could just jump up and down!" comes closer to capturing the emotional intensity of the original utterance.

Another element of performing this exercise well involves cultivating the vocabulary and the linguistic skills necessary to put people's utterances into other words. Thus, a good part of obtaining excellence in the Reflections Exercise is simply mastering fluency in the use of language.

Variations:

With young children, I like to give them one prompt where they can fill in the blanks. For example, "So you are saying _____." Then I tell them a story, which can be told in 10 or fifteen sentences. After each sentence, their job is to reflect by saying, "So you're saying _____," and filling in the blank. The story maintains their interest in the exercise if it's an exciting or interesting one.

In a slightly different variation, for older children or adults, I give them a sheet with all of the prompts for reflections on it, as listed previously. Then, as I tell a story or narrate some ideas about something, the trainee's job is to reflect each utterance, cycling through all the prompts. This introduces various formats of reflection into the person's verbal repertoire.

Another variation involves reading to the trainee and stopping every sentence or two or every paragraph to let the trainee reflect. This variation harnesses the usefulness of the Reflections Exercise as a concentration builder. I have used *Instructions on Psychological Skills* and *Programmed Readings for Psychological Skills* to practice the reflections exercise. You can also use any academic textbook.

Another variation upon the Reflections Exercise is to let family members speak to one another and practice reflecting one another's utterances. One family member is the speaker and the other is the listener. The speaker pauses after every utterance to let the listener reflect. If the reflector gets it right, the speaker acknowledges this, ideally with a tone of approval. If the listener does not get it right, the speaker tries again to explain what he really means. They continue until each utterance is eventually reflected correctly. After the speaker has come to some point of closure, then they switch roles. They continue, changing roles every few minutes.

Some speakers go on and on for so long that it is virtually impossible for the listener to reflect the main points that were made. So, the speaker must inhibit his desire to keep on talking and stop often enough for the other person to listen. This is sometimes the most difficult part of family members' doing this exercise well.

Another variation occurs when the trainee actually reads the verbal material rather than hears it. The trainee reads a paragraph from a book and then stops and reflects aloud what she has read. The trainer can give feedback upon the accuracy of the reflection.

In another variation on this exercise, the trainee sits at a computer and writes out each reflection, either after hearing a paragraph read or reading it herself. This exercise fosters several crucial skills at once: reading comprehension, concentration, typing or handwriting, spelling, grammar, composing writing, and the psychological skill that is the subject matter.

I have never seen a report of a trial of the Reflections Exercise for Attention Deficit Disorder. It would seem to me to be an extremely interesting experiment to do. If someone shows tremendous growth in the ability to produce accurate reflections for increasingly complex materials, that person is overcoming a very important element of Attention Deficit Disorder.

The challenge for the trainer, in all variations of this exercise, is to pick material that is not too hard, not too easy, but at just the right level of challenge for the trainee.

Examples:

Here's an example in which the second person generates reflections while the first person talks about his life.

First person: They say that you should not fight back when someone is bullying you. But sometimes the other options just don't work.

Second person: So you're saying that sometimes fighting back seems to be the only option that works for bullying?

First: Yes. For example, there was a kid who was taking food from a friend of mine at lunch. He told the teacher and the lunchroom supervisor, and they did nothing. My friend tried ignoring the kid, but he just kept on, day after day. Finally when he did it again, my friend grabbed his hand and twisted his finger back. He quit doing it.

Second: What I hear you saying is that the teacher and the lunchroom supervisor were no help at all, so your friend hurt the kid who was bullying him, and that seemed to work.

First: Yes. But of course, he was just lucky. Sometimes when people do that, the bully just hurts them back worse. And then if you try to hurt them back worse, they will try something still worse.

Second: In other words, sometimes fighting back just gets the other kid to fight back worse, and it keeps on and on getting worse.

First: Right. What is really needed is for the teachers and principal and lunchroom people to have all decided beforehand what they are going to do to enforce the rules, and for them to do it.

Second: You're saying that the best solution to the problem would be for the people in authority to have a plan about how to enforce the rule that people can't bully each other.

First: Yes.

Here's an example of the reflections exercise with an academic work. The trainer is reading to the trainee from *Instructions on Psychological Skills.*

First person: (Reads) How do you get yourself falling asleep and waking up earlier? The sleep researchers use the word *zeitgebers* to refer to those stimuli that reset circadian rhythms. There are four main ones to know about.

Second person: So you're saying that if you want to fall asleep earlier and wake up earlier, there are four ways to do it, and they are called zeitgebers.

First person: Excellent reflection. (Continues reading.) The first zeitgeber we have already mentioned: what time you go to bed, and get out of bed. The second is bright light. Bright light falling on the retina in the morning tends to move the circadian rhythm earlier. Bright light late in the evening tends to move it later. So if you want to wake up earlier and get sleepy earlier, expose yourself to bright light upon awakening, for at least half an hour, perhaps as long as two hours. There are a variety of companies that make bright lights especially for this purpose, if sunlight is not available or convenient.

Second person: What I hear you saying is that the first zeitgeber is going to bed and getting out of bed, and the second is bright light. Bright light in the morning moves your sleep schedule earlier, and you can buy lights that provide this light.

First person: Great reflection. (Continues reading.) The third zeitgeber is exercise. Exercise first thing in the morning also tends to move the sleep cycle earlier. It's as though exercise tells the body, "Yes, it really is time for the awake cycle to begin."

Second person: If I understand you right, the third zeitgeber is exercise, and exercise in the morning helps your body know it's time to be awake.

First person: Yes! (Continues reading.) The fourth zeitgeber is food. People with delayed sleep phase disorder tend not to be hungry in the morning, and to get hungry late at night. If you avoid eating after say 7 p.m. and try to eat first thing in the morning, you can use this to set your sleep rhythm earlier.

Second person: You're saying that eating early in the morning and not eating late at night helps you to set the sleep rhythm earlier, huh?

First person: Right!

Exercise 13: *The Journey*

What is it?

This exercise is a special case of Exercise 4: Conceptual Sharpening. The Journey Exercise is printed in the volume, *Programmed Readings for Psychological Skills*. The Journey Exercise is an eleven-chapter novel I wrote in which the characters very frequently make statements either to themselves or to someone else that are examples of the following twelve thoughts:

1. Awfulizing
2. Getting down on yourself
3. Blaming someone else
4. Not awfulizing
5. Not getting down on yourself
6. Not blaming someone else
7. Goal-setting
8. Listing options and choosing
9. Learning from the experience
10. Celebrating luck
11. Celebrating someone else's choice
12. Celebrating your own choice

In the Journey Exercise, the trainer simply reads the story to the trainee or allows the trainee to read the story himself. The trainee's job is to identify each of thought when it comes up. The version printed in *Programmed Readings* gives a choice between two alternatives for each question. If you want to make answering the questions a little more difficult, you can cover up the two al-ternatives and look at the entire list of twelve thoughts.

What's it for?

This exercise is meant to instill each of these twelve concepts into the trainee's vocabulary. These phrases help the trainee to think about her own thoughts. (This is sometimes called "metacognition.") When you can do this, it is now possible for you to pose questions to yourself, such as, "Haven't I gotten down on myself enough? Isn't it time for me to shift my energy into listing options and learning from the experience instead?" Such thoughts are much less likely if you don't have these concepts in your vocabulary.

There is a progression in the use of these concepts, just as there is in all the other concepts used in all the other conceptual sharpening exercises. The progression is as follows.

First, you practice classifying or labeling the examples that someone else has made up. For example, you might start out hearing "This is so horrible that I can't stand it!" and classify that as awfulizing.

Second, you practice making up your own examples of the various categories. For example, when asked to think of an example of awfulizing, you would say, "This means I'll never be happy again." The second activity is much more difficult than the first.

Third, you draw upon these concepts to formulate good responses to fantasy situations and to do them in fantasy rehearsals.

Fourth, you respond to real life situations at the time they take place by choosing among the different thought alternatives.

Exercise 12, the Journey Exercise, represents the first step on this progression. Exercise 13, the Twelve Thought Exercise, will give practice in the second step. Exercise 23 and 24, Fantasy Rehearsal and STEB and STEB revision, give practice in the third step.

The twelve thoughts used in the Journey Exercise and in the Twelve Thought Exercise are meant to be a brief summary of much that goes on in cognitive therapy. A great deal of psychopathology is based on the overuse of awfulizing, getting down on oneself, and blaming someone else. Too much awfulizing leads to anxiety; too much getting down on oneself leads to depression; and too much blaming other people leads to anger control problems. Of course, this is an oversimplification. But many people have vastly improved their lives simply by altering the distribution of their thoughts–away from those in the first three categories and toward those in the remaining nine categories.

In some situations, awfulizing or getting down on oneself or blaming other people is very adaptive. There are situations that need to be recognized as very bad; we all do bad things, and other people do bad things to us. The capacity to recognize danger, self-punish, and blame others would not have evolved had they not possessed some important survival and adaptive value. The adaptive value is to help us avoid or escape the bad situations.

But if the intensity of the negative emotion is too great, the emotion can get in the way or be paralyzing rather than serve as a spur to adaptive action. In such a case, the intensity of the thought needs to be turned down or the number of times it is employed needs to be reduced.

Other types of psychopathology are based on saying nothing to oneself. Very often impulsive behavior springs from simply responding to a situation with whatever behavior seems highest and strongest in the repertoire, without mediation by any thinking. Sometimes the use of some awfulizing or getting down on oneself might represent a great improvement.

For example, the teenager who is taking a thrill ride in a car at ninety miles an hour would probably do better if he would think to himself, "I could have a wreck and get killed or kill somebody and that would be just terrible." This falls into the category of awfulizing. He would also be better off if he would think to himself, "I'm doing something really stupid right now." This would be categorized as getting down on oneself. Learning to talk to yourself at all is better than simply responding without thinking to situations.

Listing options and choosing among them is a particularly useful thought pattern for people with pathology due to impulsiveness.

The Journey Exercise is a story engaging enough to be entertaining and involving for children; this makes it a useful exercise to present at the beginning of psychological skills training. An additional purpose of the story is to allow some characters to model working for nonviolence and to celebrate the achievement of nonviolent goals. It's one of only a small fraction of stories in which conflict is resolved without anyone's being killed or defeated.

How to do it well

If the trainee listens carefully and thinks hard about the Journey exercise, the trainee can probably answer all or almost all of the questions correctly. If this is not the case, the trainee may be too young for the Journey Exercise.

The trainer can also communicate that part of doing this exercise well is to pay attention to the story and become involved in it.

Variation:

In addition to the "low tech" form printed in *Programmed Readings for Psychological Skills,* a slightly higher tech form presents the text on a computer screen and provides fairly simple reinforcements for correct answers. Some children enjoy the computerized

version more, but the differences are not extremely large.

Another choice in performing this exercise is whether the trainee should hear the story read, read it himself out loud, take turns reading it out loud with the trainer, or read it to himself silently. No matter what the age of the trainee, there are advantages in the trainer's reading the story. The trainer can dramatize the dialog between the characters and make the experience more entertaining. On the other hand, some older trainees might want to speed through the exercise more quickly than a dramatic reading might allow.

Example:

Here are a few paragraphs from a random section of the *Journey*:

Just at that moment, though, there was a loud bang! Then there was a flopping sound. "Oh, no. We have a flat tire, and here we are out in the middle of nowhere. This is just awful; it's terrible," said Bo to himself. Was he

awfulizing, or listing options?

"Oh, no," said the bus driver, "I forgot to bring along a spare tire. Oh, I'm so stupid, I just can't do anything right!" Was he

learning from the experience, or getting down on himself?

When Sam saw this, he thought,
"Hmm, I learned something from this.
When I get home, if I ever get home,
I'm going to make sure I always have
spare tire that works in my car" Was he

learning from the experience, or
getting down on himself?

"Well, what can we do about this?"
said Lilly. "We can try to drive the bus
even with the flat tire. Or we can try to
go somewhere in our magic box. Or we
can start walking and see if we can find
somebody who has a phone. We can
call up the bus company or a service
station to fix the tire."

"Let's start walking," said the bus
driver. "I think I saw a house back
down the road." Were they

getting down on themselves, or listing options and choosing?

Exercise 14: The Twelve Thought Exercise

What is it?

In this exercise, you take any situation you can think of, and practice making up examples of the twelve types of thoughts taught by the Journey Exercise. You can write or say brief descriptions of the situation, for example:

It is a chess tournament, and you've just lost a game.

Or

You've just complimented somebody on a piece of art work that they've done, and the person smiles and seems to feel good about it.

Or

You have to wait for a long time in a waiting room at a doctor's office.

The situations you use for this exercise can be negative, positive or neutral.

To do the exercise, you think of something that you could say to yourself that would be an example of each of the twelve thoughts.

Here's an example. The situation is that you are an athlete in a tennis tournament, and you lose a game.

1. Awfulizing: "This is horrible. I've lost. Everyone is going to think I'm so stupid. After all the time I spent preparing!"

2. Getting down on yourself:: "How could I have hit the ball into the net like I did so many times? I did something stupid."

3. Blaming someone else: "Why did my father ever encourage me to get into this game anyway? He should have encouraged me to do something useful."

4. Not awfulizing: "This isn't the end of the world. It's just a game. It's not as though anyone was hurt or killed."

5. Not getting down on yourself: "It's true that I did make some mistakes that cost me, but I don't want to punish myself for that. It's no use in making myself feel terrible about it."

6. Not blaming someone else: "My father was trying to help me stay in shape and have some fun by encouraging me to get into this game. I don't want to waste my time blaming him."

7. Goal-setting: "What is my highest priority now? I want to behave in a good way, for the sake of my social reputation and for the sake of being kind to this other human being. I think that's the first goal. I also want the

pleasure of just relaxing. I think that's second priority right now."

8. Listing options and choosing: "What are my options at this point? I should congratulate and shake hands with the winner. I could study the video of my game and practice correcting my mistakes before I forget about it. I could talk with some of the people who watched the match. I could go home and get a shower and lie on my couch and read. I think I'll congratulate the winner and then go home and relax."

9. Learning from the experience: "Next time I don't to let up on my effort when I get ahead. I want to play just as hard when I'm ahead, so I won't blow my lead."

10. Celebrating luck: "I got paired up with a really good player who challenged me to the top of my abilities. I'm glad that occasionally I get pushed to my limits. I'm also glad that I had the time to be able to spend this day playing tennis rather than having to work in a factory somewhere."

11. Celebrating someone else's choice: "I'm glad my coach helped me get this far in the tournament. And I'm glad people set up these tournaments. They've given me a good chance to practice my fortitude skills."

12. Celebrating your own choice: "I did make some good moves. I want to remember how it felt to hit some of those aces I hit today. I'm also glad that I handled losing without getting too upset."

What's it for?

The Twelve Thought Exercise helps people take control over their thoughts. Probably most people throughout history have not chosen the sort of thoughts they want to have about a situation; they have simply responded to the situation in a habitual way. When you get to the point where you can think things like, "I want to stop blaming the other person and start thinking more about what options will make things better," you have achieved a degree of self-control that elevates life considerably.

The point of the Twelve Thought Exercise is not simply to stop doing the first three types of thoughts and do more of the last nine. Sometimes a judicious amount of awfulizing, getting down on oneself or blaming someone else is adaptive and reasonable.

For example, on a frolicsome sunny day at the beach, it might behoove a parent to stop celebrating for a while and do a bit of awfulizing and getting down on himself if he's forgotten to protect his children's skin from the sun. These thoughts would then hopefully lead to some listing of options and choosing, and learning from the experience, rather than stopping with awfulizing and getting down on oneself.

The Twelve Thought Exercise also reinforces connection between thoughts and feelings. When you do the Twelve Thought exercise, you can experience feeling different ways, depending upon which thought you are voicing at the moment. This provides first-hand experience in learning that by choosing our thoughts we can influence our own feelings.

Doing the Twelve Thought Exercise with hypothetical situations allows you to prepare yourself to be rational in a wide variety of situations. Doing the Twelve Thought Exercise requires disciplined effort with a great deal of activity from the higher cortical centers. The type of brain response that the Twelve Thought Exercise requires is much different from the sort of overwhelming emotional response that constitutes a great deal of psychopathology.

In many ways the Twelve Thought Exercise requires a great deal of creativity, especially in thinking of ways to form celebratory thoughts in negative situations and form negative thoughts in positive situations. But, it is always possible to come up with something.

How do you do it well?

One challenge in doing the Twelve Thought Exercise is to make the thought specific to the situation. It would be possible if someone were just trying to get the exercise out of the way to give generic responses like, "This is awful. I'm a bad person. It's all the other person's fault. It's not so bad. I'm

not so bad," etc., without achieving the point of the exercise, which is to generate thoughts about the specific situation at hand.

Another challenge is to avoid altering the situation to produce certain thought. For example in the tennis situation, when it comes time to celebrate what happened, you don't want to say, "Oh, I just noticed I'm not beaten after all. The other person was disqualified because of a positive drug test!" You have to stay with the situation that you're given.

Another element in doing this exercise well is not distorting reality or saying things to yourself that are clearly not true. For example, suppose that the situation presented is that a woman's husband is drinking too much and getting violent when he's drunk. It would not be a good way to celebrate luck if you said, "I'm just sure that he will quit drinking soon, and I'm so happy about that," because it probably represents practice in kidding oneself. On the other hand, celebrating luck by saying, "I'm glad that so far I've been lucky enough to escape getting hurt badly or killed," does not represent distortion of reality.

One challenge involves how to do "not getting down on oneself" when you really have done something wrong, and how to do "not blaming someone else" when the other person really has done something wrong. Let's suppose that the situation is that you've purposely pushed somebody on a bicycle and he has fallen over and skinned his knee. A beginner at this exercise might do "not getting down on himself" by saying something like, "It wasn't my fault." But given the way the situation was stated, it obviously was his fault. To deny responsibility for the bad outcome is not an adaptive way of avoiding getting down on oneself.

A better way would be to say something like, "Even though I did do something bad, I don't want to just keep on punishing myself to the point where I'm immobilized. I'd rather put my energies into figuring out how to be helpful and figuring out how to keep from making such a mistake again."

We could go through the same sort of reasoning on not blaming someone else. You want to acknowledge the truth of the other person's responsibility for bad actions, if that does exist. If someone is exploiting you or being sadistic with you, you don't want to say, "It isn't his fault."

But you want to choose to use your mental energies in ways that are more productive than simply going over and over how bad the other person is. A good example of Not Blaming Someone Else in such situations is, "Even though this person did something bad, I want to use my energy to figure out how to live my life best, rather than just keep condemning him."

How do you celebrate when bad things happen? One way is the "things could be worse" strategy. For example, a piano just fell on my leg and crushed it, but I celebrate what happened by saying to myself, "At least I'm glad it didn't fall on my head and kill me."

How would you celebrate someone else's choice in such a situation? One way would be saying something like, "Hurray. I'm glad my wife has always been very supportive of me, and I'm glad I can count on her to be supportive of me in this accident and in my recovery from it." That is, you think of people who have something to do with the situation in not such an immediate sense.

You recruit these people into the situation for the purposes of celebrating their choices, even though you wouldn't celebrate the choice of the person who dropped the piano on your leg. (Unless, perhaps, he made a choice that kept the piano from going on your head.)

How do you get down on yourself for doing good things? If I've just found a cure for a dreaded disease and won the Nobel Prize, there are all sorts of ways I can think negative thoughts. I can think to myself, "I did this for all the wrong reasons. I really didn't care about these people, I just did this for the fame and the money." I can awfulize by saying, "Nothing I'll ever do in the future can ever match this, and my life is going to be all downhill from here on." I can blame someone else by saying, "If that selfish person hadn't wasted two years of my life by suing me, I would have found this quicker, and many more people would have been saved." These responses add on to the original situation, but do not distort or change the situation as given.

Variations:

You can do the Twelve Thought Exercise with various sorts of frustrations, as follows:

Types of Frustrations

1. Not getting something you asked for: someone's saying no.
2. Someone's doing or saying something unkind or unwanted.
3. Trying to do something and failing.
4. Illness or symptoms of illness.
5. Injury.
6. Loss or damage of property.
7. Losing a competition.
8. A piece of equipment or a tool that doesn't work right.
9. Not being able to find something.
10. Having too much to do in too little time.
11. A loss of a relationship.
12. A distancing or weakening of a relationship.
13. Trying to learn something but finding it too hard.
14. Having to do something, but finding it boring or otherwise unpleasant.
15. Getting your hopes up for something and then finding out it won't happen.
16. Having to wait for something you want now.

17. Having to pass up something that is very pleasurable.
18. Loss of money.
19. Bad weather.
20. Damage to your reputation.
21. An accident.
22. Death, of loved ones, friends, acquaintances, or of oneself.

Or various types of interpersonal conflicts:

Types of Joint Decisions or Conflicts

1. Allocation of scarce resources. (Who gets to play with the toy, who gets to have the last banana, which child gets more of the adult's attention, which person deserves the parking place, whether to spend money on what the husband or the wife wants, which group should get public funds . . .)

2. Restitution for loss or damage. (Who has to replace a broken thing . . .)

3. Sensory input. (What music gets played, what smells get produced, whether lights are on or off, how hot or cold it is, whether windows are open or closed, what the house looks like, what the city looks like . . .)

4. Best action in a joint project. (Whether to have the child learn Spanish or French, whether to go to the mountains or the seashore on vacation,

whether to hire one person or another for our company . . .)

5. Action of a person on one project affects someone else on another. (One person's use of water affects the temperature for the other person taking a shower; people's use of streets for a foot race affects other people's getting where they want to go in cars.)

6. Desire for services or goods from a possibly reluctant giver. (One person thinks the other should drive him somewhere. One person thinks the other should give an earlier appointment. One person thinks the other should share money more generously.)

7. Uncertainty about terms of a prior agreement. (E.g., both people remember the original agreement as more favorable to themselves.)

8. An agreement has been made, but circumstances change for one of the people. (E.g., I thought I could build your house on time, but that was before my mother got sick.)

9. Who should have the power to decide. (E.g., a man feels his choice of job is his own decision; his wife feels she has a say. A father feels he should be able to tell his daughter when to come in at night; she feels she is old enough to decide for herself.

10. Rules of ethical conduct. (One person feels that drinking alcohol is wrong; another feels that it's right. One person is offended by the other's use of profanity. One feels that it's wrong not to report babysitters' income to taxing authorities; the other feels that it is fine not to.)

11. Who has to do the work. (Who in the family should wash the dishes? Who should put the things away? Which medical doctor has to be on call on the major holiday, to substitute for the partner who is sick?)

12. Different conventions and tastes. (One person is offended if guests do not write a thank-you note after each visit; the other doesn't go by that custom. One person comes from a culture where it's considered very impolite to interrupt another; the other comes from a culture where interrupting is the norm. One person is accustomed to being very neat; the other is accustomed to clutter.)

One of the major choice points is whether to do this exercise with hypothetical situations supplied by the trainer, hypothetical situations made up by the trainee, or real situations in the trainee's life. I've found that building up great facility in this exercise with hypothetical situations before doing it with real-life situations is a good idea.

Example:

Here's an example in addition to the one given previously.

Situation: I'm an adolescent, and I want to go to a party, but my parents won't let me go because they think there isn't enough adult supervision.

1. Awfulizing: I can't stand this. I'll never be able to have any friends.
2. Getting down on yourself. It's because I let them down before. I'm such an untrustworthy person.
3. Blaming someone else. They are just trying to keep me from growing up. They're totally unreasonable.
4. Not awfulizing. This isn't the end of the world. I would have survived if the party didn't take place, so I can survive not going to it.
5. Not getting down on yourself: I may have broken some rules in the past, but I don't want to punish myself for that now.
6. Not blaming someone else. I suppose they are just trying to look out for my best interests, even though I don't agree with them on this one. I'll choose not to spend my time condemning them.
7. Goal-setting. My short-term goal is to figure out a different way of having fun that night. My longer-term goal is to persuade my parents to give me more freedom.
8. Listing options and choosing: I could get together with another friend and go skating that night. I could invite someone to come over and visit. I could catch up on some work. I could continue reading the book I'm reading now.
9. Learning from the experience: If they are not letting me do this because I went to another person's house without telling them the last time I went to a party, then I've learned that doing that sort of thing is not something they quickly forget.
10. Celebrating luck: I'm glad that I live in a time and place where there are lots of other fun things to do.
11. Celebrating someone else's choice: At least I'm glad my friend invited me to the party.
12. Celebrating my own choice: I'm glad I decided to stay cool when they told me I couldn't go. That was a good example of fortitude.

Exercise 15: Acting Out Modeling Plays or Play Plots

What is it?

In this exercise there is either a script or a plot outline of a play that models psychological skills. The trainee, or the trainee and the trainer together, act out these plays.

I wrote a volume meant for young children, entitled *Plays That Model Psychological Skills*. One way of using this is that an adult, either the trainer or the child's parent, studies the play closely and then acts it out for the child. These plays are often much more fun if they are acted out with toy people or puppets. The child can simply be a spectator. To get more active involvement, you can put on the play for the child and then have the child put on the same play himself. Some young children will enjoy this activity; others will not.

The play plots, in contrast to the plays, are one- or two-line descriptions of the plot of a vignette to be role-played. For example, "One person has something heavy that he is trying to move; another person helps him move it." Or, "One person has a problem that he wants to talk about, but not receive advice on; the other person is a good listener." These play plots leave most of the details to be improvised by the players.

The trainers can select plays and play plots that are most appropriate for the trainee to practice, or they can simply perform them all from start to fin-

ish, especially if they enjoy this activity. Or they can pick from them randomly.

The play plots can be acted out in different ways. It's possible to follow the same play plot over and over, with very different stories.

What's it for?

This exercise is meant to provide lots of practice in the types of talk and actions that model psychological skills.

How do you do it well?

It seems this exercise gets more difficult with age. As people become older, they often develop more resistance to role-playing. Perhaps they feel that acting is childish, or perhaps they're anxious about their acting skills. But many studies have shown that even adults derive tremendous benefits from role-playing the sorts of situations that develop the skills they need most. The older a person is, the more she will want the trainer to devise situations directly relevant to real life. (That way the person has a legitimate excuse for doing pretend play!)

So a good portion of performing this exercise well is simply having the courage to do it at all. One does not have to be a great actor or actress. That having been said, the more you can really imagine yourself in the situation and thoroughly pretend to be in it, rather than just mouthing lines, the more useful and enjoyable this exercise becomes.

Another challenge is achieving a balance. You want to be creative enough to add details that make the play fun and interesting. Within the constraints of the plot outlines given, you can generate all sorts of interesting stories to act out. But you don't want to get so sidetracked from the plot that you spend a lot of time on digressions from the practice of the psychological skill in question.

Because many of the play plots for very young children involve acts of kindness, it's important to say "Thank you" or "You're welcome" to signal the end of the play.

Variations:

In one variation, therapist and client construct the play plots together. That is, they explore which situations in the client's life the client most needs practice in handling. They list those situations and construct play plots, and then practice them.

In another variation, the trainee writes out his or her own play plots to be acted out with the trainer.

Or the trainee may act out the play plots all by himself, playing all the parts involved. One of the advantages of this technique is that you can see how much the trainee improves over time independent of the trainer's input into the play.

In another written version, the trainee writes out full scripts for plays that model psychological skills.

Or the trainee or the trainer and the trainee may create audiotapes or videotapes of the plays, either from full play scripts or from improvisation from play plots. If you can create videos or audiotapes of play plots that are enjoyable for the trainee to watch repeatedly, you have found a very powerful means of practicing and modeling psychological skills.

****

The play plots that follow are two- or three-line plot outlines for plays that model psychological skills. Two people can act these out. Although the basic plot is specified, the players can improvise the details. Thus, the same plot can be acted in unlimited numbers of different ways. The person who has acted out all these plots has gained lots of practice in psychological skills.

A trainer and trainee can act out these play plots together. The first priority is for the trainer and trainee to establish a pattern of having fun doing these together. Once this pattern is established, you can add plots to the list.

If the trainee does something that is worthy of celebration, you can write a plot describing it and add that to the list. If the trainee does something NOT worthy of celebration, you can ask yourself, what would have been the desirable way of handling the same situation?

Then you can write a plot that describes this pattern of thought and feeling and behavior.

You may want to change the situation so you don't raise lot of negative feelings associated with the original situation, but at the same time you can leave intact the basic challenge that the situation holds. You can accomplish the same goal with desirable or undesirable responses observed in anyone else: the adult, fictional characters, other people observed in real life. And you can make up more play plots to embody the patterns that need to be enacted more often in real life. Your own customized list of play plots can be a repository of desirable positive patterns.

The players should feel free to imagine exotic, even outlandish circumstances for the play plots, while still keeping the basic plot intact. For example, one of the plots is that someone is moving something heavy, and someone else helps him move it. When one person is carrying something heavy, what might that thing be, and what might be the reason he wants to move it? Maybe it's a golden peacock that the Emperor of China has ordered the person to move to the site where the annual Peacock Party will be held. Someone has told the person that, if he doesn't get it moved on time, the Emperor (who also has magical powers) might turn the person into a monkey. Thus there is an embellishment of the basic plot, with the addition of another complication.

Of course it's possible to get off on tangents that lose the basic plot line and defeat the purpose of the play. It's also possible to simply act out a minimal plot line with grim determination, to get it over with quickly. Mixing fun and purposefulness in just the right proportion is the challenge for the players. If they can get this one just right, they have accomplished something worthwhile.

Videotaping the plays makes this exercise even more enjoyable. It will be fun to watch the plays again, and if watching them is fun, this provides more fantasy modeling of positive patterns.

I have acted out these plays mainly without an audience. If there is an audience, you need to select its members carefully. Sometimes an audience will reward slapstick violence or antisocial behavior by laughing, and the reinforcement will be too much for the players to resist.

In the list below, the plots in the category of kindness and those that are shorter tend to be easier. It's usually a good idea to start with the easiest ones, so that the trainer and trainee can ascend "the hierarchy of difficulty."

Play Plots

Productivity

Two people are trying to take a message or some medicine or supplies or some other type of help to someone. The travel conditions are very bad. They have a strong sense of purpose that inspires them to push on. (purposefulness)

The first is teaching the second something. The second strays off task a lot. Just as the first is starting to give up, the second somehow becomes able to stay on task really well, for reasons that you may include in the play or may leave unexplained or due to magic. There may be other back-and-forth changes in the second person, if you so choose. (persistence)

The first person has a lot of unpleasant work to do. The second has work to do too, and they decide to do it together, and be in the same room so they won't be as lonely. (persistence)

The first person needs to move something very heavy, and the second person helps the first to move it. They keep going until it's where it's supposed to go. (persistence)

The first person has a deadline to meet. The second person helps him meet that deadline. (persistence)

The first person has been teased because he can't do something well, and tells the second. The second shows the first how to work and practice at it. The first does work and practice at it, a lot. The first comes back and impresses everyone with his skill. (competence-development)

Things are all in a mess, and the second person helps the first person get organized. (organization)

The first is very disorganized, and has lots of problems because of it. The second is an elf who comes in secretly and organizes the first. The first prospers because of the elf. The first finds out about the elf and finds a way to pay him back for his help, and to continue the organizing himself. (organization)

Joyousness

The first person gets marooned on an island where there is enough food and water, but there is no one else on the island. So the first creates an imaginary person–the second person, to have fun with in creative ways. (enjoying aloneness)

The first person receives a compliment from the second person. The first person feels so good about the compliment that he works to get even better. Later, they see each other again, and the first person puts on an amazing performance at whatever the skill is. (pleasure from approval)

The first person has a skill that the other people around him don't value and even make fun of. But the first person knows that it is valuable. The first person creates an imaginary person (the second) who reinforces the first for his success in this skill, as he keeps on developing it. Finally the skill is proved valuable. (pleasure from accomplishments)

The first person is very cold. The second lends the first his coat to keep him warm. The second is a little cold, but the second feels good because of being kind to the first. (pleasure from your own kindness)

The first person is a scientist, working on a discovery. The second is the friend of the first. The second comes by and is able to help the first. Together, they achieve a big breakthrough. They then celebrate together that the discovery has been made. (pleasure from discovery)

The first person is curious about something. The second person helps the first to find the answer or tells the answer. (pleasure from discovery)

The first person is in trouble of some sort, and the second helps out the first. Later, the first comes to be rich or powerful, and returns to show thankfulness to the second in some big way. (pleasure from others' kindness)

The first person has some little problem or handicap. The second person has a much bigger problem or handicap. The first complains about how bad life is. The second tries to help the first take pleasure in the blessings that he does have. (pleasure from blessings)

The first is a dog or cat. A fairy says that the dog or cat will get a big reward if he can get a grumpy, unhappy person to pet him a lot. The dog or cat figures out a way to get the person to pet him, and when the person does so, the dog or cat seems to enjoy it so much that the person keeps on petting him. Then the dog or cat gets the mysterious reward from the fairy. (pleasure from affection)

The prince or princess is trying to decide which of two or three people to marry. They all act nice when they are with the prince or princess. The prince or princess goes out in disguise to walk around and think. The prince or princess happens to see how the two or three people treat a dog or a stranger or someone else, and this lets the prince or princess decide. (favorable attractions)

The first person is helping the second person study for a spelling test. Each time the first one gets a word right, the second one dances or sings or does something else gleeful to celebrate in a fun way. (gleefulness)

The first person never laughs for some reason. The second person tries to make the first person laugh and finally succeeds. (humor)

Kindness

The first person has something that is very interesting to use or play with. The second is interested. The first ends up sharing with the second. (kindness)

The first person doesn't know how to get somewhere, and the second helps the first. (kindness)

The first person can't figure out how to get a gadget turned on, and the second person knows, and helps the first. (kindness)

The first person has some food, and the second person has none and is hungry. The first shares with the second. (kindness)

One person has lost something, and the second helps him find it. (kindness)

The first person is caught in bad weather, and the second helps him get out of it somehow, e.g., by inviting the first person into his house, or lending a coat or blanket. (kindness)

The first person drops something without knowing it, and the second person picks it up for him and gives it back. (kindness)

The first person has lost something, and the second person helps the first person look, and they find it. (kindness)

The first person is hungry, and the second person somehow gets food to the first person. (kindness)

The first person is sick or hurt, and the second helps the first. (kindness)

The first person takes the second to a very interesting place. The second is glad to see that place. (kindness)

The first person feels bad about some part of himself. The second person points out good aspects, and helps the person feel better about himself. (kindness)

The first person is very hot. The second person has a cool house, and invites the first over. (kindness)

The first person is lost, and the second person helps him find his way to where he is going. (kindness)

The first person gets his foot stuck in something, and the second person helps him get it loose. (kindness)

The first person wants to learn how to do something, and the second person teaches him how to do it. (kindness)

The first person and the second person are eating some snacks. There is one left. The first person lets the second person have the last one. (kindness)

The first person has a little brother or sister who is getting onto the bus. The little brother or sister forgets to carry the backpack on. The first person picks up the backpack and gives it to the little brother or sister. (kindness)

The first person feels bad about how someone said something unkind to him. The second person comforts the first person and cheers up the first person . (kindness)

There is a fire, and someone helps the other to put it out. (kindness)

There is a flood, and the two people help each other not get drowned. (kindness)

The first person has something that's broken, and the second helps him fix it. (kindness)

The first person wants to sleep, so the second person is very quiet. (kindness)

The first person is swinging the second person around, and they are laughing. But then the second person has his or her facial expression and tone of voice change. The first person can tell instantly that the second person isn't enjoying it any more, and stops. The second asks why, and the first tells, and the second confirms that the first was right. (empathy)

The first person accidentally hurts the second. The first person feels bad and tries to make it up to the second somehow, and/or makes sure that the same sort of thing will never happen again. (conscience)

The first person tries to answer a question in class at school, and can't get it. A chorus of other kids laughs at him. Later the second person, who is also in the class, is nice to him, takes his side, and comforts him. (conscience)

Honesty

The first person is getting blamed for something. The second person is the one who was really responsible for it, and the second person confesses so that the first won't get falsely blamed. (honesty)

The first person is getting interviewed for a job. The boss asks a question about how good the person is at something. The second person is the person's conscience. The person has a conversation with his conscience about what to say. The conscience advises telling the truth about what he can and can't do well. (awareness of your abilities)

Fortitude

The first person asks for something that the second person can't give. The first person uses fortitude to handle it well. (fortitude)

A person wants to play the piano, but someone else is playing help the baby get to sleep. So the person has to wait for a few minutes before he can play the piano. (fortitude)

A person wants to listen to a certain station on the radio. But the other person is listening to the news. So the first person has to wait, and after he waits, he can listen to what he wants. (fortitude)

Somebody wants some attention from a babysitter. But the babysitter has to put the younger brother down for a nap first. So the person waits and gets the babysitter's attention after she has waited for a while. (fortitude)

One person wants to play with a cat. But the cat is asleep. So the person has to wait until the cat wakes up. (fortitude)

One person sees a dog, and wants to pet the dog. But the person's mom or dad says no, because they don't know that dog and they don't want to pet the dog without knowing it first. So they wait a couple of days until they see the owner, and the owner tells them the dog is very safe, and they can pet the dog then. (fortitude)

The first person wins a competition with the second and is gracious; the second person loses the competition and is also gracious. (fortitude)

The two people are best friends, but one tells the other he will be moving away. They handle it (e.g., by making a plan to stay in touch and enacting that plan). (handling separation)

Someone wants to get together with someone else. This person invites people to do lots of different things. But everyone else has some reason for not getting together. Finally, the person either finds someone, or finds some other solution. (handling rejection)

The first person hears by telephone that someone has rejected him. The second person helps the first to realize that not everyone will reject him, and is nice to him. First feels better. (handling rejection)

The first person gives some constructive and polite criticism to the second. The second handles the criticism well by seeing what he can learn that will help him. (handling criticism)

The first person makes a big mistake. The first person talks it over with the second person. The first person decides to learn from the experience and make the most of it. (handling mistakes and failures)

Someone is asked a question in class and doesn't know the answer, and is embarrassed. The person responds by studying very hard from then on. Then more questions are asked, and the person knows the answer and feels good. (handling mistakes and failures)

The first person has a challenge to meet for work or school or sports. The second helps and advises. The first person either meets the challenge or doesn't. If he does, he celebrates. If he doesn't, he not doesn't awfulize and learns from the experience. (handling mistakes and failures or pleasure from accomplishments)

The first person and the second person are brother and sister. One of the two gets all sorts of awards and recognition at a ceremony. The other doesn't. The one who doesn't win anything manages to feel good about the sibling's success and support that sibling. Someone else asks how he or she keeps from being jealous, and the person explains how. (magnanimity, non-jealousy)

One person is going to do something of pretty risky, and feels scared. That person talks to the second person about it. The second helps the first see that it's OK to be scared, that you should just go ahead and do what you have to do anyway. (painful emotion tolerance)

One person tells another about a fantasy that he has about something that he shouldn't do. Maybe he acts out the fantasy, to show the other person. The other person knows the first well enough to know he wouldn't actually do the thing, and helps him feel assured of the difference between real life and imagination. (fantasy-tolerance)

Individual Decision-Making

The first person is really nurturing and helpful and nice whenever the second one feels bad in some way. The first person doesn't pay nearly so much attention with the second one is doing well. After a while, the second one realizes he's getting in the habit of feeling bad or complaining to get the first person to act nice and be attentive. So he asks the first person not to be so reinforcing of bad feelings. (positive aim)

The first person is standing around and someone he doesn't know runs up to him and asks him to do something really quick (e.g., tackle someone else he doesn't know). The first person wants to think about it more, and doesn't do it. Then the person explains, and it turns out it would have been a bad idea. (reflectiveness)

There are two people who are being interviewed. (One person can play both parts, if desired.) A second person is interviewing both of them. When the second person asks questions such as, "Tell me, what have you been doing lately," one of the two people says things such as, "Nothing." The other can come up with things to say. The more fluent one gets the job. (fluency)

The first person says, "Boy, this was quite a situation we were in, with _____ happening." (The first person fills in the blank to describe what happened.) The first person asks, "How do you feel about this?" The second person feels at least two different ways about it, and explains why for each feeling. (awareness of your emotions)

The first person either feels guilty about something he can't control, or feels helpless about something he can control. The second person helps the first change his mind about it. (awareness of control)

Someone is sick or hurt or in danger in some other way. Someone else helps the person decide what to do. They define the problem, get information, list options, think about advantages and disadvantages, and make a choice, and see how it turns out. (decision-making)

Joint Decision-Making

One person is doing something, and the second person has some advice to give. But the second doesn't want to be too bossy. The second asks the first if he wants advice; the first says no, and the second accepts that. (toleration, non-bossiness)

The first person thinks that something should be done a certain way because it is cheaper and easier. But the second person thinks it should be done a different way because the effect on the environment is better or there are fewer health risks. They make a decision with each other in a rational way. (rational approach to joint decisions)

There is something that the two people want to use at the same time. They decide to take turns or share. (rational approach to joint decisions)

The first person has been waiting to use something. The second person has also been waiting to use it, without the first person's knowing it. They work out a plan together. (rational approach to joint decisions)

The first person in the family likes the temperature in the house hotter, and the second likes it colder. They talk to each other politely and work out the problem in a way that they can agree on. (rational approach to joint decisions)

The first person is working at a computer, and the second person wants the first person to give it up so the second person can use it. They talk together and figure out some solution to their problem. (option-generating)

The first person thinks that things should be kept very neat and orderly in a certain place. The second person isn't nearly as interested in neatness and orderliness. They make a decision with each other where they generate some good options for solutions to their problem. (option-generating)

Two people get to go someplace together. One wants to go one place, and the other wants to go another. They list options and choose, and come to an agreement that suits them both. (option-generating)

The first person is a judge. The second person plays the part of each of two people who have a dispute of some sort. The people list several options that have been generated. The judge asks about the situation and decides which option is most just, and explains why. (option-evaluating)

The first person tries to persuade a second person to eat or drink something or take a drug or do some risky activity. The second person assertively refuses to go along with the first person, without being either aggressive or passive. (assertion)

The two people have a debate or conversation in which they take opposite stands. One person is pretty sure he is right about his stand. But then he learns that he is not right. He admits this to the other person. (submission)

The first person is a young child, and the second person is a parent. Sometimes the young child whines and asks for things in an annoying way, and sometimes the child asks for things in a cheerful and pleasant way. The parent gives the child what he asks for when he asks in a pleasant way. (differential reinforcement)

Nonviolence

The first person accidentally does something that either physically hurts the second person or damages something the person owns or causes the second person to lose a lot of money. The second person handles the injury in a forgiving way. (forgiveness and anger control)

The first person is playing, and a young child comes over and grabs a toy away from the first person. The first person handles this calmly. (forgiveness and anger control)

People are in the legislature, and they are voting to start a war. The first person plays the person who listens to the people voting. The second person is the only person who votes against the war. He explains his position and persuades the others to change their minds. (nonviolence)

Respectful talk, not being rude

The first person is trying to teach the second person something, but the second person keeps messing it up and getting it wrong. The first person avoids saying anything disrespectful or rude, and keeps being patient and using non-hurtful talk. (respectful talk)

The first person doesn't bring a present to a party where all the other people have brought presents for the second person. The first person tells the second person, and the second person is gracious. (respectful talk)

The first person has borrowed something, and has forgotten to give it back. The second person doesn't want to be mean to the first. The second asks for it back in a very polite way, and the first returns it. (respectful talk)

Friendship-Building

The first person is applying for a job with the second. The second is trying to decide whether the first can be trusted to do the job right. The first has in mind some information that will shed light on this question, but the second has to work to get it. (discernment and trusting)

The first person talks to the second person about something that might be embarrassing. The second person re-sponds in a trustworthy way. (self-disclosure)

The first person sings or whistles, and the second one compliments the first. (gratitude)

The first person does a favor for the second, and the second pays the first back somehow. (gratitude)

The first person talks about something, and the second person very frequently compliments the first person. (gratitude, admiration)

The first person receives a present he doesn't really like, but is very gracious and appreciative to the second one for giving it. (gratitude)

The first person is doing something, and the second person comes up and starts a conversation with the first, in several different ways. (social initiations)

The first and second person find themselves waiting in a waiting room together. They decide to get to know each other better and have a conversation with each other. (socializing)

The first person is new to the neighborhood. The second person meets him and gets to know him and tries to make him feel welcome. (socializing)

One person is lonely, and the second makes him feel better by coming up and greeting him nicely and talking with him. (socializing)

The first person tells the second about some problem or something good that happened, and the second person uses lots of reflections to be a good listener. (listening)

Self-discipline

The first person has lots of work to do. The first person uses self-discipline to get working on it, and the second one helps out the first. (self-discipline)

The first person is a student who uses self-discipline to study very hard. The second person is a teacher who tests the first person. The first person gives the right answers and feels good. (self-discipline)

The first person tempts the second with something that is pleasant but not good for him. The second uses self-discipline to turn down the temptation. (self-discipline)

The first person is very tired. The second person could use some help on some tasks. The first person uses self-discipline to help out when he would rather rest. (self-discipline)

The first person notices he is out of shape and asks the second person for help. The second person teaches the first to exercise and eat right. The first uses self-discipline, and is grateful for the second's help. (self-discipline)

Loyalty

The first person is taking care of a younger person. Someone tempts the first person to neglect the younger person in order to do something fun. The first person remains true to his duty. (loyalty)

The first person plays the role of several people who are criticizing someone. The second person is friends with that person, and the second person disagrees with them and sticks up for his friend. (loyalty)

Conservation

The first person has some money to spend. He is tempted to spend it on junk food, but uses self-discipline. Then second person tells him about something really important that the family needs the money for, and the first person can contribute. (conservation and thrift)

Self-care

The first person notices a safety hazard, and corrects it. The second person comes by and does something safely that could have been hazardous if the first hadn't acted. The first feels good. (carefulness)

People are driving cars too fast past the first person's house. The first person is concerned about the safety of his family. The first tells the second about the problem, and they figure out something to do about it. (carefulness)

The first person has a habit that is bad for his health. The second helps the first to break it. (habits of self-care)

The first person is nervous for some reason, and wishes he had a relaxation tape to listen to. The second makes up a little relaxation monologue to help the first relax. (relaxation)

One person is trying to learn how to do something. He keeps messing up, and using self-punishing statements. The second teaches the first how to use self-nurturing statements instead. The first gradually learns to do the task better after that. (self-nurture)

Compliance

The two people are at a place together. The first is having a great time. The second is the parent, and says they have to leave now. The first does so cheerfully. (compliance)

Positive fantasy rehearsal

One person is nervous about the prospect of inviting someone for something, or asking for an increase in pay, or something else. So the second person suggests that they practice it together by role-playing. They do it, and then the person does it in real life. (imagination and positive fantasy rehearsal) The first person makes a mistake of some sort. This person responds to it by asking the second person to help him practice doing the thing the right way, in role-playing, over and over. The second person helps him. (positive fantasy rehearsal)

Courage

The first person is afraid to sled down a high hill. The second suggests he try by starting part way up. The first starts there, and gradually works his way up, and finally gets over being scared. (courage)

Two people get separated from each other, and they work to reunite with each other, while staying brave. (courage)

The first person is unrealistically afraid of something, and the second helps him get over the fear by being encouraging and supportive while the first gradually faces what he's afraid of. (courage)

The first person needs to get the second to help him on something. The first asks for help, and the second gives it. (depending)

The first person plays the part of a whole group of people who are being asked their opinions about something. They all give the same answer, and agree with each other. But the second person plays the part of the last person who is asked, who expresses a different opinion. (independent thinking)

Examples:

The two people pick the following play plot:

Two people are trying to take a message or some medicine or supplies or some other type of help to someone. The travel conditions are very bad. They have a strong sense of purpose that inspires them to push on. (purposefulness)

And here is the play that they act out:

First person: I wish those hikers hadn't gotten lost in the desert on such a hot day.

Second person: Right, and with us as the only two rescuers around. It must be a hundred and six degrees out today.

First person: Here, I'll douse you with water to help you cool off.

Second person: Thanks! That feels good! How about a little more right on my head?

First person: Like this?

Second person: Yes. Now you get to get some.

First person: Thanks! Hey, look out for that Gila monster starting to bite at your leg! (Pushes second person to safety.)

Second person: Thanks; I didn't see that little feller.

First person: These backpacks of water and fruit juice are heavy, aren't they?

Second person: They sure are. I hope we find them soon. Yodel-a-hee-hoo! Are you lost hikers out here?

First person: We've got to keep on going. Otherwise they could die.

Second person: Right, and I'm sure they have friends and family who are counting on us. We must push on.

First person: Look, there they are! Hey!

Hiker: Thank goodness you found us! We thought we would die of thirst.

Second person: So would you like orange juice, pineapple juice or water?

Hikers: Anything is fine! Thanks so much. Glug glug glug glug.

First person: We did it, partner. (They shake hands or give each other high fives.)

****

The two people pick the following play plot:

The first person can't figure out how to get a gadget turned on, and the second person knows and helps the first. (kindness)

They put on the following play:

First person: Darn it. I just don't see how you turn this computer on. It's supposed to be such a good one. But I can't get it on.

Second person: Excuse me, but would you like some help getting the computer on?

First person: Yes, please. I could use some.

Second person: Well, it's kind of strange. First you pick up the mouse with your feet and blow on it.

First person: You've got to be kidding! Oh well, I'll give it a try. Nope, it didn't come on.

Second person: Wait, I'm not through. Then you do a little dance, and while you're doing that, you pretend to sneeze.

First person: Are you just trying to make me look silly? Well here goes. Achoo!

Computer: Hello, and thank you for turning me on. My name is Hal. What can I do for you today?

First person: It worked! Thank you for helping me!

Second person: It was my pleasure!
***

Exercise 16: What's Best To Do

What is it?

This exercise presents a list of situations to the trainee, and the trainee practices saying and imagining what's best to do in those situations. This exercise is a way of practicing appropriate responses to situations. Everyone experiences recurring situations to which it's especially important to respond correctly. The list of situations should be tailored for each person's psychological skills priority list.

This exercise can be used for anyone of any age. The goal is to pick the situations that present the most important choice points. You also pick situations where there is one best answer and that answer is straightforward and unambiguous. If the answer to "What's the best thing to do?" is "It all depends," then probably the situation should be broken down into many more situations or used for a different exercise than this one (perhaps the one on brainstorming options).

A young adult who has fallen into trouble for responding angrily to criticism from his bosses might pose the question to himself "What's best to do when your boss criticizes you?" and then provide the answer for himself: "Listen carefully and seriously; reflect to make sure I got it right and then say, 'Thanks for the feedback; I'll try my best to use it." If the trainee is sure he wants to respond in this way, then he can use this exercise to drill on this response.

What's it for?

This exercise is a short and simple version of fantasy rehearsal. It takes advantage of the fact that when you rehearse doing something in your imagination, you are strengthening real-life situations. Simply verbalizing a response to a situation requires a certain degree of imagining the situation and imagining the response. Leaving out a lot of the elaboration described later in the full-blown fantasy rehearsal exercise enables this fantasy practice to progress in a quick and simple way.

How do you do it well?

The most important aspect of performing this exercise well is to figure out responses to the situations that actually are adaptive and beneficial. It is counterproductive to perform this exercise if the responses that are being rehearsed are not appropriate to the situation. Thus the trainer or other guides need to have the wisdom and life experience to help the trainee generate appropriate responses to situations. Or perhaps the trainee already has that wisdom when contemplating situations in moments of calm, and the trainee's primary task is transferring that wisdom into the real-life situation itself.

Another goal in performing this exercise is forming a vivid mental image of both the situation and the response. Like all use of fantasy rehearsal, it's also important to do it with high repetitions.

Variations:

For young children, the trainer can simply ask, "What should you do when _____ occurs?" When doing this exercise with young children, I like to take a toy person and move it along a game board series of rectangles and move the person forward one square each time the child makes an appropriate response. The exercise is over when the toy person reaches the last square.

For older people, the list of situations should be self-constructed, or jointly constructed, with the help of the trainer. The older the person is, the more it is useful for him to pose the question to himself, "What are the situations, the important choice points that I want to practice with?"

Once you've identified the situations, make a written list of them. Then the trainee can take out the list regularly and run through it, very quickly imagining the response she wants to make in the situation.

If the trainee can make a list of the most important recurring choice points for herself, decide upon a very good response to each of them, and use this exercise to practice those responses repeatedly, the benefit can be enormous.

Another variation on this exercise is to make a tape recording of the situations. Enough silent space is left for the person to imagine his response to each situation. In this way, the person can put the tape on and practice responding to the situations, hearing them presented rather than reading them.

Examples:

Here's a sample list constructed for a young child with high priority skills of social interaction and compliance and kindness.

Someone says "hi" to you. What should you do or say? (Say "hi" or "hello" etc., back to them.)

Someone gives you a present. What should you do or say? (Tell them, "Thank you.")

You find something that someone has lost. You are pretty sure you know who lost it. (Give it back.)

You want to ask to use a toy that belongs to someone else. What should you do? How should you ask for it? What word should you say? (Say, "May I use it please?")

Someone does something nice for you. What should you say? ("Thank you.")

You do something nice for someone else, and they say, "Thank you." What should you say back to them? ("You're welcome." Or "It's my pleasure," etc.)

You are leaving someone's house, where you've been playing, to go home.

What should you say to her before you leave? ("Thanks for having me over." Or "I had a good time." Or "It was good to see you.")

You are at a grocery store with your parent, and you see a friend of yours who goes to school with you. You pass very close to this person. What should you say to him or her? ("Hi," and say her name.)

Someone comes into your house to visit. What should you say to her when you first see her? ("Hi," or "Come in," or "Welcome," or "I'm glad to see you," or "Hello," etc.)

You spill your drink on the table. What should you say and do? ("I'm sorry I spilled that." Then you clean it up or help clean it up.)

You see someone who's carrying something very heavy with both hands walking toward a closed door. ("May I help you with the door?" Then hold the door open for him.)

You have been in a swimming pool, and your parent says to you, "It's time to get out now; we have to go." (Say, "OK." Then get out right away and go.)

You are playing with a friend. Another of your friends comes up to the two of you, to play with you. The person who comes up and the friend you were playing with don't know each other. (Introduce them to each other. Say something such as, "Mary, this is my friend John.")

Your parent takes you to school, and says goodbye. ("Thanks for taking

me to school. See you later. Have a nice day." And then you go inside.)

You are at school, and you have been playing with a certain toy for a long time. Someone else comes up and asks you, "May I see it?" ("Yes, I'll share it with you.")

You are not dressed yet. You are watching a videotape. All of the sudden your parent says, "Oh my goodness! I forgot that we have an appointment. If we don't hurry, we'll be late!" (Say, "OK." Turn off the videotape and get up and get dressed quickly.)

Someone offers you something that you would like to have. The person says, "Would you like some?" What should you say, if the answer is yes? ("Yes, please.")

Someone offers you something you wouldn't like to have. The person says, "Would you like some?" What should you say, if the answer is no? ("No, thank you.")

You are playing a game with someone, and you lose. (Say to the winner, "Congratulations! You won.")

You are playing a game with someone, and you win. ("Thanks for playing that game with me.")

Someone is over at your house, and you invite her to play a certain game. The person says, "No, I don't think I want to do that." (Say, "OK. We can do what you want to do.")

You accidentally bump a little child and the child falls over. What should you say and do? (Say, "I'm sorry. Are you all right?" Make sure the child isn't hurt. Perhaps help the child get up. If the child is hurt, tell a grown up.)

You are trying to get from one place to another, and someone else is in your way. If you want them to move, what should you say to them? ("Excuse me." Or, "Excuse me. Could I get past you?")

***

Here's a list constructed for college students with work block problems.

When you get a work assignment, what do you want to do? (Write it down on the to-do list. Schedule a time for it. Remind myself it's important to get it done, and that I can get it done.)

Suppose the time comes to get some work done, but it seems it would be very unpleasant. What do you want to say to yourself? (It will be much more pleasant for me in the long run if I do it now. It won't kill me. If I do it, I'll feel so good about myself.)

Suppose you find yourself saying to yourself, "I've already blown my chances of perfection, so there's no reason for me to do this work." (Every bit that I do makes my performance better. If I'm behind, I can try for a comeback. I'm not going to give up until the game is over.)

Suppose you do get started on the work and get even a little bit accomplished. What do you want to say to yourself? (Hooray for me. I've gotten going. I used self-discipline!)

Suppose you do part of the work in a way that is imperfect and not good enough to turn in. What do you want to say to yourself? (It's OK, I'm still making progress. It doesn't have to turn out perfect the first time. I can fix it up later.)

Suppose you finish the work, but you figure that somebody else probably did a better job than you did. What do you want to say to yourself? (I want to do it well enough to meet my goal. I don't need to be better than everyone else on this. If someone did a better job, that's to his credit; it doesn't take anything away from me.)

Suppose you receive some criticism on your work. What do you want to say to yourself? (Hey, maybe I can learn from this. Maybe I can use this information to do a better job next time. If the person's criticism is misguided, then I don't have to worry about it. It's not the end of the world. You can't please everybody!)

Suppose you get some praise on your work. What do you want to say to yourself? (Hooray, I got some praise! It feels good! I'm glad I did the work!)

Suppose other people ignore your work. What do you want to say to yourself? (I know I did it, and I can still congratulate myself, even if no one else congratulates me. I can be my own evaluator! Hooray for me that I did this!)

Exercise 17: Relaxation, Biofeedback or Meditation

What is it?

This refers to the use of a wide variety of techniques. What they share is taking a certain amount of time at regular intervals and attempting to turn down the level of arousal, relax muscles, and achieve a more relaxed state of mind.

There are several ways of doing this. One method focuses on tensing muscles or noticing the tension in muscles and then trying to relax that muscular tension. Another method involves imagining relaxing scenes, for example, scenes from nature. A similar method involves imagining scenes of kindness, warmth and closeness between people.

Another method includes meditation with a mantra–saying the word "one" or something else to yourself over and over while relaxing. In this technique, as well as various other techniques, one of the keys is assuming a passive attitude, letting whatever happens happen, not trying too hard to bring about any particular result. This means that when using a mantra, you should not try too hard to keep one's mind on the mantra!

Another relaxation strategy involves not trying to do anything with your mind, but simply observing what it seems to do by itself. A final strategy involves not even trying to do that, but simply resting, taking a break from whatever else is going on and letting your mind do whatever it wants.

All of these techniques involve sitting or lying down for five minutes or more. A different strategy involves trying to carry this over into real life by taking two or three seconds to relax briefly, many times during the day while you're the midst of other activities.

Biofeedback strategies often make the process of training oneself in relaxation more fun, interesting and focused. A useful parameter to measure is muscular tension via the electromyogram, or EMG. Other useful parameters are skin temperature and skin conductance. Biofeedback involves hooking yourself up to the machine and then engaging in a relaxation technique. Then you monitor the effect the technique is having on the parameter you are measuring. One of the big advantages of using these machines is that you can measure your progress in learning relaxation. If at the beginning, for instance, you could only get your muscle tension down to 4 microvolts, but then gradually you work your way down to under 1 microvolt, that's progress.

What's it for?

One of the main benefits of learning relaxation skills is attaining the ability to regulate the degree of your own emotions. The relaxation techniques allow you to turn down the degree of fear, anger and other negative emotions when they are interfering with your response to a situation. Relaxation strategies, if practiced thoroughly enough to achieve a high degree of expertise, can reduce the need for other methods of affect regulation, such as the use of sedative drugs and alcohol.

In addition, relaxation strategies can alleviate a number of physical problems, including bruxism (teeth clenching or grinding) and headaches, both tension and migraine.

The art of relaxing oneself and turning down negative emotions is particularly useful in interpersonal relationships. Injecting calmness and rationality into discussions of interpersonal issues can be extremely beneficial.

How do you do it well?

The main challenge in doing relaxation exercises well is doing them at all. Many people who could benefit from these exercises simply can't find the time to stop and practice relaxing. So any of the previously mentioned techniques the person finds palatable enough to do regularly should be adopted.

Here are a few tips for trainer and trainee in learning to relax the forehead muscles using EMG biofeedback. First, it is useful to begin with the forearm muscles because these are considerably easier to relax than those of the forehead. By tensing and relaxing the forearm muscles, you can get a taste of what it feels like to be successful in relaxing.

After this, you can address the more difficult task of relaxing the muscles of the face.

I work with an Autogenics EMG machine on which you can set the threshold at various levels of tension. Any reading below that level of tension will result in pleasant piano tones being produced. When working with a trainee, I first set the threshold at the point where he is relaxing just enough to elicit the tones. Then I gradually lower the threshold to see whether the trainee can deepen his relaxation further and thus produce the tones.

Another technique is to activate an averaging function on the biofeedback device, let the trainee relax as much as possible for about thirty seconds, and then see what the average tension was during that time. Then, on succeeding trials, you can see if the trainee can break his previous record . For most people, keeping the average reading under one microvolt for thirty seconds represents a standard of relaxation that is both stringent yet attainable.

For those who have trouble attaining this level of relaxation, however, it is usually not enough to simply practice it in biofeedback sessions. It is usually necessary to practice relaxation much more frequently by simply tensing and trying to relax the muscles in the head and face and neck as much as possible.

One way of learning to relax the muscles of the head, face and neck is to practice tensing them in pulses or bursts, one after the other, as if you were exercising these muscles. You can tighten and release and tighten and release these muscles in several ways: lifting your forehead up, pushing your eyebrows down, clenching your teeth, wrinkling your nose. You should do this rapidly for an extended period of time until you begin to feel some fatigue in the muscles of the face, head and neck. Then, when you feel that fatigue, you pretend that you are tired and that the muscles need to rest. You let them relax as thoroughly as possible. I have seen a number of people attain new lows on their EMG records when they used this technique.

I believe that some aerobic exercise, such as running, walking, or riding a bicycle before relaxation makes the relaxation task much easier. One of the reasons relaxation is so difficult for so many people in today's society is that they aren't getting enough exercise, and their bodies are really telling them to be more active.

Several audiotapes, including one I produced, take people through relaxation instructions, step by step. Some people have benefited by listening to such tapes at bedtime as they are falling asleep.

It's important not to practice relaxation only in times of headache or anxiety. It is theoretically possible to build up a conditioned association between the relaxation techniques and the negative feelings occurring at these moments. Thus, it's important to perform relaxation exercises during times when conditions are beneficial for relaxation.

Variations:

One variation of relaxation strategy is temperature biofeedback. Temperature biofeedback machines are better known as thermometers. They are much less expensive than EMG machines. You can buy an indoor-outdoor thermometer, switch it to the outdoor reading, and hold the probe between your thumb and finger, to get a reasonably accurate reading of fingertip temperature. If the temperature in the room is about 72 to 74 degrees, then the temperature of the fingertips is, to some degree, a measure of relaxation. Getting into a higher state of relaxation usually makes your skin temperature go up. Some people can raise their fingertip temperature above 95 degrees Fahrenheit.

The techniques for raising skin temperature are in many ways similar to those for muscular relaxation. In addition, I find it useful to imagine the blood vessels in the hands opening and providing lots of blood to the hands as the hands warm.

Skin conductance response (also known as galvanic skin resistance) is another parameter that is useful and interesting to measure. For many people, this is a very sensitive measure of emotional arousal.

Here's a very important variation on relaxation practice. You first practice relaxation generally. Then you try to attain a relaxed state while imagining a stressful situation. For example, someone with test anxiety first masters muscle relaxation. Then she imagines herself in the test situation, while still keeping the muscles relaxed.

Another variation on this strategy involves not trying to do two things at once. You first relax, then fantasy the stressful scene, and then go back to relaxing. You continue alternating between the two. If you can return to relaxation anytime you want to after experiencing the stress, that is almost as good or perhaps even better than experiencing the situation without getting a high degree of arousal in the first place. (Why sometimes better? Because sometimes the high arousal is useful.)

This technique of practicing relaxation and alternating this with fantasizing a stressful situation is known as systematic desensitization. The other ingredient of systematic desensitization is measuring the "subjective units of distress" that the fantasy of the stressful situation brings about and then gradually seeing if you can reduce those "SUD" units through repeated practice.

Here's an important variation for busy people (the ones who need relaxation training because they never relax, but who can't make themselves take twenty minutes off for a relaxation practice session)! In this variation, you don't set aside large blocks of time for relaxing. Instead, for about three seconds once or twice every hour, you try to relax your muscles, especially those of the jaws, head, neck and face, and assume a calm attitude. One option is to set an electronic watch so that a quiet beep goes off every hour; that beep can be the cue to spend three seconds relaxing.

Another variation you might enjoy is to listen to an audiotape of relaxation instructions. The script that follows is a compilation of relaxation suggestions that I composed. Many other people have made such tapes. You can obtain a tape of me reading the following script, or you can read it into a tape recorder yourself. Then you simply sit and listen and try to follow the suggestions. In one variation, you do this while lying in bed drifting off to sleep; in another, you do this while sitting in a chair, not falling asleep.

Here is the script.
***

The ability to relax your body and your mind, whenever you want to, is a skill that is very useful in many different ways. It allows you to calm yourself so that you can think better. It makes it easier to go to sleep. It lets you undo any tension in muscles that would be uncomfortable or painful. It has been found helpful in preventing several physical problems, including headaches and certain types of stomachaches. It gives you practice in controlling your own mood. It allows you to get rid of restlessness. It allows you to better handle and enjoy being by yourself. It is very useful in reducing fearfulness, when you want to do that. It can prepare you for getting good and thoughtful ideas. It helps you in resolving conflicts with other people that come up. It is a skill that is worth working on for a very long time if that's what it takes to master it.

One of the most important ways of relaxing is to notice any tension in your muscles, and to reduce that tension, and let your muscles stop pulling. As you sit or lie down comfortably, it often feels pleasant to let your muscles relax themselves. The more relaxed your muscles are, the more your mind will tend to drift in ways that are calm and peaceful also.

Here is one way that you can practice relaxation of your muscles. You can think about the different muscles of your body, and go through the different muscle groups one by one. You can notice the tension that is already in the muscles, or you can tense those muscles just a little bit. Then you make that tension go away, as totally as possible. If you can notice the difference between full relaxation and even a very small amount of tension in a muscle, you have a very important skill. Because as long as you can notice tension, and even make tension greater, you have the power to make that tension go away. All you have to do to produce relaxation is the opposite of what you do to create tension. When you let off the tension, you let the muscles get very loose and relaxed. You do this for all the muscle groups in the body. You notice what

happens when you relax muscles. You feel the difference that happens when you relax. When you've done this enough times, you'll know very well how to tense and relax all the muscles of your body.

You will not have to tense the muscles at all hard, but only very lightly, or maybe not at all, to feel the difference that happens when you relax the muscles.

You might start with gripping your hands into fists, not hard, but very lightly. Even if you do it very lightly, you can feel a tension in the muscles of your forearms and hands. Once you feel that tension, you can let it off, and let your forearms relax and get very loose. Pay attention to the feeling of relaxation, and how it is different from the feeling of tension.

You might next make your upper arms a little tense by trying to make a muscle as though you were going to feel the muscle in your upper arms. You do this by pulling so as to bend your arm at the elbow, but at the same time trying to straighten out your arm. Feel the tension in your upper arm muscles. Then you can let off the tension and let those muscles get loose and relaxed.

You might next make your shoulders a little tense by starting to shrug your shoulders a little, the way people do when they say, "I don't know." Then you relax those shoulder muscles.

If someone wants to make their neck muscles tense, they try to pull their head forward, and at the same time pull it back, so that the muscles are pulling against each other. Then when they feel that tension, they can relax those muscles, and let those muscles be very calm.

If someone wants to tense the muscles that are at the side of the face, the jaw muscles, they do it by biting so as to clench the teeth together, while at the same time trying to open the mouth. This produces tension in the jaw muscles, the muscles on the side of the head, and the muscles on the upper part of the neck. Then you can relax those muscles by letting your jaw relax. When you do this usually your jaw will be hanging open just a tiny bit.

If you want to tense the muscles of the upper part of your face, you lift your eyebrows and at the same time try to push your eyebrows down. Then when you feel that tension, ever so slightly, you can let it off.

If you want to tense the muscles of the lower part of your face, you push your lips together a little bit, and pull the corners of your mouth back as though you were smiling, and at the same time you try to purse your lips back as though you were trying to whistle. Then you let all that tension off, and you feel the relaxation of the muscles of the lower part of your face.

Many people find that relaxing the muscles of their face and jaws and neck is just what makes them feel the most calm and peaceful. You might try it if you want to, thinking about the muscles of your jaws, your upper face, your lower face, and your neck.

Some people like to think about their breathing as they are relaxing, and let their muscles get a little more relaxed each time they breathe out. So the rhythm is: Breathe in, relax out. Breathe in, relax out.

Now you might experiment with how to make the muscles tight in your back. If you try to arch your back like you are bending backwards, you can tense the long muscles that run down your back. Then when you feel that tension, you can let it off. If you pull your shoulders back, you can feel tension in the muscles in the upper part of your back, and then let that tension off.

You can also experiment with tensing and relaxing the muscles of your chest and your abdomen, or belly. To tense those of your chest, pull your arms as if you are going to clap your hands together, then relax that tension. To tense the muscles of your abdomen, if you are lying on your back, pretend that you want to sit up, and feel just a little tension in those muscles. Then you can let them off. Or if you are sitting in a chair, you can tense your belly and back muscles by trying to lean forward, while at the same time trying to lean backward. When you feel that tension, let it off, and as always, pay attention to the different degrees of tension and relaxation that you are feeling.

You can make the muscles in your upper legs tense by trying to bend the leg at the knee and trying to straighten it out at the same time. Then you can let off that tension, so that your upper legs are very relaxed. You can tense your lower legs by trying to push your toes down and trying to pull your toes up at the same time. Then you can let off that tension too, so that your lower legs are relaxed.

There are many muscles in the body, including some I didn't mention. It can be fun to experiment with finding out how it is that you make a certain muscle tense. Over time, you will become very much able to tense or relax any muscle in the body any time you want to.

After you go through and actually practice tensing and relaxing your muscles, you can just let your attention go first to one muscle group and then another, seeing if you can make that muscle group any more relaxed and loose and limp than it already is.

You might want to think about your breathing again, and feel the air going in and out, and each time you breathe out, feel some part of your body getting just a little more relaxed than it was before.

The skill of getting your muscles relaxed is one that will be very useful to you, for the rest of your life. It's one that people can gradually improve at over time, simply by noticing what sort of effort tends to tense what muscles, and what sort of relaxation of that effort relaxes those muscles. You will start to find which particular muscles are the most important ones for you.

Relaxing your muscles is only a part of the interesting and pleasant things you can do while you are relaxing.

Another very useful way of relaxing is to practice imagining beautiful and relaxing scenes, nice and pleasant places to be. You may want to think of the following scenes, briefly, when I mention them, and then come back to them later when the tape stops and imagine them more thoroughly. Different scenes are relaxing for different people. How does it feel when you imagine a beautiful sunset? How does it feel to imagine the sound of wind gently blowing among the tree leaves? How about the image of a bunch of beautiful flowers? How about the sight and the sound of a waterfall? How about listening to rain fall on a roof? How about imagining waves rolling in where you are relaxing on a beach? Or the image of how you feel just as you are awakening on a morning where there are no responsibilities you have to carry out? Or the image of sitting in a cool room, with a warm blanket around you, looking at a fire burn in a fireplace? Or what's it like to imagine yourself drinking cool water when you are very thirsty? Or watching snow drifting slowly to the ground? Or can you imagine a rag doll, and imagine that your body is that loose and relaxed? What's it like to imagine watching white clouds drifting by on a day in the spring? Or can you just become conscious of the chair or the bed that is holding you up, and feel yourself being held?

Sometimes the most relaxing images are not just of places, but of people, and people acting kind and gentle and loving and giving with one another. These images let people feel peaceful and relaxed.

You can imagine stories of people's being kind. For example you may want to imagine that someone is searching for something, and someone else in a very calm and kind way helps that person find it. When they find it, the people feel good about each other. If you want you can fill in your own details about where they are, what is being searched for, where they look, and what it looks like when they find it. You can do this in a different way every time if you want, or the same way every time you do it, or sometimes one way and sometimes another. You are in control of your own imagination and you can lead yourself wherever you choose.

Or you may imagine that someone leads someone else on a very interesting and pleasant journey, showing that person something that is very fun or interesting to see. If you want you can imagine your own details, about where the first person takes the second, what sorts of things they see and experience. You can imagine the faces of the first person as that person enjoys what they are doing, and the face of the other person feeling good about giving the other a pleasant experience.

Or you may imagine that someone teaches someone else something that person really wants to know. The teacher is very kind and patient. The teacher wants to let the learner learn at his own pace, and does not rush him. The learner is very grateful to the teacher. The teacher is also grateful to the learner. The teacher and realizes that someone who allows you to teach them something is giving a nice gift, a pleasant memory that the teacher will have for a lifetime. You can fill in your own details of where they are, what is being learned, and how they are learning it.

Or you may imagine that someone helps someone with a job of some sort. As you do it, imagine that the two people feel very good about one another. You can see and hear what they are doing together and what sort of words they are saying to each other, if they are saying anything.

Or you may imagine that people are being kind and loving to each other by playing together. They know in the backs of their minds that the most important thing when they are playing with each other is to be kind and caring with each other. They each take pleasure whenever they can see that they have helped the other feel good. If you want to let a story about this come to your mind, you can imagine where they are and what or how they are playing and what they are saying with each other.

Or you may imagine people showing their love and caring about each other by noticing and commenting on the other person's good acts or accomplishments. You can imagine that people rejoice and feel good when their friends and loved ones have successes. If you want you can imagine exactly what someone is doing and how someone else feels good about it, and how that person lets the other person know his pleasure.

Or you may imagine people sharing things with each other, making it so that there is enough to go around. You can imagine whether they are taking turns with some toy or tool they want to use, or whether they are sharing something to eat or drink, or someone else's attention and time, or something else.

Or, you may imagine one person showing love and caring for another by being a good listener when the other speaks. As one person tells thoughts and feelings, the other very patiently tries to be understanding.

Some people enjoy recalling the things they have done in real life that they are glad they have done. Some people like to think back about the kind things they have done for other people, or the work that they have done to educate themselves and make themselves better or the work they have done to make the world a better place, or the times that they have lived joyously, or the times that they have made good decisions and carried them out. They may want to celebrate the times that they have been honest, or the times that they have been strong and brave.

Some people enjoy thinking about the ways in which they are blessed, and feeling gratitude for those. If they are able to have any material things that make life easier, if they are able to eat and drink so that they do not have to be hungry and thirsty, if they have someone who can take care of them when they need it and be of support to them, if they have friends or loved ones that they can care for and support, they may want to feel gratitude for these blessings.

You can let your mind drift, and think about any stories or images of these things that you want to. You are perfectly free to let your mind drift in any way that you choose. Sometimes people enjoy not choosing, but simply letting the mind drift wherever it wants to go, and observing what happens.

In fact sometimes it's a very pleasant experience just to imagine that your mind is a blank screen, and to simply wait and see what comes on it, and to observe it with interest and curiosity, not trying to control it in any way. You can practice relaxing your muscles, imagining relaxing scenes, thinking of stories of people being kind to each other, or you can simply let your mind drift and see where it takes you. Or you can let your mind drift and not observe it, but simply rest. You can guide your own experience to make it pleasant, relaxing, peaceful, and enjoyable to you. As you do so you have reason to celebrate practicing such an important skill.

Exercise 18: Brainstorming Options

What is it?

In this exercise you pose to yourself a real or hypothetical life problem and then generate options for solving it. I divide these choice points into individual and joint decisions. For individual decisions, you generate options that one person could unilaterally take. In joint decisions, you generate options that two people could possibly agree upon.

This exercise seeks to separate the option-generating process from everything else involved in decision-making and conflict resolution. You simply list as many good options as you can.

There is a lot of subjectivity involved in deciding what a "good" option is. Similarly, it's a subjective decision whether one option is sufficiently different from another to be counted as a separate one. Thus, anyone trying to quantify how well a person or group of people did in generating options faces a tough task. One answer to this problem is to compare the list of options generated with a list of good options someone else has generated, and to give yourself a point for every one of the other person's options you also devised. This doesn't mean the other person has thought of all the good options. If the other person has simply generated several good options, then as a rule the more useful options you produce, the more overlap you'll have with the standard list.

It's for this reason that I've generated many options for the solution of several individual and joint-choice points. These are contained in a volume called *Options and Consequences*. You can refer to this volume if you use the "comparison to a standard list" method of measuring how well someone listed options.

Another alternative is for the trainer and trainee to decide together, or for the trainer alone to decide, what is a good option and what is a new option. Using this method, all you need to do is generate some problems on the spot rather than referring to the larger volume. But it may still be interesting to compare your list with one that someone else has generated.

What's it for?

Life is a series of choice points, and how well we live our lives depends on the quality of the choices we make at those choice points. It's impossible to choose and enact a very good option if the option never occurs to you. So, the point of this exercise is to increase one's ability to think of good responses to situations. Substantial research supports the idea that this ability is correlated with mental health.

How do you do it well?

A standard I have used in this exercise is to ask the trainee to generate at least seven options, of which at least three are options listed in the book, *Options and Consequences*.

To become proficient at this exercise, generate as many options as you can and then compare your list with the list in the book. The tendency of many trainees is to want to go on to something else too quickly rather than spending time reading or hearing the choices they didn't think of.

Another psychological skills exercise is called the Return to the Center exercise. In it, you pose a question and keep returning to it; you try to keep coming up with more answers to it, even when you think you've come up with everything you can. The Brainstorming Options Exercise can be a special case of the "Return to the Center" exercise. If it is used in this way, it is important to help the trainee realize that this is a concentration exercise–that you are stretching your muscles of concentration by continuing to dig for more answers to the question, even when you feel as if you've come up with all you can.

I've often used the analogy that, in body building or strength training, it's the last few repetitions, when your muscles have been pushed to the limits of ability, that cause further muscular development. In the same way, pushing for those last few options you didn't think you could generate really stretches the option-generating capacity.

Variations:

A competitive version of this game mimics the board game "Outburst." There are two teams; it is more fun if each of the teams has two players. The teams take turn drawing a problem in the *Options and Consequences* book. Each team generates as many options as they can in two minutes, while the other team keeps track of which options they generate. The teams earn a point for each option they think of that is included in the list in the book. The side with the most points at the end of the game wins.

Here's a cooperative game. The trainer and the trainee cooperate so as to compete against "Mr. X." The trainer and trainee take turns generating options. The options must be reasonable and good. If they can generate eight or more reasonable options, their team has beaten Mr. X on that round; if they can't, Mr. X has won that round. The one who has won the most rounds at the end of the game has won. The criterion of eight reasonable options as the threshold for beating Mr. X can be raised or lowered depending upon the skill level of the trainee.

Another variation that directs the learner's attention to options he may not have thought of is as follows: First, the learner generates as many options as possible. Then, the learner listens to the options in the book and rates each of them on a scale where 10 is best and 0 is worst.

Examples:

Below are a few samples from Options and Consequences. Following these, there are some problems to generate options for, without options listed.

Individual decision: Someone wants to get into better shape and be stronger. How can this person do this?

1. Lift weights.

2. Do pushups and situps and pullups and other strength exercises that don't require weights.

3. Go to a gym and work with weight machines.

4. Play sports that create a lot of exercise. (Each is a separate option: soccer, basketball, track, swimming, etc.)

5. Do isometric exercises whenever there is a spare moment: for example push the hands against each other.

6. Run a lot.

7. Swim laps.

8. Jump rope.

9. Walk or run on a treadmill.

10. Use an exercise bike.

11. Use a real bike.

12. Do aerobics. (Separate options: in a class, watching a tape, by yourself, with a friend)

13. Do a type of dancing that gives a lot of exercise: (Each is a separate option, e.g.,. tap, ballroom, ballet, modern)

14. Get a personal trainer and follow that person's advice.

15. Read books about how to get strong and in shape and follow the advice there.

16. Eat a good diet with lots of fruits and vegetables and whole grains and enough protein and not too much fat and sugar.

17. Do useful work that provides exercise, like construction work, moving, lifting garbage, walking fast while delivering mail, etc. (Each is a separate option.)

18. Walk to near destinations rather than driving or taking a bus.

19. Skate.

****

Individual decision: Someone cuts his finger.

1. If it's bleeding badly, press on where it's bleeding to get the bleeding to stop.

2. Wash it off with water.

3. Clean it off with a wet wipe (especially if there's no clean water).

4. Clean it off with a tissue.

5. Ask someone else to help with it.

6. Go to the hospital.

7. Go to a doctor's office.

8. Don't do anything about it.

9. Put a bandage on it.

10. Put some ointment on it.

11. If you are a surgeon and it needs stitches, try to sew it up yourself.

12. Put some antiseptic on it.

13. Get a tetanus shot.

14. Plan not to use the knife in the same way again, if it was a knife.

15. Plan not to hold the can top in the same way again, if it was a can top. (and so on, with each a separate option).

16. Rehearse in your imagination now to be more careful the next time.

****

Individual decision: You want play checkers. The checkerboard is there, but a couple of the checkers are missing, so that you don't have enough to set up the board.

1. Get some coins and use them instead of checkers, for example pennies for black and nickels for white.

2. Use coins just to replace the missing checkers, and when a couple of men get taken, you will be able to play with real checkers instead of the coins.

3. Use different types of beans instead of checkers,

4. Use paper clips and safety pins,

5. Use pieces of paper,

6. Use pieces of candy,

7. Use poker chips or any other types of pieces from another game.

8. You could look for the missing checkers.

9. You could not play checkers, but do something else instead.

10. You could go to the store and get a new set of checkers.

11. You could play checkers on a computer, if you have the computer and the software.

12. You could try playing without any pieces, but just writing down the moves and remembering how the checkerboard would look.

****

Individual decision: You have some work every day that seems boring to you, and you're having a hard time getting yourself to sit down and do it.

1. You can make up some reward for yourself that you will receive only when you have done the work. For example, you have a very interesting game that you want to play with, but you allow yourself to play with it only when the work is done.

2. You can make a routine to sit down and do it at the same time each day, so that the habit of doing it will help you get started.

3. You can get together with someone else who is a very serious worker, and help each other get psyched up to do the work, and do it together.

4. You can make up a penalty that you impose on yourself if you don't get the work done by a certain time. For example, if you don't do it one day, you don't get to eat anything sweet the next day.

5. You can get into the habit of congratulating yourself while you are doing the work, by saying things to yourself like, "Hooray for you! You're using self-discipline!"

6. You can arrange a reward or a penalty, not just with yourself, but with a friend or relative. For example, you make a deal that you will get some money each day if you have complete a task by a certain time and that you will pay money if you haven't completed it.

7. You make a list of all the reasons why you want to get this work done and all the advantages of having it done, and you post this list where you can see it and read it and think about it often.

8. If you try to make a list of all the reasons you want to get it done, and you can't come up with any good reasons, then another option may be to drop whatever project you are working on, if you have the freedom to.

****

Joint decision: One person in a family likes to listen to a certain type of music. The other hates it.

1. The person who likes it could use some earphones attached to the music player.

2. The person who likes it could listen to it only on a Walkman.

3. The person who likes it could play it quietly and get closer to the speaker to hear it.

4. The person who hates it could gradually try to acquire a taste for it.

5. The person who hates it could put up with it in return for the other person's doing something really nice for him.

6. The person who likes it could listen to it at someone else's house.

7. The person who hates it could use ear plugs.

8. They could try to find some music they both like.

9. The people can close the doors that separate them if they are not closed already.

10. The person who likes it could play it when the other is out.
****

Joint decision: Pat and Lee live together. Pat's favorite food is a dish made of fish and sauerkraut. When Pat cooks it, it makes a smell all through the house that Lee thinks is horrible.

1. Pat could cook the dish on an outdoor grill.

2. Pat could get a big fan that would pull the smelly air out of the house.

3. Pat could cook the dish only when Lee is going to be out of the house for long enough that the smell has time to go away by the time Lee gets back.

4. Pat could try to find a neighbor who really likes it and go over to that person's house to cook it and eat it together.

5. Pat could find a restaurant that makes the dish, and go out and order it there.

6. Pat could go ahead and cook it and Lee could put up with it, and in return Pat could do something nice for Lee.

7. Pat could not cook it any more, and in return Lee could do something nice for Pat.

8. Pat could try putting it in an airtight container and cooking it in a microwave oven, and see if that works in making it smell less strongl.

9. Pat could cook up a whole bunch of it and freeze it in little packets, and then heat up each frozen packet in an air-tight container in a microwave.

10. Lee could try to gradually get used to the smell.

11. Lee could go to a different part of the house, if the house is big enough.

12. Lee could use nose plugs.

****

Joint decision: A person agrees to give a speech for an organization before an audience of 200 people. The time of the speech is planned several months in advance. Just three days before the speech is scheduled, the speaker's mother gets very sick, in a town far from the site of the speech, and the speaker wants to look after her rather than give the speech. The organization people want to have their speech.

1. The speaker could find someone else to do a speech.

2. The people in the organization could find someone else to do the speech.

3. The speaker could write out the speech word for word and get someone else who is a good speaker to go and deliver the speech.

4. The speaker could make a video of himself giving the speech, and the organization could show it.

5. The speaker could find someone else, maybe a brother or sister if the speaker has any, to look after the mother for the three days until he can go to his mother.

6. The organization could postpone the meeting to a later time.

7. The organization could do something else at the meeting than have a speech -they could show a video on the same topic.

8. The organization could do something else at the meeting other than have a speech–they could have discussion groups on the topic.

9. The speaker could deliver the speech by teleconferencing.

More Problems for Listing Options

Individual decisions:

1. A person is very slow at adding, subtracting, multiplying and dividing. This causes the person to do poorly on tests in a math course he's taking, even though he understands the math as well as other people do.

2. A person wants to lose fifteen pounds but wonders how to do it.

3. A woman gets married to a man she doesn't know well. After she is married, she discovers that her husband drinks too much and yells abusive things at her and hits her.

4. A man finds that his family does not have enough money to save anything. This produces a lot of stress and worrying about whether bills can be paid.

5. A person is trying to keep from getting sunburned. But even when she uses sunscreen, she still gets burned a little when she is outside much of the day.

6. A doctor goes to work for a clinic. Because the business people who run the clinic ask her to see so many people for so short a time and so infrequently, she can't give care to her patients in the way she thinks is right.

7. A person finds that his mood is irritable and low too much of the time.

8. A person wants her computer program to do something, but she can't get it to work right.

9. A person wins a lottery, and now has so much money that she is not sure what to do with it.

10. A woman wants to work so she can make a big contribution to the world and do interesting things. But her children seem to behave much better when she spends more time with them.

Joint decisions:

1. One person in a family wants the family to buy only organic food, because that person is worried about the effects of pesticides on people's bodies. The other person thinks this is expensive and inconvenient.

2. Two parents have a baby. One thinks the baby will become a more well-adjusted person if they go to her and comfort her whenever she cries. The other thinks it's best sometimes best to let the baby cry herself to sleep at night so the parents can get their own sleep.

3. One person in a family wants to spend a vacation in Las Vegas having some fun in gambling casinos. The other person feels that this is a decadent waste of money and that the money should be given to charitable organizations instead.

4. A boss at a furniture factory thinks that it's very important to build lots of furniture quickly. The head of the workers' group thinks the boss should allow more time so that the workers can take pride in doing their jobs very well rather than rushing to

make furniture that might be second-rate.

5. One person in a couple wants to be a social drinker of alcohol. The other person thinks that, because alcohol causes so many problems in society, they should be models for their children and other people by not drinking it at all.

6. One person in a couple wants to keep a gun in the house in case of entry by a robber or kidnapper. The other person feels that this creates more dangers than it solves.

7. One member of a couple believes they should not use the family's money to finance slaughterhouses, where cruelty to animals prevails. So this person feels that the family should become vegetarian. The other family member has always enjoyed eating meat and wants to continue to do so.

8. Two children like to have sleep-overs with each other. But when they do so, one wants to go to sleep early, whereas the other likes to stay up very late.

9. A boss likes to have prayer meetings each morning with any of his workers who want to join in. One of the workers, who is an atheist, feels that the boss should not do this, because this favors workers who agree with the boss's religion.

10. One of two sisters often thinks up fun things to do with their father, such as little gymnastic moves. Almost every time this happens, the other sister says, "Can I have a turn?" The first sister wants to keep doing what she thought up without having to be interrupted by her sister.

Exercise 19: Brainstorming Consequences

What is it?

This exercise is very similar to that of Brainstorming Options. The difference is that, rather than thinking of possible options of things to do, you think of possible consequences that could result from a particular action. A section in this volume lists several possible actions and several possible consequences.

As with the options exercise, you can contrast the consequences the trainee generates with the list in the book, *Options and Consequences*. You can measure skill in generating consequences by seeing how many of those in the book were mentioned by the trainee. For challenges, you can use the same criterion–thinking of at least seven reasonable consequences, three of which are in the book.

You can play the types of games I listed in the section on brainstorming options: the Outburst-like game and the cooperative game against Mr. X, where you take turns and generate a certain number of ideas to beat Mr. X for the round. As with formulating options, you can let the trainee devise her own actions from life experience, list the consequences and add these to the storehouse in the book.

What is it for?

Brainstorming Consequences, like Brainstorming Options, is an antidote to impulsive actions. Carefully considering the consequences of options most under consideration is a mental maneuver basic to the careful decision-making process. Accurately predicting the consequences of actions obviously helps you in deciding whether or not to take those actions.

How do you do it well?

The trainee in this exercise thinks creatively of many consequences that could possibly occur but does not waste time listing consequences that are unlikely to occur.

The answers given in *Options and Consequences* are meant to be a model of performing this exercise well.

Like the Brainstorming Options exercise, the trainee will reach a point where he feels he has run out of ideas; it is usually possible to generate more after that point, and doing so provides a good concentration exercise.

Variations:

The same variations that we mentioned with the Brainstorming Options can be used with the Brainstorming Consequences exercise. The most useful variation occurs when the trainee takes actions from his own life, adds them to the list, and then lists consequences for these actions.

Examples:

Below are some sample actions and consequences.

Action: Someone is going to a party. Before going, she spills food on her shirt, and it makes a big stain. She considers just going ahead to the party anyway, without changing clothes.

1. The people at the party might think that she's a sloppy person and like her less.

2. The people at the party might thinking nothing of it, and it could have no consequence.

3. Some people at the party could think bad things about her, and others might not.

4. Someone at the party might not notice the stain until she had been there for a while, and might think she spilled food on her there. That person might offer to help her get it off.

5. Depending on what the food is, it could start to smell bad after a while, and this might turn off people she sees at the party.

6. Depending on what the food is, it could irritate her skin after a while.

7. The stain could be harder to get out later, as opposed to washing it out before it sets.

8. Someone at the party might accidentally spill more on her, and she would be glad that she just dirtied one shirt rather than two.

9. If this is the only nice shirt she has, even with the stain, it might look better than whatever she has as the alternative.

10. She might feel embarrassed if people looked at the stain or talked about it.

11. If she went into a bathroom and washed it out, she might have a wet spot instead of a food stain.

12. The person who gave the party could feel hurt, thinking, "She doesn't care enough about me to wear clean clothes to my party."

****

Action: A father is planning to pay the fee for a 12-year-old boy to take a course in typing/keyboarding at school during the summer. The boy considers asking his father to give the fee to him, instead of the school, if the he can teach himself this skill. The boy considers using a book to teach himself and proposing the money be given to him only if he can pass a test on typing at a certain speed and accuracy by a certain time.

1. The father could say no.

2. The father could agree. Trying to learn it on his own, the boy might put off working and never get around to gaining the skills he wants.

3. If the boy tries doing this and fails, he might figure out how to use self-discipline when teaching himself things, and eventually succeed.

4. If the boy tries doing this and succeeds, he might have an experience that makes him more likely to try teaching himself other things later on.

5. If the boy tries doing this and succeeds, the boy will be able to write much faster than before.

6. If the boy succeeds, he will be able to do some homework assignments a lot faster.

7. If this experience starts the boy off on becoming really good at teaching himself things, he might save more money in the future by teaching himself subjects from books rather than having to take courses.

8. If the boy becomes good at teaching himself things, he might teach himself some other things in the future that would do a lot of good for other people or himself.

9. The boy might miss out on meeting some friends he would like in the summer course.

10. The boy might learn some very useful skills in tolerating being alone by doing the course on his own rather than being with other people.

11. The boy would miss out on developing some useful socializing skills by doing the course alone rather than with other people.

12. By doing the course at home rather than at school, the boy would spend less time going back and forth to school.

13. If the boy did less traveling on the road, he would lower his risk of being in a traffic accident.

14. If the boy did less traveling, he would have more time to spend in other ways.

*****

Action: A 15-year-old girl is overweight. She considers the following plan: writing down what she eats, looking up the number of calories, adding the calories up as she goes, and stopping eating for the day when she reaches the number of calories a book says will enable her to lose about a pound a week. The plan includes eating lots of vegetables, fruits, and grains, making sure she eats some protein foods, and exercising for at least 30 minutes a day.

1. While she is on this diet she probably wouldn't feel very hungry and deprived and uncomfortable because the amount of weight she is trying to lose per week is not enough to require starving herself.

2. She might be able to follow this plan for long enough to lose the weight.

3. She might find it's too much work writing down what she eats, and she might go off the plan.

4. If she sticks with the plan, she might be able to change it just enough so she can keep off the weight once she has lost it.

5. People who see her trying to use this plan might feel she has generated some smart ideas.

6. People who see her writing down what she eats and looking up how many calories might ask her what she is doing.

7. If she does lose the weight, she might feel good about her accomplishment.

8. If she does lose the weight, she might feel more attractive.

9. If she does lose the weight, more boys her age might be interested in dating her.

10. By exercising 30 minutes a day she would get in better shape.

11. By exercising, she might get better at sports.

12. She might get so interested in sports that she earns a sports scholarship to college.

13. She might learn some self-discipline techniques that would help her accomplish other goals in her life.

14. By exercising, she might injure herself.

15. Dealing with the numbers of calories so often might make her better at mathematics.

16. Getting in the habit of following this type of diet and exercise program might prevent a heart attack or a stroke.

17. Such habits of eating and exercising might help her live longer.

18. She could become so preoccupied with her weight and appearance that she neglects other goals more worthy of her effort.

*****

Some more actions, without consequences listed

1. A person thinks up an idea for a new type of business. She has enough money saved up to live on for one year. She considers quitting her job and working on her new idea for a year.

2. A person is not getting along with a spouse. The person considers getting a divorce.

3. A lawmaker considers a law that puts a big tax on gasoline, to discourage people from using so much of it.

4. A person is at a party, and someone offers him a pill to take. "It will make you feel really good," the person says.

5. A couple consider eliminating television from their home.

6. There is a child at school who gets teased and bullied a lot. Another child considers joining in the bullying, because the child being bullied isn't very nice at all.

7. A person doesn't like his nickname at school. When someone calls him that nickname, he considers saying, in a very exasperated tone, "Don't call me that!"

8. A person has an illness. A friend has some medicine. The friend says, "I have some extra medicine. Why don't you try it? It might work for you."

9. A person finds school pretty easy, even without doing homework. The person considers doing a couple of hours of homework each night, working toward teaching himself things that aren't even assigned in school.

10. A person isn't getting along well with her stepdad. She considers trying to avoid him and stay away from him as much as possible.

Exercise 20: Advantages and Disadvantages

What is it?

This is very much like the Consequences Exercise. The trainee is given a situation and a possible action in response to that situation. The trainee's job is to list advantages and possible disadvantages for that action. You can use the actions in the *Options and Consequences* book or come up with your own hypothetical actions.

What's it for?

This is a basic exercise for decision-making skills.

How do you do it well?

The goal of this exercise is not to generate as extensive a list as possible, as in the options and consequences exercise, but to make a list of advantages and disadvantages that's of ideal length. The goal is to include the major advantages and major disadvantages in a way that would make it most easy to decide whether to choose the option.

Variations.

As with all these decision-making exercises, older trainees can write the answers as well as present them orally.

As with the others, a very important variation allows the trainee to come up with the choice point and the possible actions and to list the advantages and disadvantages.

It is especially useful to list one situation and two or three possible options, as well as the advantages and disadvantages for each option, since this is the way decisions are made in real life. Then the ratio of total advantages to total disadvantages can be compared among the different options.

Example:

Action: I am an adult with an aged parent who has Alzheimer's disease. She has been in a nursing home. I am thinking of bringing her back to my family's home to live with us.

Disadvantages:

Her care will take a lot of time we could put into other things that might be more useful.

Since she doesn't seem to recognize us any more, her being with us will probably not make her any happier than being with the people at the nursing home.

We will not be able to use one of the rooms of the house for what we were using it for before.

There may be conflicts over the work that needs to be done, which might make our family less happy.

I may hurt my back trying to lift her.

A lot of the work will be unpleasant, such as changing diapers.

It will be more difficult to get her to a doctor or to get a doctor to see her.

Advantages:
Since she can't walk any more, we don't need to worry about her wandering into the street.

We will have a chance to be with her a lot more.

It will be good for us to spend more time taking care of someone and less time indulging ourselves.

If the children do some of the work for her, they may learn good work habits.

The family will save money by not having to pay the nursing home.

She may be happier being in a home than in an institution.

There may be some recognition of us, and that may make her feel good.

***

Action: I am a 9-year-old child, and I am trying to decide whether or not to accept an invitation to a sleepover party.

Disadvantages:
It's likely that we won't get much sleep. I'll be tired the next day.

I may get a migraine headache if my sleep schedule is thrown off, since that has happened to me before.

It may be that getting more headaches now will make me more likely to get more later.

If I try to get other kids to go to sleep or be quiet, they may be irritated with me or not like me as much.

I may be angry with the other kids for keeping me awake.

Advantages:
I may have fun at the party.

I would not have to have the embarrassment of turning down the invitation. But it won't be very embarrassing if I explain the reason openly; I think my friend will understand.

I may get left out of other things if I don't accept the invitation, and going to the party might prevent this.

It's possible that I can take a nap the afternoon before and after, and learn a technique of staying up late without bad consequences.

Exercise 21: Decision-Making

What is it?

This exercise calls upon the trainee to combine several mental maneuvers that have been practiced separately so far and to practice making good decisions at choice points.

The trainee is to pick a choice point from his own life or to make up a choice point. (By choice point, I mean a situation where one has to decide what to do, think or feel.) Then the trainee is to go through six steps. The first step is to describe the choice situation; this means that you describe to someone what is going on so that someone else can understand what sort of decision you have to make. You tell the story up to the point where you have to make a choice.

The second step is to state your goals for handling the situation. What are you trying to do?

The third step is to list some options for things you could do, think or feel in this situation.

The fourth step is to list advantages and disadvantages for the best options. Usually the advantage takes the form of good consequences for the option and disadvantages take the form of bad consequences for the option.

The fifth step is to say what you choose, or if you don't want to make a final choice, at least what set of options seems to be your first choice right now.

The sixth step occurs when you don't have sufficient information to make a decision now with certainty; you decide how you are going to get more information to make the decisions.

What's it for?

The quality of our lives equals the quality of our decisions. Life is an endless stream of choice points, and we are constantly deciding how to handle each one. Going through these six steps gives the trainee practice in being rational and thoughtful about life decisions.

How do you do it well?

Here is a checklist for conducting the decisions exercise well.

1. Enough description of the situation. Was there enough information about the situation so the reader or listener could understand it?

2. Leaving out irrelevant details. To what extent were inconsequential details omitted from the description so as not to clutter it up?

3. Sensible goal statement. To what extent were the goals suitable and sensible for this situation?

4. Enough good options. To what extent were reasonable and good options listed? For this exercise the crite-

rion is met if there are four good options listed.

5. Accurate advantages and disadvantages. How reasonable was the analysis of advantages and disadvantages of the best options, based on a realistic prediction of consequences?

6. Choice. Did the person state a choice that was consistent with the analysis of advantages and disadvantages?

7. Ideas for more information. Were there good ideas for getting more information to make this decision?

Variations:

The situations in this exercise can be situations the trainer supplies, situations the trainee makes up or real situations in the trainee's life. If they are real situations, they can be those from the distant past, those from the recent past or those currently facing the trainee. Thus, there is a whole spectrum of situations–from totally fanciful to totally real and immediate.

As with so many exercises, you can perform this one by speaking or by writing. I believe the written form of the Decisions Exercise can help people make good decisions for themselves throughout their lives.

Example:

The choice point: I've been learning to play the piano for about three or four years. I've been taking lessons. But I don't put in enough practice time to get really good at it. I learn more and more songs, and then I forget them afterward, because I don't keep playing them. What do I want to do about my piano playing?

The goals: My goal is to figure out ways of using my time to make me happiest and also allow me to serve other people the most. I want to pick those activities that will have the highest payoff.

Options: I could drop the study of piano. I could keep doing what I have been–working at it every once in a while but not very hard. I could allocate a certain amount of time to practice every day. If I did that, any amount of time, up to perhaps an hour a day, is an option worth considering. I could think of ways to motivate myself to work more at it. I could play songs on some regular schedule for the people at the nursing home. I could work to the point where I'd be able to play at a church or some other place for money. I could stop piano until some of the other time-consuming activities I'm pursuing end, and then start back after that.

Advantages and disadvantages: It's good practice in concentration skills to play the piano, and that concentration skill might carry over to other activities. If I can get good enough that I can play songs for my family and they gather around the piano and sing with me, that would be lots of fun. I might be able to entertain the people in the nursing home, with only a little more practice than I'm doing now. All these are reasons to keep doing it.

A disadvantage of continuing to do it the way I have been is that I'm falling into a habit of doing a mediocre job. Another disadvantage is that I often feel guilty over not practicing more. Also, I feel we're wasting money on the lessons when I don't practice much. If I were to practice just fifteen minutes a day, I think I could probably get about ten songs polished well enough to play them for people. That would not take too much time away from other activities, but it would let me entertain people at the nursing home and would let me play songs for people whenever they're in the mood.

Choice: I want to try out practicing just fifteen minutes a day, every day, and working toward the point where I can play ten songs really well. I want to start playing regularly for the people at the nursing home then.

More information: My guess is that, if I really do fifteen minutes of practice every day, I'll get good at those ten songs fairly quickly. I don't know how fast I'll be able to make progress in my playing. By conducting this experiment, I'll see how much I'll accomplish in this time. If this isn't enough time,

I'll find that out, and then I'll again decide what to do.

Exercise 22: Joint Decision Role-Play

What is it?

There are seven criteria for positive processes of communication in joint decisions. These are:

Checklist for Joint Decision-Making

1. Defining. Each person defines the problem from his or her point of view, without blaming and without telling what the solution should be.

2. Reflecting. Each person reflects to let the other person know he understands the other person's point of view.

3. Listing. They list at least four options.

4. Waiting. They don't criticize the other's options until they've finished listing.

5. Advantages. They think and talk about the advantages and disadvantages of the best options.

6. Agreeing. They pick one to try.

7. Politeness. They don't raise their voices or put each other down or interrupt.

In the Joint Decisions Exercise, the trainee practices having joint decision-making conversations that meet these criteria as closely as possible. You can use hypothetical problems from the *Options and Consequences* book, or you can come up with your own.

What is it for?

The process of joint decision fostered by this exercise emphasizes rationality, thinking and using the mind. This process contrasts sharply with the countless real-life situations in which attempts at joint decision-making erupt into anger or violence. If this exercise were a part of universal education and all people learned it so well that its processes became automatic, the prevalence of violence and other harmful discord would probably be greatly reduced.

Why does this exercise require you to wait until the options are all listed before starting to evaluate them? This is based upon the principle that the brain's information storage capacity is limited—it is difficult to do everything at once. Once we get into evaluating a certain option, we often forget to come back and finish listing options. Very often people can become so sidetracked with evaluating the merits of one option that they fail to generate options that would solve the problem well.

How do you do it well?

The essence of conducting this exercise well is captured in the checklist; meeting the seven criteria is the major challenge.

Another key to performing this exercise well is making the conversation realistic, being a good actor and not just doing a perfunctory job in order to get the conversation out of the way as soon as possible. Another element not captured in the checklist is the quality of the options. You have to try very hard to come up with creative options that will really be acceptable and useful for all involved.

Variations:

As with all these exercises, there are ways to make it easier or harder. To make it easier for young children, I supply a very concrete, two-person problem and role-play the problem-solving conversation with the trainee, aiming at only the last two criteria: agreeing and politeness. Once the trainee is able to do this, we can start to incorporate the other criteria as well. Role-playing these conversations and attempting to meet all seven criteria is useful throughout one's life.

I find it useful to ask the trainee to play both parts in joint decision conversations. This variation gives the trainee practice in seeing both points of view in a problem situation.

This version of the Joint Decision Exercise can also be a written exercise; the trainee writes a dialogue meeting all seven criteria.

Another variation, as with many of these exercises, occurs when the trainee does not depend on the trainer to devise or supply a situation. The trainee comes up with his own imaginary situation or a real life situation.

Another variation is to ask family members to practice joint decision conversations among themselves. These can be either hypothetical situations or real life joint decisions. It's good for family members to start with hypothetical situations that do not arouse a lot of emotion. Then they graduate to real situations of minor importance. Then they work their way up to the more emotionally charged joint decisions.

Another variation involves videotaping or audiotaping these joint decision-making conversations and then having family members observe these conversations and rate them according to the seven criteria. This exercise, like many others, can be done with groups. People can divide up into pairs and practice the joint decision-making role-plays, or they can divide up into triads, with two people practicing the role-plays and a third one rating each participant according to the seven criteria.

Another variation on this exercise occurs when the trainer or someone else interacts with the trainee in a way that does not meet the seven criteria and does not provide a very good example of joint decision-making skill. In other words, the person the trainee has to interact with is immediately dismissing options, getting off the subject, using problem definitions that dictate what the solution should be, interrupting and so forth. The trainee's task is to meet the seven criteria himself, even though the other person is not meeting them.

Example:

First person: Do you have time to talk with me about a problem now? It's about the dog.

Second person: Yes, I do.

First: The problem is that I think the dog isn't getting nearly enough exercise and opportunity to be out. I think too much of his time is being spent cooped up in the house.

Second: So you're feeling that we are not giving the dog enough of a chance to live a happy life, because he's being confined and ignored too much, huh?

First: Right.

Second: I'm glad that you're concerned about his welfare. I totally agree that he's being neglected. I have just been too busy lately to worry much about him. Problems at work have just taken first place in my mind.

First: So it sounds as if you are concerned about this problem too, even though other things have kept you from spending time on it lately.

Second: That's right.

First: Want to think about some options to address this?

Second: Sure. One option is to admit that we made a mistake and try to find a different home for the dog.

First: Another is to try to hire some kid in the neighborhood to take the dog out.

Second: If in the next few years we move to a place in the country where the dog can run loose, that will solve the problem.

First: Another option is to teach the dog to run on a treadmill, to solve some of the exercise problem.

Second: Another option is just making a schedule and making the time for the dog to be taken out and walked, and seeing if we can follow it, getting everybody in the family involved.

First: Another idea is finding another family in the neighborhood who wants to have a dog, and enter into a dog-sharing agreement where both families take care of the dog and own it together.

Second: Sounds like some good ideas. Shall we think about advantages and disadvantages?

First: Sure. Getting into a dog-sharing arrangement with another family might bring us closer to another family. The disadvantage is that finding a family willing to do this might be hard, and we might get into conflict with them.

Second: The treadmill idea is a novel one. I think that it doesn't meet the dog's more basic need to have more stimulation and opportunity to explore, but it does provide exercise. And it wouldn't be too hard to teach.

First: Hiring a kid in the neighborhood to help would cost some money. But it would be worth it, in my mind. And I know a girl who would probably jump at the chance.

Second: I think that hiring a kid in the neighborhood is the best option for now. How about you?

First: We can always give it a try, and keep our minds open to the other ones if it doesn't solve the problem. Let's try it.

Second: Good. Do you want to ask her?

First: Yep, I'll give her a call tonight.

Second: Sounds good.

Exercise 23: Concentrate, Rate, and Concentrate

What is it?

This exercise was inspired by the biofeedback paradigm. In biofeedback, you measure whatever you are trying to change, so that you can gradually learn to control it. In the Concentrate, Rate, and Concentrate exercise, you measure your concentration on a given task. You alternate between doing the task, noticing how well you concentrated on it, and then concentrating again.

This exercise differs from biofeedback in that, rather than having a physiological measure of concentration, you have a performance measure of it. If you are doing mathematics problems, how many you get right in a minute is probably a better measure of your concentration than any physiological measure we have at this point.

But in the Concentrate, Rate, and Concentrate activity, the trainee doesn't just receive feedback. The trainee first rates his own concentration. Only after rating his own performance does the trainee get more objective feedback on the performance.

Thus, the trainee has the opportunity to gradually improve his self-monitoring ability by comparing his own ratings to the more objective measure of performance.

One way to do this exercise is with some computer programs I've written. One of these computer programs presents mathematics questions to the trainee to answer as quickly and as ac-

curately as possible. Another program is meant to give the trainee practice in touch-typing. This program presents letters or combinations of letters and the trainee types them with the proper fingers as fast as possible. After the trainee completes a round, the program prompts the trainee to rate his concentration.

The program then provides objective feedback on the trainee's speed and accuracy in completing the task. Then the next round begins. At the end, the program computes a correlation coefficient, a number that summarizes how closely the trainee's ratings corresponded to the objective performance measures. You can select the length of the rounds. From thirty seconds to three or four minutes is the range I've found best.

Beyond these two programs, a variety of other computer programs provide mentally demanding challenges with quantifiable measurements of performance. Several shareware programs include drills on naming the notes of the musical staff. *Chessmaster 8000* provides chess drills of different degrees of difficulty, that can be solved quickly. With all these you can acquire quantitative measurements of concentration performance.

I tend to prefer these sorts of practical tasks to more meaningless concentration tasks, such as continuous performance tasks. Continuous performance tasks involve such things as looking at a long succession of letters flashed onto a computer screen and, for example, hitting the space bar every time an "a" is followed by an "x." With more useful types of tasks, you emerge from many trials of concentration training with some handy skills, in addition to practice in concentrating.

The Concentrate, Rate, and Concentrate activity is not limited to activities with computers. It can be done with any activity that requires concentration. You can also use more subjective ratings of the trainee's concentration, as rated by the trainer.

The trainee can, for example, work on ordinary homework. You can set the timer for a five-minute trial. The trainee works as efficiently and productively as possible. When the timer goes off, the trainee stops working and rates his concentration on the task. The trainer, who has been observing him, rates him independently. Then they compare ratings. They talk about why the ratings were what they were. If the concentration was good, they celebrate and examine how the trainee did such a good job. Then the next trial begins.

In this activity, the job of the trainee is not simply to concentrate and rate and concentrate. The trainee is also asked to try to remember "what he did with his brain" on the most successful trials of concentration. That is: some of the trials will be more successful than others. On some, the performance will be very good, and on some, the performance will be not so good. But, if the trainee can try to capture in memory what it felt like to attain the best performances, then the trainee now has a resource he can use on future trials. He can recall that mental maneuver or that feeling or "what he did with his brain" and use that recollection to more readily reenter that mental pattern.

This procedure is based on the same idea used when basketball players benefit from having a "personal highlight" video made for them. From videotapes of games, someone chooses the player's most successful and most proficient moves and places them together on one tape. The player then observes this tape repeatedly in order to strengthen those patterns in the mind. In the Concentrate, Rate, and Concentrate exercise, the trainee is asked to capture his personal highlights of concentration in memory.

What is it for?

Obviously, this exercise is meant to teach concentration skills. It directly applies the principles of monitoring, practice, reinforcement, and fantasy rehearsal to the skill of concentration. Of the huge numbers of children who are treated for Attention Deficit Disorder, I would wager that a very small fraction of them ever receive any direct training in the skills of attention and concentration.

How do you do it well?

It is important to communicate to the trainee that concentration skill means the ability to do work:

at greater speed,

with greater accuracy

for a longer period of time

with more complex or boring materials.

The trainee performing this exercise should gradually learn to extend his ability to concentrate along each of these dimensions.

One of the biggest challenges for the trainee is to come up with accurate ratings of concentration. At the beginning some trainees will find it difficult to rate themselves as anything other than perfect.

Variations:

One important activity is a drill very useful in teaching children to read. The student looks at words, one at a time, and says the individual sounds of the phonemes in that word. Then the child blends those sounds together to say the word. This exercise can be used in the Concentrate, Rate, and Concentrate activity, as well as in learning the crucial skill of reading.

Another activity that can also be used for this purpose is a typing and spelling activity. The student looks at a list of spelling words, and types them into the computer. The student earns points for typing the words correctly.

The Reflections activity, discussed earlier, is a special case of the Concentrate, Rate, and Concentrate activity.

The Concentrate, Rate, and Concentrate activity can also be conducted with a wide variety of tasks, including motor tasks, such as shooting a basketball into a basket, and musical tasks, such as performing a song on a musical instrument. It's probably a good idea to start this activity with tasks the trainee enjoys doing and then progress toward tasks the trainee finds more difficult and challenging.

The following is a scale on which the trainee can rate his concentration.

0=none
2=very little
4=some but not very much
6=pretty much
8=a high amount
10=a very high amount

This scale can be used to answer the question; "How much did you concentrate during this last trial?"

Exercise 24: Fantasy Rehearsals

What is it?

In this exercise, you encounter in your imagination a situation you would like to practice handling well. Then you imagine the thoughts, emotions and behaviors you would like to use in responding to the situation. You imagine this situation and your response as vividly as you can. In one version of this exercise, you do this silently; you can then report afterward to the trainer what you imagined. In another version, you speak out loud what you are imagining.

When you perform these verbalizations, you speak as if you are encountering the situation in the present. You speak in the first person rather than describing this experience as happening to someone else. (One exception to this occurs when you are imagining something that is scary for you. In such a case, it is often helpful to imagine someone else doing it first, as a less scary intermediate step before imagining yourself doing it.)

What is it for?

A great deal of research shows that practicing in imagination produces effects much like practicing in real life. With Fantasy Rehearsal, you can engage in repeated and concentrated practice in handling situations well. You can practice enough times that you really have a good chance of building up good habits.

How do you do it well?

The first prerequisite for a beneficial fantasy rehearsal is to come up with a good response to the situation. It's counterproductive to spend your time fantasy rehearsing a bad response.

Often the best responses to situations that have caused very intense negative emotion still involve some negative emotion, only with much less intensity. For example, if a child says something impudent to me, and I have been in the habit of flying into a huge rage at such a remark, perhaps in my fantasy rehearsal I might still feel irritated. But my irritation would be nothing close to the intensity of anger I felt during the real-life experience.

Another aspect of performing Fantasy Rehearsals well is including your thoughts and emotions, as well as your overt behaviors, in your response to the situation. And when you've handled the situation well in fantasy, it is helpful to celebrate internally by, for example, saying, "Wow, I handled that situation well! Hooray!"

The mnemonic STEBC is useful for fantasy rehearsals. The letters stand for Situation, Thought, Emotion, Behavior and Celebration.

How do you generate thoughts that are useful, adaptive and appropriate for situations? The Twelve Thought Exercise prepares you to come up with thoughts that are useful for fantasy rehearsal. The key to handling a situation well often lies in choosing well among the twelve types of thoughts.

To conduct fantasy rehearsals well you must imagine the fantasies as vividly as possible. This means trying to see and hear very specifically what is going on

As with all of these exercises, the most difficult part of doing fantasy rehearsals is simply performing enough of them. Like push-ups and sit-ups, they do produce results, but only if they are repeated regularly and often.

Variations:

As I've already mentioned, fantasy rehearsals can be silent and then reported later, or they can be done out loud. They can also be written out. They can also be recorded onto audiotape. When they are written or recorded, the trainee can then read or listen to the fantasy rehearsals repeatedly after that.

When the trainee is just beginning to learn how to conduct fantasy rehearsals, it's useful to perform an exercise in which the trainer supplies the STEB and simply lets the trainee express that as a fantasy rehearsal. Or, the trainer can supply a positive modeling story and let the trainee translate that into the first person, present progressive tense in the format of a fantasy rehearsal.

In another variation, the trainer and trainee refer to lists of types of kind acts, types of frustrations, types of self-discipline situations, or types of conflicts. (Such lists are presented in an-

other book in this series entitled *Lists and Charts for Psychological Skills*.) Together they look at each category, and each of them performs a fantasy rehearsal of an example in that category.

For example, one category of frustration is having someone turn down a request. The trainer imagines that someone has rejected an article he has written and then fantasy rehearses handling that well. The trainee then imagines handling it well when a friend turns down an invitation to visit his house and socialize. Trainer and trainee continue until they have conducted fantasy rehearsals of all the different categories.

In another variation, the trainer and trainee examine at the list of sixteen skills and principles, or the larger list of sixty-two individual skills, and determine the set of skills that are the highest priorities the trainee. They then pick perhaps four or five skills to target.

Then the trainee imagines a specific situation and performs a fantasy rehearsal that exemplifies one of those psychological skills. The trainee continues until he has engaged in a fantasy rehearsal of each of the target skills. This is an exercise that can then be repeated many times.

Another variation is fantasy rehearsal of other people's positive behaviors. The trainee can be on the lookout for examples of other people's positive behaviors in real life of in stories, books, movies or television shows. I have referred to this as the "scavenger hunt for positive models."

The trainer's role would be to provide feedback on whether he agrees that the thought, emotion and behavior the character exemplified were really appropriate and ethical in the situation. If they are, the trainee can turn that situation into a fantasy rehearsal.

Another variation is fantasy rehearsal of celebrations. Previously we discussed the Celebrations Exercise. This involves recalling and recounting the things you've done that you're glad you've done. In this variation, you turn these celebrations into fantasy rehearsals in order to maximize the chance that you will do them again.

The last variation is fantasy rehearsal of replacements of situations in which you did something you regret, or in which you could have responded more effectively. This variation is important enough that it gets listed as a separate exercise called STEB and STEB revision.

Example: Here's an example of a fantasy rehearsal from someone who is working on anger control:

Situation: I'm thinking it's really nice that I've been able to keep my new car nice and clean. Now I'm picking up a friend of my parents, to take this person back to our house. Now the person is getting out of the car, and I notice that he had mud all over his shoes and there is now mud on the carpeting of my car.

Thoughts: Wait a minute. This is the type of situation that, in the past, would have caused me to lose my temper. But I don't want to do that. I want to stay cool. I'm reminding myself, this isn't the end of the world. I can clean this up. The weather is bad, and he couldn't help it. I want to relax my muscles. I can say something to him before he tracks mud into the house, or I can just keep quiet and let my parents handle that. I'll say something in a very polite way. I can learn from this experience to get something to put over the carpeting in bad weather.

Emotions: I'm feeling a little irritated, but it's only 1 on a scale of 0 to 10. I'm also feeling proud of myself for stopping and thinking.

Behaviors: As we go inside, I'm saying to him, in a very calm and polite voice, "I think I'm going to take my boots off just inside the door; it's hard to get all this mud off, isn't it?"

I'm planning to clean up the mud later without being obvious about it and without trying to make him feel bad. I don't need to punish him; I just need to get the carpet clean.

Celebrations: I'm really glad I handled this well. This was a real success.

Exercise 24: Fantasy Rehearsals

****

Here's another fantasy rehearsal. This time the person is practicing courage skills before giving a speech.

Situation: I have a speech to give. It's a few minutes before the speech. Lots of people will be watching and listening.

Thoughts: This is an opportunity to handle a situation well that before has been scary for me. If I mess up, it won't be the end of the world. It may be scary again this time, but if I'm able to read my speech well, that will be a success. I want to relax my muscles. All I have to do is read it. I've practiced many times and have done fine. I'm recalling one of the practice sessions where I did a great job; I'll just do it again. I'm recalling another time I delivered a speech like this successfully; I want to visualize that time and just go right into that pattern.

Emotions: I'm feeling excited, but I'm not feeling terrified. I feel confident that I can do this well enough.

Behaviors: I'm standing up and reading my speech. I'm speaking loudly enough and very clearly.

Celebration: Hooray, I'm doing this well.

Exercise 25: STEB and STEB Revision

What is it?

STEB and STEB revision is really a special case of fantasy rehearsal. First the trainee describes a situation that he responded to in a way he would like to improve upon. In reporting this, he recounts the situation as it happened in real life and the thoughts, emotions and behaviors with which he responded in real life. This is the same process that was followed in the Identifying the STEBS exercise. If the person's response to the situation was maladaptive, inappropriate, unethical or incompetent, it will take a great deal of courage for the trainee to recount the STEB. The trainer should be sure to reinforce such courage appropriately.

Then the trainee, with or without the help and suggestions of the trainer, generates a revised set of thoughts, emotions and behaviors that would constitute a more desirable response to the situation. This involves decision-making. Listing options, thinking about advantages and disadvantages, and thinking about ethical principles and goals will be very helpful in deciding upon the best response to situations.

Once the more desirable response is conceived, then the trainee puts that new STEB into fantasy rehearsal format and conducts a fantasy rehearsal of the new and better response.

What is it for?

With the combination of STEB and STEB revision and the fantasy rehearsal of Celebrations Exercise, you can make use of nearly all of your life experiences for self-improvement. For each thing you do, you are either glad you did it or you aren't. If you're glad you did it, it's worthy of celebration, and you can perform a fantasy rehearsal of it. If you're sorry you did it, you can conduct STEB and STEB revision. In this way you learn from your successes, and you learn from your mistakes. STEB and STEB revision are the quintessence of learning from mistakes.

How do you do it well?

One of the hardest parts of this exercise is recalling and recounting the mistakes you have made. It's usually embarrassing to report your mistakes to someone else. This is an exercise that must be done in the context of a very trusting and usually quite confidential relationship. Even in these circumstances, it's not easy to report the details of mishandlings of life situations.

The next big challenge is devising replacement thoughts, emotions and behaviors that would be appropriate to the situation. Again, everything that has been learned in the Twelve Thought Exercise, in the Decision Making Exercises, and in study of the Skills and

Principles, should be brought to bear on this decision.

All the other considerations that apply to conducting fantasy rehearsals will also apply to conducting the fantasy rehearsal of the STEB revision.

Variations:

As with other exercises, one of the most important variations is STEB revision in written format. Written records of both celebrations and STEB and STEB revisions can be the complementary parts of a diary the trainee keeps.

Examples:

STEB:

Situation: I'm practicing the piano. I make three mistakes in a row.
Thought: I'm an idiot. I can't do anything right.
Emotion: Discouraged, angry at myself.
Behavior: I keep on trying to play the same thing for a while, keep making mistakes and getting more frustrated, and then get up and kick the piano and walk away.

STEB Revision:

Situation: I'm practicing the piano. I make three mistakes in a row.
Thought: This seems to be hard for me. What are my options? I think I want to play just one hand at a time rather than trying to play both hands. Also I want to play a lot slower. And before I even play it I can go through and practice naming the notes. That way I'll break it down into little steps. I can take it one step at a time. And even if I still don't do it perfectly, it isn't the end of the world.
Emotion: Proud that I figured out a better strategy.
Behavior: I practice the small steps, and after each one I feel good.

***

STEB:

Situation: My friend is showing me his hunting trophies. He doesn't seem to realize that I'm not enjoying this. He keeps talking about how he got this animal and that.
Thoughts: I'm not interested in this at all. In fact, I'm disgusted by it. How can he be so inconsiderate?
Emotions: Angry, bored.
Behaviors: I keep waiting for him to finish, with a very sullen look on my face.

STEB Revision:

Situation: My friend is showing me his hunting trophies. He doesn't seem to realize that I'm not enjoying this. He keeps talking about how he got this animal and that.

Thoughts: I'm not enjoying this. What do I want to do? I want to communicate to him that I want to do something else. My goal is to begin some other activity. I don't want to antagonize him, but, if he is offended, I can handle that.

Emotions: Confident, determined.

Behavior: I say to him, "It sounds as if you've had some times you've enjoyed. I think I've seen enough of the hunting trophies, though. Different people are into different things. How about a little walk around outside while there's still some light out?"

**

STEB:

Situation: I'm sitting in the kitchen chatting with someone in my family. I see a box of honey-roasted peanuts.

Thought: Those would taste good.

Emotion: Pleasant anticipation.

Behavior: I munch down about half a cup of honey-roasted peanuts while we continue to talk.

STEB Revision:

Situation: I'm sitting in the kitchen chatting with someone in my family. I see a box of honey-roasted peanuts.

Thought: Those would taste good. I want some. But wait a minute. Let me think. I'm trying to lose weight. I want to limit myself to 300 calories of food per day beyond what I eat at meals. And I've already had that much today. It would taste good. But I'm not starving; I'm not even very hungry. It won't hurt me to do without these. I'll be using self-discipline if I do.

Emotion: Determined, proud.

Behavior: I put the box of peanuts away in a cabinet. I invite my family member to go into the living room and chat with me, away from all this food.

Exercise 26: Goal-Setting and Planning

What is it?

In this exercise, you record your thoughts about a goal you want to achieve.

It's good to record these goal statements somehow: the trainer acts as a transcriber, or the trainee tape records them or writes them down.

The exercise asks you to choose a goal for yourself or to speak or write about a goal you have already set. It also asks you to record thoughts about:

the reason why this is a worthy goal,
the criteria for the goal's being met,
the plan for meeting the goal,
the obstacles that might interfere with the plan
and the ways of overcoming those obstacles.

What's it for?

If you don't know what you want to accomplish, it's less likely that you'll accomplish anything worthwhile. Almost all people do too little thinking about the questions, "What do I want to accomplish?" and "How am I going to accomplish that?" Choosing goals and making plans are very important "executive functions" of the brain; they are the opposites of impulsivity. They are one secret of achieving your objectives.

This exercise involves not just choosing goals but selling yourself on them. It involves thinking about why is it worthwhile to work toward the selected goal. People who do not have these selling points in mind find it more difficult to muster the self-discipline to accomplish the goal.

How do you do it well?

In performing this exercise you answer the following questions.

1. Choose a goal for yourself. Make it something you want to accomplish, something you have a realistic chance of achieving. State the goal clearly.

2. Why is this a worthy goal? Why should anyone spend time working toward this? What is the "sales pitch" you will use to convince yourself to keep working on it?

3. Describe the specific criteria for the goal's being met. How will you know you've accomplished this goal when you have done so?

4. Describe your plan for meeting the goal:
What are you going to do to accomplish the goal?
How are you going to do these things? How much time are you going to spend on it and how often?
Are there are steps and stages in meeting your goal? If so, what are the

dates by which you must complete the various stages?

Are there other people or other resources you will call on to help you? If so, who or what are they?

5. What obstacles can you anticipate that might interfere with your plans working?

6. How do you plan to overcome these obstacles?

Conducting this exercise well requires answering these questions well. This exercise demands a good deal of patience. The temptation when goal setting is to simply list several goals and be done. Doing this exercise well requires the patience to think about each goal in great detail.

When someone performing this exercise reaches the part about why this is a worthy goal, she may conclude the goal is not particularly worthy. This can be very useful! A person who decides that it does not really benefit humanity for her to set the world record for the longest time standing on one foot has saved herself a lot of effort. She can then channel that effort into helping children learn to read or building houses for homeless people or working on a cure for a disease, or improving her own psychological skills. It takes lots of courage to discard goals. Abandoning unworthy goals is one of the most important ways people save their time for more worthy goals.

Variations:

In one variation, the trainee is simply asked to generate with goals out of the blue. In another variation, the trainee is helped in goal selection by being shown the following list of possible areas for goal-setting and possible types of goals:

Menu for Goals

Personal development
What would you like to do to improve yourself?
How would you like to make yourself a better person?
What psychological skills do you want to get better at, at this time? (Looking carefully at the menu of psychological skills will be helpful in making this decision.)

Relations with family members
Are you pleased with the way you get along with each person in your family?
Which member of your family would you like to get along better with?
What would be happening less often, and what would be happening more often, if you got along better with that person?
Is there someone in your family you would like to spend more time doing fun things with?

Social Life, Relations with friends

Would you like to make more friends?

Would you like to have a best friend you are closer to?

Would you like your time with a friend to be more fun?

Would you like people you don't know really well to like you better?

Athletics and/or Health and Fitness

Any accomplishments you want to make in sports?

Any sport you want to get more skilled at?

Any particular sports skills you want to acquire?

Do you want to get more exercise? If so, how?

Do you want to improve your eating habits? If so, how?

Are there other health habits or attitudes you want to strengthen, such as non-use of alcohol or tobacco or others?

Hobbies

Do you want to take up any new activities, such as playing a musical instrument, learning to use a computer well, reading and learning about a new subject, hiking, cycling, etc.?

Are there particular skill goals you have in any activity?

Or do you have a goal of simply spending time enjoying some activity?

Religious or Philosophical involvement

Would you like your religious or philosophical life to be improved in any way?

Career Development

Are there work competencies you would like to get or to increase?

Are there changes in your career you want to work toward?

Would you like to be more productive in some way?

Are there particular work achievements you would like to complete?

School Achievement and/or Learning

Are there any subjects you would like to become stronger in?

Would you like to be better organized in your schoolwork?

Would you like to earn better grades in general?

Would you like to be able to study better?

Is there something you would like to learn about or learn to do?

School Behavior

Are you making life pleasant for your teacher? Would you like to do this more?

Are you making life pleasant for your classmates? Would you like to do this more?

Do you have a good reputation at school for behaving reasonably? Would you like to do this more?

Service to Humanity, Making the World a Better Place

Would you like to be of more service to humanity?

Would you like to be of service in some particular way?

Would you like to learn more about how to be of service to humanity?

Are you interested in a cause such as nonviolence, reducing poverty, improving the environment?

The written version of this exercise is an easily repeatable exercise that gives good practice in writing skills, as well as in goal-setting.

In a slight variation on this exercise, the trainee is asked to think separately about goals to be accomplished within the next month, within the next year, within the next five years and at some point during his lifetime.

Once goals have been listed and written down, it is very important not to call the exercise over and forget about them. You return to the goals list frequently and update it, and you ask yourself another very important question: what percent of the way am I toward completion of this goal? If these estimates are getting higher and higher all the time, that is progress.

Example:

1. State the goal.

My goal is to develop my ability to do independent work. This means deciding what I want to accomplish and accomplishing it, without needing to have someone prodding me to do it.

2. Why it's a worthy goal.

If I can develop this ability, I'll be able to teach myself almost any subject I want to know about, without even needing to take a course in it. I'll be able to take control of my own education. I can save lots of money by educating myself rather than, for example, going to an expensive private school. And I can get into habits that will let me keep on educating myself once school is over.

In addition to that, I can accomplish much more in other areas of life, not just school. If I want to write a book, for example, I can do it if I have enough independent work skills, but I could never do it without them. If I want to start a business and run it myself, I'll need lots of independent work skills because I won't have a boss telling me what to do.

3. Specific criteria

When I am in the habit of working on something independently for at least three or four hours a week, that's a criterion. Or when I have taught myself to do something worthwhile that takes more than fifty hours of work. Or when I have taught myself the equivalent of a one-semester course, independently.

4. Plan

I'm going to start by teaching myself to type at least forty words a minute. I already know which fingers to use on which keys, but I'm slow now, typing probably about ten words a minute. My plan to learn faster typing is to look through books of great quotations and mark the ones that seem the most worth remembering. Then I'll practice typing them into a computer file. I'll do this for at least a half an hour each day. My guess is that this will get me typing faster, by itself. If it doesn't, I'll practice typing the same sentence over and over, working for more speed. I'll time myself on a test passage every couple of weeks or so.

Another part of my plan is to keep a record, every day, of how much time I spend in independent work. Each week I'll total up the amount. If the total is over, let's say five hours, I want to do something really nice for myself to celebrate. Maybe I can call up my friend who lives out of state and talk on the phone long distance as a prize for doing this.

I'm hoping to accomplish the typing goal by three months from today.

After that, I want to take on the goal of teaching myself psychological skills by independent work on these writing assignments. I want to write one of these assignments every day. I'm going to get a good person to review what I've written and give me feedback every so often, let's say every week. I think my dad would be a good person to do that. I'll ask him if he would help me in that way. I want to keep going on this program until I've completed at least five of each of the assignments, and have done them really well.

Some time in the future, I want to try to teach myself a course and take a test on it, like the CLEP test or one of the tests given by Excelsior College. I'll make a schedule for myself and do some work on it almost every day until I'm ready to take the test.

5. Obstacles

One of the obstacles is that my brother likes to be with me, and he finds it very hard to leave me alone to do independent work. And I enjoy being with him, too. We can usually come up with something to do together that is more fun than independent work.

Another obstacle is that I'm the type of person who likes to be with people. I just naturally tend to gravitate toward activities that put me with people, not those that require independent work.

6. Overcoming obstacles

I could talk with my brother about whether he wants to set the goal of increasing independent work skills too. If he does, we could perhaps work together. We could each work on something on our own, at the same time. Then, at the end of the time, we could celebrate with each other over how much we have accomplished. If we were in the same room, an obstacle might be our temptation to talk to each other. We might overcome that by being in different rooms.

A way of overcoming my tendency not to be alone is simply to get more practice at it. I could practice doing activities I really enjoy doing alone, like reading novels. Maybe this would be a good preparatory step toward doing things that require more self-discipline, like doing psychological skill-writing assignments.

Exercise 27: Reading *Instructions on Psychological Skills*

What is it?

My book *Instructions on Psychological Skills* gives whys and hows for each of sixty-two psychological skills. For instructions on psychological skills in the more generic sense, there's a great wealth of information other people have provided on how to do various psychological skills well.

The essence of this exercise is that the trainee reads the book, and reflects upon it.

What is it for?

The rehearsal and role-playing exercises described here are meant to provide practice in psychological skills. However, there is a lot of knowledge that is best obtainable by reading or hearing direct instructions. *Instructions on Psychological Skills* is meant to give the trainee the ideas and knowledge that complement the other practice exercises.

How do you do it well?

The job of reading these instructions well is to study them thoroughly and to incorporate them into your ways of thinking. This involves understanding what you have read and recalling it. It involves being able to apply that knowledge and those ideas to new situations in life.

Some parts of *Instructions on Psychological Skills* involve complex and abstract ideas. Trainees who are young or who have not had much experience reading complex ideas in this area may benefit from working on the vocabulary and comprehension of language necessary to understand the words in this book. This book, in addition to serving its direct purpose, also serves the goal of vocabulary building.

Variations:

Instructions on Psychological Skills can be used for the Reflections Exercise. The trainee reads a paragraph and then summarizes the main idea of that paragraph, either orally or though typing out the summary. It's often more fun if the trainee and the trainer take turns reading and reflecting.

In another variation, the trainer and the trainee take turns reading this book to each other. They stop whenever they wish to discuss what they've read.

In another variation, the trainee and the trainer read the book silently, and then, after each section or each page, they stop and discuss what they've read.

By discussing, I mean raising questions about what was read and trying to answer those questions. The most important question to be raised is "How can I use this to make my life better?" Other topics for discussion include, "Let me see if I understand this correctly: The main point is

_____." Another way of discussing it is to say, "Here is another example, I think, of what is being talked about: _____ "

Another variation upon this exercise is simply assigning this text in an educational format and giving tests on it, or giving essay assignments to write about as in a traditional school.

A final variation helps both trainer and trainee break through the "intimidation factor" of a six-hundred-page book. This variation may be called "Find a take-home message." In this version, the trainee starts reading anywhere he wants. He can choose the starting point by a quick peek at the index or table of contents. Or the trainee can thumb through the book until a certain section looks interesting. Or the trainee can open the book to a random place, put his finger down, and start reading there. The trainee reads until he has gotten in mind one idea that might be useful to him. When this idea is in mind, he states it out loud to the trainer, who might transcribe it, discuss it with the trainee, reflect it, or simply acknowledge it. Then the exercise is over. You can usually do this exercise in five minutes or less. It's a great way of breaking your way into thick, intimidating books in general.

Exercise 28: Telling or Writing About Your Life

What is it?

In this exercise, trainee's job is to talk about his or her life.

If you're performing this exercise, you might want to talk about things that have happened to you, things that might happen and things that you think will happen or won't happen. You can talk about things that you do, people in your life, places you've been, what home is like, what school or work is like, what activities you like, your thoughts and feelings about events, and your ideas. You can talk about any experiences you've had, feelings about experiences, problems you're facing, and your thoughts about those problems. You can think about your goals in situations, obstacles to those goals and how to overcome those obstacles. You can talk about anything at all.

But you want to talk about things that are interesting to you and are useful for you to think about. You want to think about things that happened in the past and how you can use that information in the future. It is especially useful to talk out loud about decisions.

In one version of this, the trainee simply talks while the trainer is a nondirective listener. The trainee uses responses such as "Um hmmm", "Okay" "Oh" and "Is that right?" The trainer tries to be rather inactive and nondirective and to let the trainee do the work.

What's it for?

One of the purposes of this exercise is to overcome the "OK-Nothing" approach to thinking about one's life. That is:

How are you doing?
OK.
What have you been up to?
Nothing.

It's not without reason that in all forms of psychotherapy, one of the central tasks of the client is to generate information about what is going on in her life–what sorts of situations are coming up, what sorts of feelings they invoke, what she thinks about them, what happened next, what principles seem to be at work, what motives are operating, what the goals are, what the obstacles are, and so forth.

Being able to put into words what is going on in one's life is one of the most basic steps to changing things for the better.

This exercise has an agenda that is broader and less specific than other exercises that have sought to bring out the trainee's expressiveness about his life. The Guess The Feelings Exercise, the Celebrations Exercise, the Decisions Exercise and others, including the Goals Setting and Planning Exercise, all give preparation for the Telling About Your Life Exercise. In the Telling About Your Life Exercise, the trainee can choose among any of these different agendas for talking or others, and can use the time as he or she wishes.

By learning to do this exercise well, he learns to examine his life and reflect upon it and to use words to help understand it.

How do you do it well?

Here's a rating scale for a trial of telling about your life.

0=None
2=Only a little
4=Some but not much
6=Pretty much
8=High amount
10=Very high amount

1. Things to say. The trainee was able to think of things to talk about.

2. Depth of Exploration of a single topic. To what extent was the trainee able to stay on a single topic long enough to think about it thoroughly before going to another topic or stopping talking?

3. Interest to the trainee. To what extent did the trainee seem interested in the subjects he or she was talking about?

4. Usefulness or pleasantness. To what extent did the trainee talk about things that seemed either useful to think about or pleasant to think about?

5. Past and future. To what extent did the trainee think about the relevance of past experience for future experience?

6. Decision making, versus just recounting. To what extent did the thoughts help the trainee reach a new place? This means to evolve to a new perspective, make a new decision, start looking at something a new way, rather than just relaying facts and memories?

6. Talk about feelings. To what extent did the trainee either talk directly about feelings, or talk about events that generate some feelings?

7. Talk about hypothetical situations. To what extent did the trainee talk about options, consequences or situations that were not physically present? In other words, to what extent did the person use fantasy and imagination?

Variations

Doing this exercise in writing is a wonderful way to practice writing as well as to explore one's own life. It's also much cheaper than psychotherapy.

It's useful to separate several goals with which one can approach this exercise:

1. To make a decision

2. To generate choice points, for later decision-making

3. To take the time to think about events that one has not previously had time to process–to have a richer experience of life

4. To entertain yourself

5. To be thankful for accomplishments and others' kind acts and blessings

6. To work through and get over unpleasant events of the past

7. To set goals, or to have pleasant daydreams that may be useful for setting goals

Example:

Here's an example written by an adult:

Today I want to think about the problem of how overcommitted I am. People ask me to do things, and I say yes, because the projects and activities sound fun and worthwhile. I'm taking my kids to tennis and piano lessons and Boy Scouts and baseball games. I'm teaching a Sunday school class, trying to exercise often, plus working, plus being on the board of directors at my kids' school. Because of all these commitments, I don't take the time to go through all my mail, and I don't organize my things, and things tend to pile up in disorganized clutter that is really stressful to me. When I think about attacking that big backlog of paper I have to process, it makes me feel really bad. I think all this stress makes me get headaches, and getting headaches takes time away from being able to organize myself more. Also, the house gets to be a mess, and that bothers me too. When I'm in a lousy mood, it affects the emotional climate of the family.

What do I want to do about this? I need to cut back on my commitments. I want to set aside a regular time each day for all my kids and me to work together on cleaning up the house and organizing things. I want to set up a regular time each day to organize papers and tasks. I think that right after supper would be a good time for both of these activities. I'll talk it over with my family today.

I need to stop certain commitments. The term on the board of directors of the school doesn't run out for another year; I'll give them a month's notice and quit that; they can find someone else without difficulty. I'll stop doing Sunday school teaching in three months when this year ends. Neither of my kids likes playing the piano, and it's a big hassle to get them to practice; I'm going to quit that immediately. They can learn it later if they want. I want to put lots of effort into training my kids to help out with the work of the household.

I feel good about these decisions. I want to see if this reduces the number of headaches I get and helps me feel better about life.

***

Here's an example from the point of view of a child:

I want to take this time today to think about how lucky I am. First of all, I could have been born a mouse instead of a person, and I could have just gotten caught and eaten by our neighbors' cat. My one chance to be alive could have ended just like that, in a very scary and painful way. But instead I get to be a human being. Second of all, I could be a human being in the middle of a war or a famine, or I could be getting beat up every single day very badly by people who are very mean to me. But none of these things is happening. I could be hungry every single day of my life, and eventually die of starvation. That still happens to lots of people. But I'm lucky enough that this isn't happening to me. Not only all these things, but I've got a friend I get along with really well. Whenever we get together, we have a good time. Plus I really enjoy reading and writing. Even if I were in prison, if I could read books and articles and try to write them, life would be really worth living. So even though there are lots of problems in my life, there are lots of good things that make me a lucky person. It makes me feel good to think about these.

Exercise 29: Pleasant Dreams

What is it?

In this exercise, the trainee is to make up something that is like a story, except that it shouldn't have a traditional plot based on conflict. It's like a dream, except that the trainee isn't asleep. The trainee is to make up a stream of images. The trainee imagines himself somewhere and imagines things happening and describes what is happening.

In this exercise, the images are to be pleasant, safe and relaxing. The images resemble a very pleasant dream, and not a scary one. The images are of kindness, relaxation and beauty. For example, you imagine people helping one another, speaking nicely to one another, giving each other happiness; you imagine relaxing scenes; you imagine the beauty of nature or beautiful artistic creations. You don't include imaginings of violence, hostility, danger or emergency. You don't have the scenes change in a jarring way–change takes place gradually and gently. There is plenty of time for everything–no sense of time running out. The senses are not overwhelmed, for example, by loud noises.

One way of putting this is that all the elements that television uses to grab our attention–violence, abrupt shifts of scene, hostile words between people, constant attempts at surprise, loudness–are absent. Instead there are images of kindness, relaxation and beauty.

What's it for?

The theory behind this is as follows.

1. Our minds are seldom inactive; they are usually generating ideas and images of some sort or another.

2. When we are not consciously trying to do something, our minds generate ideas and images on "automatic pilot."

3. The types of images and thoughts our minds generate when on automatic pilot make a great difference to what our lives are like. If we need to work to keep the automatic pilot from scaring us or tensing us, our lives are much different than if the automatic pilot tends to give a secure and warm feeling.

4. Constantly responding to the urgent demands of life can create habits of tension, fear, and irritation.

5. The types of thoughts that go through our minds while we are sitting and relaxing, waiting for something, going for a walk, lying in bed before going to sleep, or while we are dreaming, provide a measure of what the automatic pilot tends to do.

6. We can influence the contents of our automatic thoughts by practice. If we practice thoughts of kindness, relaxation, and beauty, these will tend to show up more often in our freely flowing consciousness.

Thus, part of the point of this exercise is to make it more likely that pleasant images will pop into our minds when we are not asking our minds to do anything in particular. One of the practical purposes of this exercise is to make relaxed sleep and pleasant dreaming more likely. The Pleasant Dreams Exercise is one that is often pleasant to do while lying in bed waiting for sleep to come. It's also useful for those who tend to be tense during the day and who find it hard to relax. It may turn out that the Pleasant Dreams Exercise is useful for those who clench their jaws, for example.

The Pleasant Dreams Exercise is also an antidote to constant stimulus seeking. Some people get themselves into trouble by being too strongly driven to seek excitement, thrills, and novelty. If they can learn to enjoy the lower-stimulation images of this exercise, they may overcome some of the problems of stimulus seeking.

How do you do it well?

The following checklist presents criteria for performing the Pleasant Dreams Exercise successfully.

Criteria for the Pleasant Dreams Exercise

0=None
2=A little
4=Some but not much
6=Pretty much
8=High amount
10=Very high amount

To what extent is each of the following statements true about the stream of images you produced?

1. You could easily come up with things to imagine and say. You could keep up a flow of talk or writing.

2. There were images of kindness, warmth and friendliness between people or other living beings.

3. Images of hostility, anger, violence or attempt to hurt, between people or other living beings, were ABSENT from the stream of images. (0=very much hostility, 10=totally absent hostility)

4. The images were of safety; images of danger, threat or emergency were absent from the stream of images. (0=very much danger and threat, 10=no danger and threat.) (Count images as non-dangerous if they are things that would ordinarily be dangerous but are rendered non-dangerous in this stream of images. For example: a lion that is cuddly and friendly, a tornado that gen-

tly wafts someone along in the air without any threat of dropping her, a volcano in the distance that is fun to watch, like a fireworks display.)

5. You seemed to enjoy low stimulation, to enjoy soothing or relaxing images, as contrasted with needing a frenetic pace of stimulation. For example, you could take pleasure in listening to the sound of a burbling brook or watching a snowfall or feeling the warmth of a fire.

6. You seemed able to enjoy beauty. For example, the narrator takes pleasure in a beautiful sunset or takes pleasure in watching a sculptor create a beautiful sculpture before your eyes.

Variations:

It's almost always useful for the trainer to model how to do this exercise first. Then the trainee does it aloud, while the trainer listens. The trainer can also provide the trainee with written examples of the Pleasant Dreams Exercise. The trainee can also write out versions of this exercise, which then may be useful for other trainees.

The Pleasant Dreams Exercise can be a meditation technique. As with other meditation techniques, I find it useful for the trainer and trainee to simply sit silently together as both of them to do the exercise. Then, after both of them have done it for a certain period of time, they can talk about the experience.

Example:

I'm lying on some soft moss. The moss feels great. I've been sleeping very peacefully, and, as I'm waking up, I look through a clearing among the trees around me to see a glorious sunrise. The colors gradually come into the clouds, more and more–purple and pink and red, brighter and more beautiful. I look around me more, and I see a spring, where water flows from the ground. This water is absolutely pure and clean and cool. I'm thirsty, and I drink the water, and it feels great to drink it. I follow the stream down a hillside, and it becomes bigger, big enough that I can get into it and float, and let the current gently carry me along, until it becomes a river. As the river carries me along, I see men and women along the side of the river, working. They wave to me, and I see that they are friends of mine, people I've known for a long time. I stop and help them. I help one of my friends unload sacks of grain from a boat onto a wagon. We talk and laugh and then wave good-bye. Then I get into the river and float some more. I see another friend, and I get out and help her as she takes clothing from a truck and carries it into her store. She tells me a funny joke. Then we say good-bye for now. I go down the river farther, and then I see another friend who waves to me. I get out and help him as he cooks oatmeal for breakfast. Then my other friends all come and he serves it to all of us. We sing a song to-

gether before we eat, harmonizing with
one another.

Exercise 30: Evaluation of Appointment Calendar and To-do List

What is it?

This is an exercise that is best done as "homework" rather than in the session with the trainer. The trainee takes his appointment calendar and to-do list book (or whatever he uses for these functions) and tries to record all the events and activities that are scheduled and make a to-do list of what should be done in the remaining time. The "to-dos" are ordered in priority, and they are checked off as they are completed. Then the trainer examines the appointment calendar and to-do list.

What's it for?

The use of an appointment calendar and to-do list (preferably combined in one book that serves both functions) is at the core of organization skills. The use of paper (or a computer chip if you want to go high-tech with this) as a "brain extender" makes organization much easier. If you have appointments, deadlines, and assignments written down in a very organized way, you are much more likely to meet them. If you have a to-do list written down in an organized way, and if you refer to it often, you're likely to accomplish more.

How do you do it well?

Here is a checklist for rating the appointment calendar and to-do list after examining it.

Rating Scale for Appointment Calendar and To-Do List

0=None
2=A little
4=Some but not much
6=Pretty much
8=High amount
10=Very high amount

1. The appointment calendar reflects all deadlines, assignments and appointments.

2. The appointment calendar clearly indicates the date and time for all deadlines, assignments and appointments.

3. The appointment calendar is organized well enough that it is possible to find fairly quickly what is scheduled for any of the dates it covers.

4. The appointment calendar is legible and clearly decipherable.

5. There is a master to-do list that records the goals the person sets. These include both short-term and long-term goals.

6. There is a daily to-do list made nearly every day that tells the person

what is to be done with discretionary, unscheduled time that day.

7. As items on the to-do lists are accomplished, they are checked off.

8. The to-do list items are numbered in order of priority (they are not necessarily physically placed on the page in order of priority).

9. The to-do list is legible and clearly decipherable.

Variations:

For students, the appointment calendar and to-do list are often in the form of an assignment book. The assignment book has more to do with deadlines and tasks that would go in the appointment section. The to-do list section is where the student writes down the activities he wants to accomplish during some discretionary time. Then the student checks them off when they're done. These can have to do with schoolwork, or they can also have to do with practicing music lessons, arranging social appointments, doing housework or other useful work, and other things. Sometimes it's useful for students to learn to make an appointment calendar out of their assignment books.

I like to combine the appointment book and to-do list in one monthly, pocket-sized spiral notebook that I carry in my hip pocket. I use one page for appointments and the facing page for the to-do list. I strongly recommend that people carry their "brain extenders" and a writing tool with them at all times. If you have to go somewhere to get it or look for it its usefulness is much reduced.

Exercise 31: Purpose and Direction Questions

What is it?

In this exercise, the trainee answers the following questions:

Questions on Direction and Purpose

1. People have sometimes spoken about their purpose in life or the meaning in their lives or the general direction they want their lives to take. Sometimes they think in terms of the general goals for their entire lives. Please tell me your thoughts about this, as it applies to you: do you assign meaning, purpose or goals to your life, and if so, what?

2. Please imagine that you are a very old person and your life is nearly over. What would you like to be able to look back and say about your life?

3. Please try to think of someone you know about, either in real life, or someone you've read about, or some fictitious person, for example from a story or a movie, anyone who is a good example to you, someone you admire, someone whose life seemed to have meaning, purpose, and direction. Please tell me about this person. Who is it, and what did the person do?

3.1 Is there anyone else? What others can you think of?

3.2 Anyone else?

4. How do you want things to be different because you lived? In other words, what effect would you like your life to have?

5. What qualities would you most like to have? What sort of person do you most want to be?

6. Some people develop an illness or have an injury that causes them a lot of constant pain. Some of these people can think to themselves, "I still think that life is worthwhile, even with the pain, as long as _____ ." Can you fill in the blank? Is there anything that would make you feel that life is worthwhile even with lots of pain every single day?

The answers to these questions can be given orally or can be written down.

What's it for?

A sense of purpose and direction in life is a very important antidote to many forms of psychopathology, especially if the purpose is a worthy one. It has been said that if you have a why, it is much easier to find a how. In other words, if you have a very strong reason for living and living well, it will be much easier for you to find the techniques for you to do it.

As an example, many people with eating disorders become obsessed with how thin they are. If you wish very strongly to make the world a better place, if you are intently focused on trying to improve the world, it is harder to divert yourself to a pathological degree of worrying about whether you're thin enough. Similarly, if you have a very intense desire to make the word a better place, you have a more intense reason to stop drinking alcohol the moment it interferes with such a direction and purpose. You have more of a reason to get over being depressed. You have more of a reason to conquer fears that get in the way of your activities.

How do you do it well?

One of the challenges in doing this exercise well is simply to give a meaningful answer to these questions rather than have them "not compute" or be seen as "stupid questions."

Evaluating other people's thoughts on purpose in life is a very subjective and inexact undertaking. I believe most worthy purposes and directions have something to do with increasing others' happiness and taking care of one's own happiness. I believe that the best answers to these questions give no evidence of destructive wishes: the wish to destroy a certain group of people, or to get revenge on a certain person or groups of people.

Variations:

In one variation of this exercise, you write out or dictate, in as much detail as possible, the answers to these questions at a certain time each year. For example, you answer them on a certain holiday or on your birthday. These are kept in one place where you can read the progression of thoughts over the years. I believe it is useful to start doing this exercise in this way with children when they are fairly young.

Example:

Questions on Direction and Purpose

1. Purpose assigned to life:

The purpose I would like to assign to my life is to make the world a little better place by my having lived, and to take pleasure and happiness from fulfilling that goal.

2. Old person looking back:

When I am old and looking back, I would like to be able to say that I did not pass up opportunities to make contributions to the world that would produce a big payoff. I'd like to say that I enjoyed being alive and that I did not forget to have a grateful heart for the chance to take part in the adventure of life. I'd like to say that I persisted in one area long enough to make a big contribution, rather than just dabbling around.

3. Person I know of:

One person I have read about is named Aaron T. Beck. He did lots of work on developing cognitive therapy. This is a way of making your life better by consciously choosing what types of thoughts you want to think. He worked with lots of people who needed help. He wrote lots of books and articles on this topic. He taught lots of other people to do what he had figured out. His work helped a lot of people to get over being depressed and anxious and to live happier lives.

3.1 Another person:

Another person I admire was Carl von Ossietzky. He was a journalist who lived in Germany before World War II. He was very courageous in writing about what a bad idea it would be to give power to Hitler. He kept writing in opposition to Hitler's ideas even when they threatened to put him in prison. Finally, they put him in prison and told him they would let him out if he would never write about government again. He refused. He won the Nobel Peace prize while he was in prison. He finally died in prison. I think that, even though he died in prison, he was able to take a great deal of satisfaction from knowing that he had done his best to oppose something very evil that was happening.

3.2 Another person

Another person I admire is Louis Pasteur. He was a scientist who made great discoveries about infectious diseases. He came up with the way of vaccinating people against rabies. This saved lots of lives. He came up with the process of heating milk to kill the germs in it. He helped a great deal in advancing the very basic ideas of how disease results from germs and how vaccination works. I understand that he had to face some opposition from doctors for some of his discoveries. This was because he was not a medical doctor, and some doctors felt that the things he was doing should be left to doctors. He had to work very hard and long and come up with great ideas and do so in the face of some opposition. And I understand that, after achieving as much as he did, he was not at all arrogant to other people, but was humble and unassuming.

4. Effect of my life

I want my life to have a very large positive effect on a few people I love the most, my family members, my spouse and my children. I want them to be able to remember me as a model of the qualities that make life better.

I want to leave behind me some methods of teaching people, some things that are very helpful for them to know. I want to write these methods down and see these methods used by lots of people, perhaps even after I die.

5. Qualities

I want to be productive and joyous and kind. I want to be the sort of person who is able to make the most of whatever situation life deals out to me. I want to have a real sense of priorities and to be able to distinguish what is really important and what will have a big payoff from those things that are trivial and time-wasting.

6. Worthwhile with pain as long as

As long as I am able to do things that make my loved ones happier, my life is worthwhile. As long as I can do things that better the human condition, even by a little bit, my life is worthwhile. As long as I can see people made happier by my actions, and as long as I can model for other people a courageous approach to living, life is worthwhile.

Exercise 32: Making and Following Resolutions

What is it?

In this exercise, you form a resolution to do something. This resolution can be written down in the appointment calendar and to-do book, or it can be written down elsewhere, or it can be simply remembered. Then, after making this resolution, you keep it. You actually follow though on what you intend to do!

This kept resolution then is a very celebration-worthy event. It is handled like all other celebrations. (For example, you can enter it in the Celebrations Diary, use it for a fantasy rehearsal of celebrations, or just periodically recall it and feel good about it.)

The resolutions should start out easy. For example, I might resolve to have breakfast this morning, despite the fact that I do this every morning. Or I resolve to attempt to call up one friend and chat on the phone. I resolve to exercise for one minute today. The important concept is to establish the sequence of resolving and following through. If you can develop this habit with easy resolutions, you can more easily work your way up to more difficult ones.

This is an exercise that the trainee usually does as a homework assignment and reports to the trainer, rather than doing it in the trainer's presence. However, it may be possible and useful to perform the exercise within a training session, for quick resolutions. This may be especially appropriate for training sessions held on the telephone.

What's it for?

We might think of the personality as having two parts: one that gives directions to the other, and one that carries out those directions. For very many people, those two parts of the personality conflict greatly with one another. Sometimes the part that gives directions or makes resolutions is overly harsh, punitive, exacting, and demanding. And sometimes the part that carries out the directions is like a rebellious child defying the other part. Or perhaps it's like a sneaky child, avoiding following the directions as if the other part won't find out.

Eric Berne has written about such internal conflicts, using the terms "rebellious child" versus "critical parent" to refer to the parts of the personality. These parts of the personality often have their counterparts in real-life interactions that have been acted out between a critical parent figure who was trying to get the child to do something, and a real-life rebellious child who did not want to do those things.

For superior psychological functioning, however, the parts of the personality that make resolutions and the parts that follow them should be in a cooperative, harmonious and friendly relationship with each other. The part that gives directives takes care not to set up unreasonable expectations. The part that follows directives realizes that the resolutions are constructed to be in his best interest. The resolution exercise is meant to achieve a healthy relationship between these two parts of the self.

It has always fascinated me that Benjamin Franklin, an example of a very high achiever and apparently a happy individual (although not without his faults), prayed every morning for a healthy relationship between the resolving part of the self and the part that carried out the resolution. Here was his prayer:

"O powerful Goodness! Bountiful Father! Merciful Guide! Increase in me that wisdom which discovers my truest interest. Strengthen my resolutions to perform what that wisdom dictates. Accept my kind offices to thy other children as the only return in my power for thy continual favors to me!"

How do you do it well?

The hardest part of this exercise is to remember to keep on doing it. Another challenge is to make the resolutions not too hard, not too easy, but just difficult enough for the stage you currently occupy.

The most important part is to follow though with the resolutions and to perform them. Many people will realize at the beginning of this exercise that they have habitually followed through with very few of their resolutions. To do this exercise well, the percent follow through should be close to 100 percent.

Variations:

It may be very useful to form a resolutions diary. You write the date and the resolution and then write what happened in attempting to follow the resolution. The trainer and trainee go over this diary each time they meet.

Example:

12-6-2001: I resolve that today I'm going to say "Good morning!" in a cheerful and pleasant way to everyone in my family when I first see them.

Follow-up: I did it. I usually do this anyway, but I'm trying to get the momentum going with this exercise. It felt good to keep a resolution.

12-6-2001: I resolve that today I'm going to sit at my desk and work for at least an hour.

Follow-up: Yes, I kept it. I ended up working for about three hours. I knew I would have to work for a long time to finish my project. Again, I wanted to make a resolution I knew I would keep.

12-6-2001: I resolve to get at least fifteen minutes of aerobic exercise today.

Follow-up: Shot basketball, running around a lot, for forty-five minutes with my sister.

12-7-2001: I resolve that today I will spend at least five minutes organizing and cleaning up in the morning.

Follow-up: Slept later than I intended to, but I could still get in five minutes just to follow the letter of the law. I got a fair amount done in that short time.

12-7-2001: I resolve that today I will eat little enough to take in fewer calories than I use up.

Follow-up: It's hard to say whether I succeeded or not. Perhaps the next resolution I make in this area should be more easily measurable.

Exercise 33: Affirmations on Psychological Skills

What is it?

An affirmation is a short sentence you say to yourself. The affirmation brings to mind the image of achieving a desired goal and associates that image with a good feeling. Through affirmations you quickly bring to mind images of positive functioning and psychological fitness.

The following are examples of affirmations for the sixteen psychological skill groups:

1. Productivity. I want to work hard to make the world a better place. I want to better myself and prepare myself in the skills I need for this great goal.

2. Joyousness. I want to take pleasure and joy in the wonder of life and living. May I have a heart that is grateful for being able to take part in the great adventure of life.

3. Kindness. I want to treat people as I would like to be treated. May I be unselfish and forgiving and work to make people happier.

4. Honesty. I want to keep my promises and tell the truth, without lying, cheating, or stealing.

5. Fortitude. I want to be strong when things don't go my way. I want to put up with hardship when necessary.

6. Good decisions. I want to think carefully and systematically when important choice points arise. In my joint decisions with other people, I want to work thoughtfully to find a just and good option.

7. Nonviolence. I want to hold sacred the right of people to live without being hurt or killed by others. I want to work for the day when this right is available to all.

8. Respectful talk (not being rude). I want to consider carefully the effect my words have on others and to let my words support and nurture people.

9. Friendship-building. I want to build and maintain good relationships with other people, for my sake and for theirs.

10. Self-discipline. I want to do what is best, even when it is not the most pleasant thing to do. I want to give up pleasure and tolerate discomfort when necessary to achieve my higher goals.

11. Loyalty. I want to value the continuity of relationships. I want to stand by those who have earned my continuing loyalty.

12. Conservation. I want to use scarce resources wisely, without wasting them. I want to protect the earth for future generations.

13. Self-care. I want to be appropriately cautious and protect my own health and safety and welfare.

14. Compliance. I want to comply with authority when it is right and reasonable to do so.

15. Positive fantasy rehearsal. I want to rehearse in my imagination the

thoughts, feelings, and behavior patterns I consider good and right. I want to avoid taking pleasure in images of another person's misfortune.

16. Courage. I want to be courageous enough to do what is best and right, even when that involves some risk.

The following are affirmations for all sixty-two psychological skills.

Group 1: Productivity

1. Purposefulness. I want to work for the highest and best purposes, reasons for living that I can feel proud of.

2. Persistence and concentration. I want to develop my power to concentrate for longer and longer times, so that I can accomplish more that brings happiness to others and myself.

3. Competence-development. I want to take joy in developing my own skills and abilities: schoolwork skills, skills in arts, recreations or sports, and especially the skills that will let me be productive.

4. Organization. I want to be organized in my decisions about how to use my time, how to use my money and where to place my papers and objects. I want to use organization skills to realize the greatest yield from the effort I expend.

Group 2. Joyousness

5. Enjoying aloneness. I want to find joy in the work and play that I do by myself, as well as from the things I do with other people. I want to have a good balance between doing things alone and doing things with others.

6. Pleasure from approval. I want to enjoy it when I receive compliments and approval, especially from the people I consider wisest about what is good and worthwhile.

7. Pleasure from accomplishments. I want to congratulate myself, thank myself, and celebrate in my mind when I do something smart, good, or worthwhile. I want to help myself to feel good, even if nobody else notices.

8. Pleasure from my own kindness. I want to arrange my mind and my thoughts so that I feel very happy over making someone else happier.

9. Pleasure from discovery. I want to take joy in discovery, in finding out things about the world and how to live life.

10. Pleasure from others' kindness. I don't want to take for granted what other people have done for me, but to feel gratitude and happiness over whatever kindness comes to me from other people.

11. Pleasure from blessings. I want to be aware of the many blessings I have, the many ways in which I've had good luck and good fortune, and feel good about those things.

12. Pleasure from affection. I want to feel good in giving and receiving affection in a way that is kind and good

and mindful of the best interests of the giver and receiver.

13. Favorable attractions. I want to be attracted to the sort of person with whom I can be happy over a long period of time, the sort who is wise and good.

14. Gleefulness. I want to nurture the ability to be gleeful and to take joy in letting the childlike part of myself come out.

15. Humor. I want to enjoy laughter and humor; I want to help other people enjoy what is funny in our lives.

Group 3: Kindness

16. Kindness. I want very often to do kind acts, acts that make other people happier in the long run.

17. Empathy. I want to become aware of what other people are thinking and feeling. I want to see things from other people's points of view. I want to see how my actions affect other people.

18. Conscience. I am glad that I have a conscience and that I cannot harm other people without getting signals from my conscience. When I have harmed another person, I want to listen to my conscience telling me that I should make amends if possible and should avoid inflicting further harm in the future.

Group 4: Honesty

19. Honesty. I want to tell the truth, and not deceive people, even when it is very hard to be honest.

20. Awareness of my abilities. I want to have a true idea of my own skills, abilities, and potentials. I want to be confident in how much I can learn to do if I really try. When I am not very skilled at something, I want to be honest with myself, as a first step in improving if I wish to.

Group 5: Fortitude

21. Frustration-tolerance. I want to handle it when things go badly, and not think things are worse than they really are. I don't want to feel overly bad about little things that go wrong.

22. Handling separation. Sometimes I may lose someone I've come to depend on or love. At those times, I want to find the strength inside me that lets me handle my loss and return to being happy.

23. Handling rejection. I want to handle it well when people reject me or don't want to be friends with me. If they don't like me because of a fault I can correct, I want to try to correct it. If they don't have a good reason for rejecting me, I want to go on being happy.

24. Handling criticism. When someone criticizes me, I want to learn all I can from what they are saying. If they have something good to teach me, I want to learn it respectfully. If they are criticizing me without a good reason, I want not to let it bother me too much.

25. Handling mistakes and failures. When I make mistakes or fail at things I try, I want to honestly admit to myself

that I made a mistake. I want to think about what I can learn for next time and what I can do to make things better now, and not waste too much energy condemning myself or blaming someone else.

26. Magnanimity, non-jealousy. I want to be glad when other people have good things happen to them, even when I don't have those good things happen to me. I want not to be overly jealous when someone else experiences something good.

27. Painful emotion-tolerance. I want to be brave in handling the situations in which I feel bad. I want to try to learn as much as I can from those situations. I want to tolerate the pain that should be tolerated and avoid the pain that should be avoided.

28. Fantasy-tolerance. I want to be aware of the difference between thinking and doing. Even though I think about many things, I will choose to do only some of the things I think about.

Group 6: Good decisions
6a: Individual decision-making

29. Positive aim. I want to keep myself focused on making things better, for others and myself. I don't want to make things worse by trying to get sympathy, consolation or revenge.

30. Planning before acting. I want to think and plan before acting, devoting more thought to important decisions and less thought to less important ones.

31. Fluency. I want to make full use of words as tools to express what is happening around me and within me. I want to use words to make life better for others and myself.

32. Awareness of my emotions. I want to be aware of what I am feeling, and why I am feeling what I am, and thus be better able to make decisions and live happily in the world.

33. Awareness of control. I want to be able to figure out how much power I have to change things. When I do that, I can know what to try to change and what to try to tolerate.

34. Decision-making. When I have an important decision to make, I want to take several steps: think about what the problem is; work to get the information I need; think of several options; think what will probably happen when the options are tried; assess the desirability of the things that might happen. I might also think about the advantages and disadvantages of each option. In this way I want to make as good a choice as I can.

6b: Joint decision-making, including conflict resolution

35. Toleration. I want to be able to enjoy a wide range of what people do and say, without needing to boss them around.

36. Rational approach to joint decisions. When I have a problem or joint decision to make with another person, I want to work to find a solution that makes us both happy, if such a solution

exists. I want to think hard about how I want to act, rather than being ruled only by emotion.

37. Option-generating. When I have a problem to solve, I want to be creative in thinking of options for its solution.

38. Option-evaluating. When I have a problem to solve, I want to recognize the best and most reasonable options.

39. Assertion. I want to be able to take a strong stand, stick up for my own way, or continue to work against those who don't agree with me when it is wise to do that.

40. Submission: I want to be able to give in to another person's wishes, admit I was wrong, or allow myself to be led when it is wise to do that.

41. Differential reinforcement. I want to focus enthusiastically on the good that other people do, since that is almost always a good way to bring it out and encourage it.

Group 7: Nonviolence

42. Forgiveness and anger control. I want to be able to forgive those who have harmed me, not only for their sakes, but for my own. I want to avoid burdening myself with unnecessary anger.

43. Nonviolence. I want to commit myself to the principle of nonviolence and to work to foster this principle for the world.

Group 8: Not being rude (Respectful talk)

44. Not being rude, respectful talk. I want to be very sensitive and aware, and always notice when I get the urge to use words, vocal tones or facial expressions that are accusing, punishing or demeaning. I want to avoid these unless there is a very good reason.

Group 9: Friendship-Building

45. Discernment and Trusting. I want to accurately appraise other people and not distort my images of them with prejudice, overgeneralization or wish-fulfilling fantasies. I want to decide wisely what someone can be trusted for, and trust when it is appropriate.

46. Self-disclosure. I want to be able to reveal myself and share intimate thoughts and feelings with another person, to the degree that it is appropriate and wise to do so.

47. Gratitude. I want to be able to communicate to others my gratitude, admiration and approval.

48. Social initiations. I want to initiate friendly talk with others frequently and comfortably.

49. Socializing. I want to give joy to other people and myself by talking with them and hearing what they have to say, and doing fun and useful things together.

50. Listening. I want to be a good listener. I want to take the time and effort to understand the other person's

point of view, and to let the other person know I understand.

Group 10: Self-discipline

51. Self-discipline. I want to tolerate discomfort, pass up the temptation of certain pleasures, and expend tough effort when necessary to make good things happen.

Group 11: Loyalty

52. Loyalty. I want to stand by the people who have earned my loyalty, and keep my commitments to them.

Group 12: Conservation

53. Conservation and Thrift. I want to preserve resources for ourselves and future generations. I want to resist the temptation to waste resources on unnecessary luxuries. I want to be thrifty to the degree that is best.

Group 13: Self-care

54. Self-nurture. I want to think kind thoughts to myself, just as I wish to say kind things to other people.
55. Habits of self-care. I want to take the best care of my body and my mind that I possibly can. I want to avoid any drugs or toxins that I know will hurt my body or mind in the long run. I want to eat, sleep and exercise in ways to take care of my body.

56. Relaxation. I want to become expert in relaxing and calming myself when I wish to.
57. Carefulness. I want to be aware of real danger when it is present. I want to protect others and myself, and try to make us safe.

Group 14: Compliance

58. Compliance. I want to feel good about obeying reasonable and trustworthy authorities at times, especially when they tell me to do something I don't feel like doing but which I know is best to do.

Group 15: Positive fantasy rehearsal

59. Imagination and positive fantasy rehearsal. I rejoice in the use of my imagination as a tool in rehearsing or evaluating a plan, or adjusting to an event or situation. I want to practice in fantasy the patterns that are useful to me and avoid the ones that are harmful.

Group 16: Courage

60. Courage. I want to be confident and brave when I wish to be, especially when there is no danger present. If I feel unrealistic fear, I want to face what I fear, and thus take a step to conquer the fear.

61. Independent thinking. Sometimes people model wrong decisions or try to persuade me to enact wrong decisions. I want to think for myself and do what is right.

62. Depending. When I need help from someone, I want to be brave enough to ask for that help and to feel comfortable in receiving it.

****

The technique of affirmations is widely advocated by inspirational speakers. Almost all of them believe the affirmation statement should be phrased as if the goal had already been completely achieved, for example, "I am comfortable in every social situation," or, "I am at my ideal body weight, and I find it easy to maintain this weight."

By contrast, I think it's best to speak, not as if the goal had already been achieved, but of what you want to do or be. There are several reasons for this. First, "the truth shall set you free." Suppose I'm NOT at what I define as my ideal body weight, and I imagine if I get there, it will take lots of effort to maintain it. If I say to myself, "I want to maintain my ideal body weight," I am honestly stating an earnest wish to do this. I think the precedent of not lying to myself is important enough that I'm willing to give up whatever advantages people think come from making the affirmations as if the goal were already achieved.

I also think that we should phrase affirmations in ways that don't set unrealistic expectations. For example, being totally comfortable in all social situations is not possible for most individuals, nor is it desirable. (For example, being held up by a mugger is a social situation.)

What's it for?

Affirmations are meant to be a pleasant way of bringing to mind the mental images of a desired goal. Each time those images come to mind, we are fantasy rehearsing the goal and making it more likely to be achieved. Also, simply being reminded of the goal tends to keep us on course and working toward it. If we can express affirmations in a relaxing, pleasant and positive way, this might also help alleviate conflict between the resolution-making and the resolution-following parts of the personality I spoke of earlier.

How do you do it well?

For some people the main challenge in the Affirmations Exercise is avoiding undercutting oneself by negative self-statements. Here's NOT what you want to do: "May I do productive and useful things that are worthy of my efforts, (but there's little chance that I'll ever do it if I keep up as I am now)." If you feel the irresistible urge to undercut the self-statements of the affirmation by awfulizing or getting down on yourself, it's probably best to practice the Twelve

Thought Exercise to work on more conscious control of these thoughts.

Variations:

A variation for a very busy person is to carry a written version of the affirmations in a pocket or a purse and read them at regular times.

In another variation on this exercise, you make an audiotape for yourself. First, you record pleasant instrumental music. I think that baroque music fits this purpose nicely. Then you record a voiceover of the affirmations with the music in the background. The result can be a tape that is very pleasant and relaxing to listen to.

Exercise 34: Self-Run Contingent Reinforcement

What is it?

This is a project you carry out over time and report to the trainer, rather than performing it in a training session. In this exercise you devise a reinforcement program for yourself. You use concrete reinforcements for certain behaviors. You allow yourself to get what you want, contingent upon doing what you should do.

The tasks should be something that you really want to do but are hard to get yourself to do. Examples may be exercising, following a diet, completing household chores, remembering to floss your teeth, refraining from teasing your sister, going to bed and/or getting out of bed at a certain time, working on the book you're writing, or remembering to use the appointment book and to-do list.

The reinforcements that you give yourself for doing these sorts of tasks are the pleasures that are almost classifiable as vices. These might include watching television, watching videotapes, playing chess against a computer, eating sweets or sugar, buying things that aren't necessities, surfing the internet, going out to a restaurant rather than cooking at home, and so forth. Going to an amusement park, going to a movie, going to an athletic contest, and having somebody read to you from a novel also might be reinforcers that are useable in such a program.

After you've decided what tasks you want to do and what reinforcers you want to earn for doing them, then you have to figure out your rate of payment. How much of the reinforcer do you get for how much of the work task that is done? If you pay yourself too liberally, you'll get all of the reinforcer, so that it no longer motivates you for the tasks. If you are too miserly in reinforcing yourself, you make it too likely that you'll say to yourself, "It isn't worth it, I'll just do without." Another decision is how to measure both the work and the payoff. For example: Are you going to measure your writing by the number of hours spent writing or by the number of pages written?

Once you've made all these decisions, then the really hard part begins: the act of withholding from yourself the reinforcement unless you've earned it. The very strong temptation is to cheat and to "steal" the reinforcer. If you can learn to follow the rules you have made for yourself, then you have achieved a wonderful degree of self-discipline. If you can develop the habit of following your own rules on such contingent reinforcement programs, you can help yourself achieve all sorts of things.

What's it for?

The theory behind this exercise is that people seem to be happiest under conditions of contingent reinforcement. Animal research, done or summarized by Martin Seligman (in his 1975 book entitled *Helplessness: On Depression,*

Development, and Death) indicates that working for rewards and getting them is more satisfying than getting rewards for free. For example, animals at zoos who simply have their foods dumped into their cages at regular intervals seem to be less vibrant and alive than animals in the wild who have to work to get their food.

In our lives, many tasks that should be done are not particularly fun. In addition, many enjoyable activities don't accomplish anything worthwhile. If we can link these two types of activities in a contingent relationship, we run a good chance of finding balance between delay of gratification and consumption of gratification. We make the delay of gratification tasks easier by reinforcing them with consumption of gratification. We also keep the consumption of gratification from getting out of hand by controlling it and delivering it to ourselves only in measured amounts.

How do you do it well?

Contingency programs are made or broken in the details, and self-run contingency programs are no exception to this rule. It's important to set goals for the work tasks that are not too hard, not too easy, but just at the right level of difficulty. That way, you will have a good chance of acquiring the reinforcer, but you will have to work for it.

The hardest part of this exercise is obeying your own rules. Doing the Resolution Exercise, getting on good terms with the resolution-making part of yourself, and getting into the habit of following your own resolutions is an important prerequisite for the Self-Run Contingency Program exercise.

Variations:

If you'd like, you can recruit somebody else to play some role in your self-run contingent reinforcement program. In one variation, the role of the other person is simply to lend an ear when you periodically report honestly what you have and haven't done in the program.

In another variation, you actually give the other person some power over the reinforcers. For example, you give a deposit of money to the other person, which the other person will send to you depending on your finishing the tasks. What you don't receive by a certain date will be sent to some charity or organization that to you represents throwing away your money. (For example, for many people a donation to the Internal Revenue Service would be aversive enough a consequence to provide some motivation. You don't want to pick a consequence you can't ethically tolerate, e.g.,. a donation to the Ku Klux Klan.)

Exercise 35: Tones of Approval and Enthusiasm

What is it?

In this exercise the trainee practices saying various phrases with any of three degrees of enthusiasm and approval:

No approval and enthusiasm
Small to moderate approval and enthusiasm, or
Large approval and enthusiasm.

Sometimes these degrees are abbreviated by calling them "none, small to moderate, and large."

In this exercise the trainee first practices discriminating degrees of approval and then practices producing them. The trainer chooses a phrase such as, "I like that" or "Way to go" or "That was good." The trainer speaks the phrase with one of the degrees of approval and enthusiasm. The trainee practices discriminating whether it was none, small, or large.

For no approval, the trainer speaks the phrases mechanically, like a robot. For small to moderate approval, she speaks the phrase in a pleasant, conversational tone. For large approval, she sounds very excited and says the phrase with much greater intensity. The trainer should first model the three degrees of approval and identify them; then the trainer gives the trainee several examples to classify.

Once the trainee can do this accurately, then the trainer might hand the trainee a sheet of paper with a list of phrases, each one with a certain degree of approval and enthusiasm. For example:

"Good idea." (with small approval and enthusiasm)
"Good idea! (with large approval)
"Good idea." (with no approval)
"That sounds good." (with no approval)
"That sounds good!" (with large approval)
"That sounds good." (with small approval)

The trainee goes down the list, and the trainer does not look at the list. The trainer guesses what degree of approval the trainee was trying to convey. If the trainee is doing the exercise well, the trainer is able to guess easily and accurately.

In another variation, the trainee makes up the phrases and the degrees of approval and lets the trainer know whether the guess was right or wrong.

Here are some phrases you can use to practice with in this exercise:

Nice job.
Look at that.
Oh, my goodness.
Look what you've done.
Did you do this?
Who gave this to me?
What is this about?
This is really something.

Who was it that did this?
So this is your work?
It's all done now.
Oh ... I see.
What brings you here?
Come on, look at this.
Let's get back on task.
I don't want any, thanks.
Come in.
How did you do that?
Please pick up that thing.
I don't know.
You're finished with it now.
What an outfit you have on.
You did it, yourself?
You are an unusual person.
I did it.

What's it for?

Much of people's success in human relations depends on the messages of approval that people send to one other in their tones of voice. People who convey approval to one other in their tones of voice tend to be better liked than people who don't. People who convey enthusiasm tend to be better leaders. Many people in the world are extremely hungry for the approval and enthusiasm of someone else. People who are able to meet this need of their fellow human beings can do lots of good. This is especially true if they give such approval when their fellow human beings attain their highest and best behavior or take a step in that direction. Because strong relationships are built upon the meeting of mutual needs and desires, people

who give approval can also strengthen relationships they have with others.

This is an important exercise for parents of young children. Young children are probably much more responsive to the tones of voice in the messages they get from their parents than they are to the semantic content of those messages.

Many young children seek to elicit a show of excitement and emotion from their parents, even if the emotion is negative. This is especially true for children with temperamental traits of sensation-seeking. But suppose a parent provides excited approval after positive behavior and avoids excitement in response to negative behavior. Now the parent can still shape the child toward positive behavior even when the child is a sensation-seeker.

There is another important element of this exercise: using tones of approval and enthusiasm in self-statements, or what you say to yourself. Just as the reinforcing value of things you say to others depends on your tone of voice, the same principle applies to things you say to yourself. So if I say to myself, in robot monotones, "Good–You've gotten started on your article–It's a start,"–I will probably take less pleasure in that thought than if I say to myself, "GOOD! You've gotten STARTED on your ARTICLE! It's a START!" I believe that one of the antidotes to depression is learning to give positive reinforcement to yourself, not only with words but also with the tones of voice you use.

How do you do it well?

In this exercise, it's usually fun for the trainee to practice the bland and emotionless statements of no approval and the high-intensity excitement of large approval. Small to moderate approval is the one that's most frequently appropriate in real life. It's important for people to make a very clear distinction between small approval and no approval.

Transferring the important learnings of this exercise to real life is a big job. The Tones of Approval and Enthusiasm Exercise is an acting exercise. In real life, you actually have to work up the positive emotion that goes along with these tones of voice in order to be genuine. This involves being clear in your own mind about just why something you did or someone else did is worthy of your excitement and approval.

When someone learns something, you can contemplate how many years the person has to use the skills she is learning. You can think about what an accomplishment it will be if you can impart a skill the person will use well for the rest of her life.

If the act that the person did has anything to do with kindness and helpfulness, you can think about the violence and hostility that prevail in the world and about how wonderful it is that kindness exists where it does exist.

If the person is a child, or if the person has been kind to a child, you can think about how the emotions of childhood experiences are evoked by events throughout the rest of life. You can think about how providing a child with some good memories will help the child feel good throughout her lifetime.

If a person has been kind to you, you might contrast this to the times when people have been unkind to you; this may help in not taking the person's act of kindness for granted. If you are being kind to someone else, you might think about the kind acts you've received from others that have stood out in your memory, to help yourself realize that these are important.

In other words, you think the thoughts that make yourself feel the emotions of approval and enthusiasm; you don't just mouth the tones.

Do you want to approach this exercise from a musical point of view? If so, we can think about what musical qualities of the utterances convey emotion and enthusiasm. Larger approval tends to involve: higher pitches; greater differences between the lowest pitch and the highest pitch; and pitches that rise from the beginning to the end of the utterance. Sometimes, but not always, volume also rises with greater enthusiasm and approval, and often the tempo is faster. There is often greater difference in the duration of notes, as some ideas get much greater emphasis than others. The most essential elements, I believe, are variations in pitch and duration of notes, the elements that make an emphatic melody rather than a diffident one.

Variations:

As I've already mentioned, there is a discrimination exercise and a production exercise. In the production exercise, you can give the trainee a list or the trainee can make up his own phrases and degrees of approval. The trainer can guess after every utterance the trainee makes, or the trainer can wait and give feedback after the end of the list.

A very interesting variation on this exercise involves going to the celebrations diary and letting the person practice "celebrating my own choice" with real-life behaviors he has done, using any of the degrees of approval. This exercise will help the trainee realize how tones of voice influence the effectiveness of self-reinforcement.

Another very important variation involves purposefully recognizing and producing tones of disapproval as well as approval. The chart then becomes:

Large approval
Small to moderate approval
No approval
Small to moderate disapproval
Large disapproval

Here are some hypotheses about these degrees of approval. First: if you could tally up all the approval and disapproval that occurs in various families, in each of these five categories, you would find that the happier families give more approval and less disapproval to one another. Second: the amounts of approval and disapproval people give to themselves, in their self-talk, correlate with the approval and disapproval they give to others. Third: the amounts of approval and disapproval in self-talk correlate with people's happiness and psychological functioning.

This reasoning suggests that, to become psychologically healthier and happier, you should try to express a lot of approval to other people, and you should try to express a lot of approval to yourself in self-talk.

A separate exercise connected with this concept is attempting to monitor the proportion of your utterances to family members or other people that fall into the various categories of approval and disapproval. You can start out by taking a wild guess. For the five categories listed above, what percent of your utterances made to each important person in your life fall into each category? How would the important person in your life answer this question? Is it possible for you to change, by conscious effort, the distribution of approving and disapproving utterances you make to other people and to yourself? If you can, you should celebrate that. For many people, this variable seems to governed by reflex and habit, not by conscious choice.

Example:

Trainer: I'll say one of the phrases on the list, and you tell me whether you think it's

large approval
small to medium approval
neutral
small to medium disapproval
or large disapproval.

OK?
Trainee: OK.

Trainer: Here's the first one. *Nice job!* (In very sarcastic voice.)

Trainee: Large disapproval?

Trainer: Yes! That's exactly what I was trying for. How about this: Nice *job*!

Trainee: Large approval?

Trainer: Yes. How about this one: Look–at–that. (In monotone)

Trainee: Neutral?

Trainer: Right. Now how about this one: Look at that. (In pleasant voice.)

Trainee: Large approval?

Trainer: I was trying for small to medium approval. How about this one: Look at that! (In very excited voice)

Trainee: Now it's large approval.

Trainer: Right. Now it's your turn to do some, and I'll guess.

Trainee: Oh, my goodness. (In tone of disgust.)

Trainer: Large disapproval?

Trainee: Yes. Oh, my goodness.

Trainer: Small to medium approval?

Trainee: I was trying for large approval, but I think I can muster some more excitement. How about this: Oh, my goodness!

Trainer: Great! That's larger approval.

Exercise 36: Handling Criticism

What is it?

In this exercise the trainee practices receiving a criticism and practices responding to it with four types of utterances.

Reflection
Agreeing with part of the criticism
Asking for more specific criticism
Planning to ponder or problem solve

Here's an example:
Suppose that one family member says to another family member, "I don't think you're pulling your weight around this household." Here are examples of the four types of utterances.

Reflection: "So you feel that I'm not doing enough work and other people are having to do my work for me."

Agreeing with part of criticism: "I'll admit I haven't attained perfection on household work."

Asking for more specific criticism: "Is there anything in particular that prompts you to say this?"

Planning to ponder: "I'll give some thought to what you've told me about this.

Planning to problem solve: "I want to hear more of your thoughts about this, and then let's list some options and choose among them to try to solve this problem."

What's it for?

These sorts of responses are not meant to be a universal formula for handling all criticism. But they are very useful responses to have in the repertoire. They are especially useful when attempting to foster a climate of cooperation and good will. They are good responses to be able to use, however, even when a climate of cooperation and good will is impossible for the moment. They are very useful in helping you feel that you are being reasonable. They are also very useful in helping you feel you don't need to defend yourself against every criticism. Thus, sometimes these responses are appropriate even with the most malicious and adversarial criticism. Agreeing with part or all of criticism is sometimes the best "defense" against unfriendly criticism.

For example, imagine that children have been singing together in music class, and one student says to another student in a loud voice, "You sound like a sick cat!" If the criticized student gives a little smile and a shrug and says, "You're right. I'm not a great singer. I never pretended to be," then he gives the other person the message, "This is not an issue that I'm vulnerable on. You can criticize me all you want, and it won't devastate me." The critic, who was probably looking for stimulation and entertainment in the criticized person's response, doesn't find it and is not reinforced.

How to do it well

One of the most difficult challenges in doing this exercise well is eliminating self-defense or counterattack from the response. Sometimes defensiveness can work its way into responses that fit the format of the category. For example: The critic says, "You don't do enough work around this house." Consider the following responses:

Reflection: "You, of all people, are telling me I don't do enough work?" (Embedded message: "You do even less work than I do.")

Agreeing with part of criticism: "It's true that I could do more, but I already do an awful lot." (The second part of the sentence is defending oneself.)

Asking for more specific criticism: "Just give me three examples of what you're talking about." (Embedded message: "I bet you can't think of anything.")

Planning to Ponder or Problem solve: "Well, whatever. I'll think about it, I guess." And then the person makes a remark to someone else about a different topic. (Embedded message: "I'll not give it another thought.")

In order to avoid these types of responses and to perform the exercise in a more sincere way, it's useful for the trainee to give himself a cognitive "subtext." The subtext is the set of assumptions that guide the utterances. These are self-instructions along the following lines: "If I have a bad habit, I want to explore it and eliminate it. If the other person has a problem with something I'm doing, I want to see whether a good solution can be found." With these thoughts, even if they are unexpressed, it is much easier to do this exercise. In fact, it may be useful for the trainee to actually express these ideas out loud before going through the four types of utterances.

Variations:

As with almost all of the exercises, this lends itself to a written exercise. The trainee can compose and write down a criticism and then write down the four responses to it.

This exercise has two other variations—one in which the critic words his criticism in constructive ways and another in which the critic uses a more punishing and insulting form of language. Of course, responding in appropriate ways to the more punishing and insulting language is more difficult for the trainee.

Example:

Here is another example. The first person says, "You talk for so long without quitting; it can really be annoying."

Here are examples of the four types of response.

Reflection: "So I don't yield the floor often enough?"

Agreeing with part of criticism: "I can go on for a long time sometimes; that's for sure."

Asking for more specific criticism: "Is there any more you want to tell me about this? Any specific examples or anything?"

Planning to ponder or problem-solve: "I'll try to be aware of what you said. Let's sit down and talk about it again if I'm not able to solve this."

Exercise 36 B: Less Friendly Ways of Handling Criticism

What is it?

The world is not always a happy family. School, in particular, is a place where people often have to withstand vicious attacks upon their reputations and self-esteem. In many other settings, including at times even in the best of families, there is criticism that deserves not to be listened to but to be non-reinforced, punished or exposed as wrong.

In this exercise, the trainee practices coming up with a response that is an example of each of the following:

> Criticizing the critic
> Debating the critic
> Ignoring the critic
> Silent eye contact
> Humor

Here's an example. The situation is that someone sits on a school bus and another kid says to him, "That's a dorky shirt you have on, queer face." Here are some possible responses.

Criticizing the critic: "Is that how you try to feel powerful and important? Go out and find somebody to insult for no reason? Why don't you grow up and find something more constructive to do?"

Debating the critic: "Sounds like you really think it's important how shirts look, huh? Can't you think of anything else more worthwhile to think about?"

Ignoring the critic: The criticized person makes a slight shrug or a slight lift of the eyebrows; then he turns to the person sitting next to him and says, "So how was your day at school today?"

Silent eye contact; The criticized person looks straight into the eyes of the critic, with a facial expression of pity, sadness, disdain, curiosity or any of a variety of other emotions other than indignation or fear, which the critic expects and wants.

Humor: The criticized person makes a funny face portraying mock surprise, grabs his shirt and pulls it out with his hand and looks at it, and then says, "It's dorky? Oh my! It's dorky!" Or as another example: "Not like that non-dorky shirt of yours, huh? In fact, ladies and gentleman, I'll bet this shirt that he has on is about the un-dorkiest one on the whole face of the planet."

What is it for?

The point of this exercise is to get more responses to criticism into the repertoire. These responses are meant to have the effect of either punishing the critic, not reinforcing the critic, or getting the onlookers on one's own side.

Responding to criticism with humor can sometimes disparage and punish the critic. But it can also be a more friendly response that transforms the situation. It can replace stimulation by hostility with stimulation by silliness.

Responding with silent eye contact is meant to avoid the game that sometimes gets played when the criticized person tries to ignore the critic. In this game, the critic realizes that the other person is trying the ignoring strategy and escalates the harassment or criticism. The critic engages in a game of "I bet I can get you to pay attention to me." Silent eye contact makes this game difficult. It confronts the critic nonverbally. At the same time, it avoids a verbal rejoinder. This avoids giving the critic a chance to play the game of "I'll attack and you defend."

Debating the critic should never be undertaken with much hope of persuading the critic himself. Rather, the purpose of this is to persuade the "audience" of the rightness of the criticized person's point of view. Another reasonable purpose sometimes is to make the consequences of criticizing unpleasant for the critic.

How do you do it well?

In criticizing the critic, it's important not to descend to the level of the critic or beneath it. The more valid, constructive and truthful your criticism of the critic is, the more effective it will be.

In debating the critic, one of the challenges is deciding which question to debate. The criticized person should not fall into the trap of debating whether he or she is a good person. If the critic can define the question for debate as "Resolved: my opponent is a bad person," then the criticized person is nearly defeated before beginning. The criticized person debates some other topic, such as "Resolved: the critic is someone who likes to attack people for no good reason."

In the example above where someone's shirt was criticized, the person defined the debate issue as "Resolved: the appearance of shirts is not something worth spending much energy on," instead of "Resolved, my shirt is not dorky." He is debating with the critic, not about his judgment upon the shirt, but about his judgment on what is really important in life. He defines the debate in terms of whether the fault makes any difference, not whether it exists.

In order to do ignoring well, you must do it with nonchalance. Sitting silently and frowning, or glaring and avoiding eye contact with the critic is what some people do when they try to use ignoring. In so doing, they look wounded, yet defenseless, encouraging the malicious critic. Proper ignoring entails continuing with one's business unaffected by the critic.

In silent eye contact, the facial expression and nonverbal messages are crucial. Any of the emotions I listed above, rather than impotent indignation or fear, allow this response to be effective.

Humorous responses to being attacked require quite a bit of skill. If one has some talent as a comedian, it's possible to practice applying it to this situation. If one lacks this talent, it might be best to leave this response well enough alone. The more good-natured and friendly the humor is, the less risk there is of retaliation.

Variations:

It's possible to do this as a written exercise, although it may be difficult to describe some of the nonverbal responses in writing.

In another variation, the trainee is given various situations involving criticism, and the trainee decides whether to practice the five responses for less friendly responses or the four responses aiming at greater cooperation.

Exercise 37: Ranking of Options

What is it?

This is another decision-making practice exercise. The trainee is given a situation and three different ways of responding to it. The trainee's job is to rank the options as the best, the worst and the middle.

Below are some examples of questions for this exercise.

1. Someone has problems at work, and they are bothering him; he can't sleep. He could:

Get up and write notes to himself about what to do about the problems.
Drink some of an alcoholic drink to put himself to sleep.
Get up and watch whatever is on television.

2. Someone has an appointment with someone for the first time. They are to meet in an office at a big building. The person comes to a door and tries it, but it is locked. She could:

Go home.
Sit outside and wait.
Check to see if a different door is unlocked.

3. A kid wants to use something his sister is using, and only one person can use it at a time. He could:

Grab it away.
Say, "May I use that after you're done with it?"
Forget about it, and do something else.

4. A person loses a file on the computer, something he has been writing. He could:

Write it again quickly before forgetting it.
Go outside and take a walk to cool off.
Hit the wall with his fist.

5. Someone is at a party where she doesn't know anyone and wants to make a friend, but she feels shy. She could:

Interrupt someone who is talking to someone else and try to talk or play with that person.
Start crying in front of everyone and beg her mom to take her home.
Watch for an opportunity to start talking or playing without interrupting someone.

6. Somebody wants to be the star of a play, but gets chosen for a more minor part. He could:

Have a fit, screaming and crying and saying it's not fair.
Quit the play.

Enjoy doing the minor part.

7. Somebody loses a chess game. She could:

Say congratulations to the winner.
Not say anything at all.
Say, "I could have won if I had been feeling better today. You aren't so good."

8. There are some mice in the house, probably because people leave food out a lot. They could:

Move out of the house.
Put rat traps around the house.
Clean up the food.

9. Somebody is harassed by her brother. She could:

Hit him.
Yell at him.
Go into a room to be away from him.

10. Someone is bored. He could:

Harass a sibling.
Talk to a friend on the phone.
Watch a scary movie.

What's it for?

This exercise allows practice in another maneuver of the decision-making process. Quickly deciding where an option ranks on the hierarchy of appropriateness is very useful for life decisions.

This exercise also allows the trainer to take a measure of the trainee's judgment.

How do you do it well?

Doing this well in the simplest variation means ranking the options in the "correct" order.

In a more complex variation, the trainee not only ranks the options, but also tells the reason why he ranked them as he did. Explaining these reasons can rely on advantages and disadvantages, consequences and the sixteen ethical principles.

In an even more difficult variation, the trainee adds to the bank of situations and options for this exercise by composing them. Doing this well entails devising situations that are new, interesting or relevant, and options that clearly stand in a certain order of appropriateness.

Variations:

To summarize the variations already mentioned:

The trainee can simply rank the options.

The trainee can rank the options and explain his choice.

The trainee can create new situations and options for other people. Either the trainer or trainee can do the secretarial work for this one.

Exercise 38: Sentence Completion

What is it?

In this exercise the trainer presents the trainee with several unfinished sentences. The trainee's job is to finish them in a way that discloses something about the trainee. The following unfinished sentences can be used in this exercise:

1. It makes me happy to
2. One thing I'm proud of is
3. I like to
4. I am sorry that
5. I wish that
6. I wonder about
7. It's a challenge to handle it when
8. One thing about me most people don't know is that
9. I would like to learn more about
10. Sometimes I worry that
11. If I had a lot more money I would
12. One thing I fear is
13. One of the hardest things for me is
14. One of my main goals is
15. One of the qualities of people I admire most is
16. Before my life is over I would like to
17. One thing I never want to do is to
18. It really bugs me when someone
19. One time I felt really successful was when
20. It was scary when
21. I like it when
22. I want to know about
23. I am sorry that
24. Boys usually
25. A mother should
26. I would greatly fear
27. I don't think I can
28. Other people
29. The future looks
30. One thing I need is
31. I am at my best when
32. What bothers me a lot is
33. School for me is
34. A thought about my father is that
35. I don't tell most people that
36. Most girls
37. A great worry of mine is
38. I don't like it that
39. When I daydream, I think about
40. Years from now I will be
41. I am happiest when
42. I feel sad when
43. People in my family
44. I am at my worst when
45. It is fun to imagine that

***

What's it for?

This exercise provides practice in the skill of self-disclosure, a subskill in the friendship-building group.

This exercise is derived from sentence completion "tests," typically given by a tester who hardly knows the testee and who will not have a continuing relationship with the testee. These tests are meant to encourage self-disclosure in a situation where the tested person might be appropriately wary about self-disclosure.

This exercise is meant to be done in the very different context of an ongoing relationship between the trainer and trainee. It is meant to be selected at a time in the relationship where the trainee has come to trust the trainer enough to self-disclose.

As in all these exercises, it's best that the trainee know what the purpose is. If the trainee chooses to give the funniest, most creative or most unusual possible responses, the exercise will be very different in character from an exercise in which the trainee gives the most serious, dull or ordinary responses. Also, before doing this exercise, the trainer and trainee should talk about whether the trainee would like to practice the skill of self-disclosure. If the trainee strongly wishes not to work on this skill, this is not the exercise to do.

It takes some time to build up the requisite degree of trust for working on the skill of self-disclosure. In most cases, the trainee is not ready to do this until he has had several meetings with the trainer.

In addition, if true self-disclosure is to occur, the trainee must be assured about the confidentiality of her responses. It would not be wise, for example, for the trainee to be extremely open and forthcoming if the answers were to be shared with a group of untrusted peers. The trainer should make very clear exactly who, if anyone, will be told the answers to these questions.

How do you do it well?

The object is to complete the sentences in ways that really reveal something about yourself. It is very possible to respond to any of them in ways that reflect external or public or superficial events. For example, let's imagine that the stem is "I hope that . . ." A response fairly low on the self-disclosure scale would be "I hope that the Pittsburgh Pirates win their next baseball game." Higher on the self-disclosure scale would be "I hope that someday I have a happy marriage." Even higher perhaps might be "I hope that someday I can marry John Smith."

Yet, doing this exercise well does not necessarily mean jumping to the most intimate and private details immediately. The most appropriate degree of self-disclosure depends on how far the trainee has progressed on the hierarchy of self-disclosure skills. For many trainees, simply a sincere disclosure about a hope about a baseball game may be a great step up on the hierarchy of self-disclosure skills.

The person doing this exercise need not restrict the response to finishing the one incomplete sentence. It's great to add other sentences for a more complete disclosure.

Here's the broadest definition of what it means to do this exercise well: The trainee can consciously choose what degree of self-disclosure he feels comfortable with at this particular time and can then select responses that correspond to that choice.

Variations:

The trainee can perform this exercise either orally or in writing. If the trainee performs it in writing, she can first explain what degree of self-disclosure she wants to use in the exercises.

Of course, writing these answers down brings up the possibility that some undesired person could read them. This is also a possibility when the trainer writes them down. Thus, in another variation, the responses are not recorded in any way other than in the trainer's and trainee's memories.

Example:

1. It makes me happy to be able to help someone solve a problem. This is especially true if I feel what I've done has really made someone a lot happier than he was before. Often when I've done this, it has involved teaching someone to do something that he couldn't do well before.

2. One thing I'm proud of is writing an article that was very hard to write. I used self-discipline and made myself get it done. I think it helped some people.

3. I like to sing and play my guitar. But lately I haven't taken much time to do this. I guess that's because my life is so full of other activities that are also fun and useful to do.

4. I am sorry that one of the conditions of life is that we gradually get feeble as we get older, and that we eventually have to die. But then again, I'm glad that we get to live in the first place! Although the deal isn't perfect, it's good enough, and I'll take it!

5. I wish that the settlers who came to the United States had treated the Native Americans better. William Penn was one of the few who were kind and truthful to them, but there were not enough like him.

6. I wonder about what sort of changes in human society will take place in the next fifty years. Things have changed so rapidly in the last fifty years. I think lots of the changes have been for the good. I'm especially happy about the movements that have worked toward non-oppression and acceptance of minority groups.

7. It's a challenge to handle it when there's something very pleasant to do, but it's not a good thing to do. One example is the temptation to eat a lot of junk food.

8. One thing about me most people don't know is that I had a very strong Southern accent for the first part of my life. I like some Southern accents very

much. But when I heard myself on tape,
I didn't like my own accent. So I
changed it. And I've liked the change.

9. I would like to learn more about
ordinary people–not famous ones–who
have done brave, good, self-disciplined
or otherwise imitation-worthy things.
I'd like to have a long book about the
smart and good things they've done that
have made their lives better.

10. Sometimes I worry that the pesticides that people put on their lawns
may do some damage to people in ways
that are hard to figure out. What if these
chemicals caused an increase in learning problems among children?

Exercise 39: Good Will Meditation

What is it?

In this exercise, you start with the following incomplete sentences:

May _____ become the best _____ can become.

May _____ give and receive compassion and kindness.

May _____ live happily and productively.

In doing this exercise you usually sit silently and close your eyes. Then you let these sentences go through your mind, filling in the blanks with the names of various people. Some people like to begin by wishing these outcomes for themselves:

May I become the best I can become.
May I give and receive compassion and kindness.
May I live happily and productively.

After wishing these things for yourself, you then imagine someone else and bring the image of that person very clearly to mind. Then you wish each of these three things for that person.

I find it's appropriate to apply these meditations to people you're in conflict with, as well as to people you have a positive relationship with. It does require a certain degree of self-discipline to wish someone self-fulfillment, compassion and happiness when sometimes you feel like crushing, defeating or punishing him. But, that is the sort of self-discipline that this exercise is meant to strengthen.

What's it for?

This exercise aims to improve skills in two major areas. One is kindness. The root of kindness is good will: the wish for the other person to be happy.

The other skill area is concentration, persistence and sustaining attention. I categorize these as a subskill under productivity. Following the discipline of keeping your mind on the task, clearly visualizing one person after another, wishing for the desired outcomes without becoming distracted, is indeed a concentration challenge.

How do you do it well?

It is fairly easy simply to fill in the blanks of these sentences. What is more challenging is sincerely wishing for these outcomes for the person. It's also useful to have some sort of mental image of the person achieving the outcome, although the outcomes can be achieved in many different ways.

It's probably best to imagine more than one particular way in which the person becomes the best he or she can be. That way you don't get yourself into a fixed idea of what the other person should do. If you're wishing for your son to become the best he can be, for instance, you don't want to restrict yourself to an image of his going to Harvard. (Who knows, he might want to go to Yale instead.)

As mentioned before, another aspect of doing this exercise well is simply keeping on task with it. Five or ten minutes will permit a very large number of good wishes for many people.

Variations:

One variation is to say the sentence to yourself and then to talk further to yourself about possible ways in which this outcome could come about. In other words, the imaginings involve several possible concrete images. For example:

"May Jane Doe live happily and productively. I hope that she is able to stop having so many headaches. I'm imagining her relaxing and being easier on herself. I'm imagining that she learns to forgive herself more for what happened to her son."

This more extended and detailed version of the good will meditation can be written out, as well as spoken.

Exercise 40: Graphing of Self-Discipline

What is it?

To do this exercise, you first select a task that challenges your self-discipline skills. It can be a physical task, such as seeing how long you can hold a handgrip tightly squeezed together. You can see how many times you can lift certain weights overhead, or see how fast you can run two miles. You can use an intellectual task, such as skip counting. It can be a computer exercise in math facts or touch-typing or naming musical notes.

The self-discipline challenge can also involve longer-term projects that are, nonetheless, quantifiable. If the long-term project is losing weight, the number you put on the graph might be your weight, measured every Sunday morning. If the long-term task is doing better in schoolwork, the quantification might be the number of hours you work on schoolwork each week.

Once you have a self-discipline task, you give it your best shot, time after time, for repeated trials. You measure how you do on each trial and make a graph of how you do. The object of the exercise is to produce a learning curve in which you gradually do better and better over time. Or, for certain tasks, such as doing hours of school work, the goal might be to keep the graph above a certain threshold. The point of this exercise is to consciously make the graph go where you want it to go.

What's it for?

We develop self-discipline skills and fortitude skills by pushing ourselves to the limits of our endurance on repeated occasions. Many people have never had the experience of discovering that if they push themselves repeatedly, they can substantially improve their performance. Finding out that you can progress along a learning curve is an extremely valuable life experience and a prototype for many future experiences of skill acquisition.

How do you do it well?

The major challenge in this exercise is continuing and persisting even when the graph is flat or headed in the wrong direction. It's easy to maintain morale when the learning curve is headed on an unmistakable upward slant.

The other key to doing this exercise well is learning how to try as hard as you possibly can on any given trial. Giving close to 100 percent effort on anything requires self-discipline. Sometimes the only way to make the learning curve go up is to reach for greater and greater amounts of self-discipline.

Variations:

It's good to start with tasks that produce a learning curve in repeated trials fairly quickly. Learning to skip

count, for example from zero to seventy
by sevens, is usually an example of
such a task. With repeated trials, the
time needed to accomplish this task
usually falls substantially. From this,
you can work your way up to the more
difficult tasks of losing weight, writing
a thesis or increasing the time devoted
to schoolwork.

Exercise 41: Thinking Ahead in Strategy Games

What is it?

By strategy games, I'm referring to games such as Chess, Checkers, Connect Four, Mancala, and–the one I've used the most for this exercise–Tic-Tac-Toe.

In this exercise the trainee is given a position in a strategy game and makes a plan for play that involves thinking ahead. You don't just think, "This looks like a good move. I'll move here and see what happens." You think about your possible moves; you think about your opponent's possible responses; you think about your own response to those responses. You are learning to think one to several "moves ahead." You are also thinking of your eventual goal and moving backward from that goal to the current position.

The advantage of using tic-tac-toe is that it's a simple game in which you can plot out the strategy all the way to the end of the game. In this exercise, you plot out your strategy, name it in words, and tell exactly what's going to happen, before you make your move.

In doing this exercise, I have used a shareware tic-tac-toe program that is just smart enough to be the perfect opponent for this exercise. The program never makes blunders like overlooking two in a row, but it fails to look far enough ahead to prevent itself from being defeated by someone who can look several moves ahead.

I have used a "level-one" challenge and a "level-two" challenge in tic-tac-toe. For the level-one challenge, the trainer makes the first two moves against the computer, and the computer responds. For the level-two challenge, the trainer makes only the first move against the computer, and the computer responds. The trainee's task in each case is to plot out and to say in words the strategy that will win the game, and then execute that strategy.

Here is the fact about tic-tac-toe that makes this possible. If the player who moves first moves to any corner, and the player who moves second moves any place other than the center, it is then possible for the first player to force a win.

The computer makes this exercise more fun. But you don't need a computer; you can present the positions on paper. Here are examples of level-one positions:

Problem 3.

1	2	3
X	O	X
4 O	5	6
7	8	9

Problem 1.

1	2	3
X	O	X
4	5	6
7	8	9 O

It's X's move. Where do you think X should move, and why?

It's X's move. Where do you think X should move, and why?

Problem 2.

1	2	3
X	O	X
4	5	6
7 O	8	9

Problem 4.

1	2	3 O
4	5 X	6
7 X	8 O	9

It's X's move. Where do you think X should move, and why?

It's X's move. Where do you think X should move, and why?

Here are examples of level-two challenges:

Problem 5. (Level 2)

1	2	3
X	O	
4	5	6
7	8	9

It's X's move. Make a plan for how X can win, even if O plays as well as possible.

Problem 6. (Level 2)

1	2	3
X		
4	5	6
		O
7	8	9

It's X's move. Make a plan for how X can win, even if O plays as well as possible.

Problem 7. (Level 2)

1	2	3
X		
4	5	6
7	8	9
		O

It's X's move. Make a plan for how X can win, even if O plays as well as possible.

Problem 8. (Level 2)

1	2	3
4	5	6
	X	O
7	8	9

It's X's move. Make a plan for how X can win, even if O plays as well as possible.

Here's how the trainee might respond to the first level one challenge:

I'll move to cell number 7. That gives me winning cells at 4 and 5. Whichever one he moves to, I will win at the other one.

Here's an example of how the trainee might respond to problem 5, the first level two challenge:

I'll move to cell number 7. That will force him to move to cell 4. Then I'll move to 9, and that will give me winning cells at 5 and 8. Whichever one of those he moves to, I'll win with the other one.

If you use this planning ahead strategy against the computer, you'll find you can beat the computer on every occasion, other than when the computer responds by moving to the center. This means you win about seven out of eight times. If you do not plan ahead, the computer will win or draw a much larger portion of the time. Thus, you witness a very clear demonstration of the value of planning ahead.

After the trainee has exhausted the possibilities for tic-tac-toe, the trainee can progress to more complex strategy game tasks. For those trainees who enjoy playing chess, learning to solve "mate in one" and "mate in two" give great exercise in planning ahead. A book by Laszlo Polgar (*Chess: 5334 Problems, Combinations, and Games*,

Black Dog & Leventhal Publishers Inc., New York, 1994) presents enough chess problems to occupy almost anybody for a long time. A book by Bruce Pandolfini (*Chess Target Practice*, Simon & Schuster) presents another challenging batch of chess problems requiring you to think two or three moves ahead. Just as in the tic-tac-toe exercise, you decide upon a strategy and say it in words before executing it. Two computer programs, *Chessmaster 8000* and *Maurice Ashley Teaches Chess*, have enough chess drills and exercises for extensive practice in thinking ahead.

What's it for?

The more moves you're able to think ahead, the more likely you are to win strategy games. In many ways, the same is true of life. The more you can think ahead and make detailed contingency plans, the more likely you are to be successful at achieving goals. Thus, this is an anti-impulsivity exercise. It is an exercise in planning before acting, in careful decision-making.

How do you do it well?

One of the challenges in this exercise is holding moves in memory. Suppose you find yourself thinking of an option and predicting the responses, and then you start to think of responses to those. What if in the middle of all this, you forget what the first move was? I suggest using pencil and paper as an aid to memory. Getting into the habit of jotting things down on paper to aid memory is a very useful skill in itself.

Another key to performing this exercise well is persisting and continuing to think of options when the problem seems insoluble. This involves cultivating fortitude skills. It also involves cultivating systematic search strategies rather than waiting for the answer to pop up out of nowhere.

For many trainees, the major challenge while doing the computer exercise is keeping the hands off the keys until the plan has been made and stated. You can often see the trainee battling the impulse to act before thinking. When the trainee prevails in this struggle, he gets practice in overcoming such impulses.

Variations:

In addition to the variations that I've already mentioned, one important variation on this exercise is for the trainee to find or create his own problems. This is fairly easy to do with computer strategy games. For example, you play Chess or Connect Four against a computer, using a program where you can back up to undo and replay various moves. You play against the computer until the point where the computer either beats you or achieves a major advantage over you, or vice versa. Then you back up to the point in the game where that decisive advantage is foreseeable, but only by thinking ahead carefully. You find the choice point where the player could have avoided the fatal outcome through sufficient thinking ahead. You print out the position at this choice point and write the question and its answer. Then, you can go back later when you have forgotten the answer and solve the problem again.

If the trainee can become a composer of many of the exercises, as well as simply an answerer, the benefit is multiplied.

Exercise 42: Some Now, vs. More Later; Some Now vs. More For Work

What is it?

This is a paradigm Walter Mischel and colleagues devised to measure delay of gratification or self-discipline skills in children. It also is a good strategy for exercising these skills.

In the Some Now vs. More Later Exercise, you simply offer to the trainee a small amount of some reward that can be acquired immediately, vs. a larger amount of a more desirable reward that can be obtained by waiting longer. So, for example, you say to the trainee, "Here are some thin-mint cookies. If you want to eat half a cookie now, you can. But you won't get any more if you do. If you can wait without eating it until thirty minutes from now when our session ends, you will get two whole cookies."

In the Some Now vs. More For Work Exercise, the trainee not only has to wait in order to get the larger reward–he also has to work. For example: "Here are thin mint cookies. You can have half a cookie now if you want. However, if you are willing to wait until you've completed 200 points on the computer reading program, you will get, not half a cookie, but two whole cookies."

Both of these exercises can be conducted with tangible objects or money as rewards, as well as food.

What's it for?

Walter Mischel and his colleagues found that the skills of waiting for the larger reward, when measured in preschoolers, predicted various positive outcomes later in life, including higher SAT scores and greater ratings of maturity during the teen years. The ability to wait or work for larger rewards, rather than consuming immediate gratification, is central to the notion of self-discipline or delay of gratification skills. These skills are very important for attaining success in a wide variety of activities. Success in these exercises is trainable. In view of the correlation between success in these exercises and later success, it makes sense to give people extensive experience in successfully waiting for or working for delayed rewards.

How do you do it well?

Mischel and his colleagues found that distracting yourself from thinking about the immediate reward was helpful in overcoming the temptation to consume it immediately. They also found that thinking about abstract elements of it, such as its shape and size and diameter and so forth, helped to withstand the temptation. But imagining the concrete properties of the reward, such as how good it would taste, made it more difficult to resist temptation.

Other helpful techniques in overcoming the temptation include reminding yourself that this is a test of self-discipline and reminding yourself that self-discipline is an extremely desirable skill. Another helpful technique in performing this exercise well is using internal reinforcement for withstanding the temptation. For example, the trainee says to himself, "Hooray. I'm being tough and strong. I'm withstanding the temptation. I'm using self-discipline skills!"

Another technique is to envision models of self-discipline such as a track runner or a figure skater you admire. You visualize the self-discipline this person used, and then you imagine yourself using the same self-discipline in resisting the temptation.

Variations:

There are close to an infinite number of ways to conduct this exercise, if you consider the variations in the types of reward and the circumstances of waiting or working. The rewards can be food, money, objects or experiences, and the type of activity to be done while resisting temptation can be waiting with nothing do, waiting while looking at the reward in front of you, waiting with other activities to do without the reward in front of you, or working to complete a task in math, writing, reading or typing.

In another variation, the trainee himself organizes the whole project, playing the role of both the giver and the receiver of the reinforcers. For example, the trainee gets a box of cookies and puts it in front of him and resolves that, if he can keep working long enough to make 400 points on the typing program, he will give himself two cookies, but if he stops before that, he will only get half a cookie. He does this on his own and writes up a description of what happened and then brings this and reports it to the trainer, rather than doing it under the eye of the trainer. This variation represents a move toward an exercise previously discussed, the Self-Run Contingency Program.

Here's another variation that I especially like. The trainee works at a self-discipline task to earn an edible reward, such as a piece of cookie. If the trainee can hold the cookie on his tongue for thirty seconds *without eating it*, then the trainee gets that piece of cookie and also a bigger piece in addition. But if the trainee fails to delay gratification and gobbles the first piece down, then there's no additional piece. If the trainer is there to watch the trainee during the whole 30 seconds, tell how much time is left, and cheer the use of self-discipline so far, the trainee will be more likely to succeed at this.

I believe that frequently repeated successes in this exercise give the brain an exquisite experience of the benefits of self-discipline. It would be very interesting to observe the long-term effects of giving children this type of experience frequently from an early age.

Exercise 43: Responsive Utterances

What is it?

In this exercise, the trainee practices using seven types of responsive utterances as follows:

Reflection
Follow up question
Facilitation
Positive reinforcement
Follow up statement
Tracking and describing
Silence

The trainee practices generating one or more of these responsive utterances in response to either hypothetical situations, utterances from the other person, or real situations or utterances.

Let's quickly review what each of the responsive utterances is.

A reflection is stating what you head the other person communicating in order to make sure you got it right. For example, "What I hear you saying is that you're just thrilled to have your new puppy."

A follow up question is asking for more information about something the other person has already started talking about. For example:

First person: I just got a new puppy!
Second person: Oh! What kind is it?

A facilitation is a brief utterance that gives the message, "I'm listening to you, and I'm still interested; please go on." Facilitations include utterances such as:

Hmmm. Oh. Is that right? What do you know? Yes. I see. Wow.

Positive reinforcement is thanking, congratulating, praising or otherwise reinforcing something that the other person said or did. For examples:

I'm glad you told me about that.
Thanks for mentioning that.
Those flowers you're planting look pretty.
You're working hard.
I appreciate your interest in this subject.
Wow! I didn't think you could do that, but you did.
I appreciate your being open with me about that.

A follow-up statement offers information about the topic the speaker is addressing. For example:

First person: I love this type of dog!
Second person: I do too. My neighbor had one of those, and it was a great one.

Tracking and describing means putting into words the physical action the other person is doing. For example, the first person is chasing around with the dog. The second person says, "You're getting a lot of exercise playing chase with that puppy."

Another important responsive utterance is silence. For example, the first person says, "I'm not sure what I should do," and looks as if she is thinking hard. The other person remains silent. After a while, the first person says, "Maybe I could write her a letter."

In one variation of this exercise, the trainer poses hypothetical utterances or situations and the trainee makes up responses that exemplify any of the seven responsive utterances appropriate to the situation.

In another variation, the trainer conducts a conversation with the trainee, and, every time the trainer speaks, the trainee responds with one of those seven responsive utterances

What's it for?

In interacting with others, some are too bossy or directive. The opposite of such directiveness is responsiveness. With responsiveness, rather than trying to get the person to do something, you are responding by acknowledging what the person has already done. Or, in the case of silence, you are simply giving the person space to do whatever she wishes.

Many problems in human relationships develop when people are too directive of one another. The cumulative effect of receiving constant suggestions, advice, questions and other directive utterances can often lead to mounting feelings of frustration and aversion. Sometimes the person can't really explain why this feeling is building up. But conversations characterized by the more responsive utterances often give the recipient a more relaxed feeling, a feeling of freedom and acceptance. If people lack these responsive utterances in their repertoires, this exercise is a good way to develop them.

How do you do it well?

We've spoken previously about how to do reflections well.

The key to performing follow up questions in a responsive manner is to ask about things the speaker is already interested in discussing.

The key to using positive reinforcement is to constantly keep an eye out for positive statements you can respond to with sincere appreciation.

The key to making follow-up statements is to wait until the speaker has finished communicating before becoming the discloser and communicating something about yourself.

The key to using silence is to notice that the other person is working on something or pondering something and needs to be allowed to continue.

Another key to conducting this exercise well is to tell yourself, "I want to let the other person do his own thing," or, "I want to let her follow her own lead."

Variations:

In addition to the variations previously mentioned, another very important variation involves an older person playing with a pre-schooler or toddler. A third person keeps a tally sheet on the reflections, follow-up questions, facilitations, etc., the person uses while playing with the child. Most children greatly enjoy play sessions in which the older person many responsive utterances. In addition, responsive utterances elicit positive language use from the younger child as well as positive affect. Therefore, it's great for parents of young children to conduct this exercise.

Example:

The following is an example of a written variation of this exercise. Here the trainer makes up a dialogue using responsive utterances, and then asks the reader to tell which one was used.

First person: I've been reading a lot about the different options people now have for educating themselves. It's really exciting what is going on.

Second person: What sort of options are you talking about?

(Was that a follow-up question or reflection?)

First person: I'm talking about ways of getting a college degree without going to college, but by teaching yourself. Several colleges, for example, will give you credit for coursework if you pass a certain test.

Second person: So you can just teach yourself the course, and take a test, and you don't have to go to classes?

(Was that a reflection or a facilitation?)

First person: That's right. The College Board gives some of those tests. Plus, some colleges grant credit based on independent study. One in New York, called Excelsior College, makes up its own course outlines and tests, and allows you to get credit by taking those tests after you've studied some textbooks on your own.

Second person: Humh!

(Was that a positive reinforcement or a facilitation?)

First person: Plus, many universities offer correspondence courses, allowing you to earn credit by studying on your own and sending in papers and tests.

Second person: What's the advantage of doing it this way rather than the usual way?

(Was that tracking and describing or a follow-up question?)

First Person: You can save more than a hundred thousand dollars by getting a degree that way! Plus, you get practice at educating yourself, which is a really important skill.

Second person: This is interesting. I'm glad you told me about this.

Exercise 43: Responsive Utterances

(Was that a facilitation or positive reinforcement?)

Exercise 44: Self-Assessment with the Psychological Skills Inventory

What is it?

The Psychological Skills Inventory comes in several different forms. There is a sixteen-item version that asks people to rate themselves (or to rate someone else) on the sixteen skill groups. There is a sixty-two-item version that asks the person to give a rating for each of the individual sixty-two skills.

These inventories simply attach a 0 to 10 scale to the lists of psychological skills.

In one version, the question is "How much skill do you have at this?" The second version asks, "How much do you want to improve in this?"

In this exercise, the trainee looks at the inventory, goes through the items one by one, and talks about each item. The trainee thinks over examples in her life and thinks aloud about how proficient she is or how much she wants to improve in that skill. Then she gives herself a rating and goes on to the next skill.

What's it for?

This is an exercise in the skill of self-disclosure, as well as in Skill 21 on the long list, awareness of your own abilities. To conduct an honest inventory of your strengths and weaknesses in the various psychological skills takes courage. It helps greatly in making decisions: you don't want to promise to do something you don't have the proficiency to accomplish.

This exercise also helps you identify which of the other exercises you want to spend the most time and energy on. If you need to improve in joint decision skills, do the joint decision exercise; if you need relaxation skills, do the relaxation exercises.

How do you do it well?

Anybody can go through a questionnaire and put down numbers on it. But those numbers may not be meaningful. The first task is to fully understand what the psychological skill concepts mean. This is accomplished by doing the "Guess the Skill or Principle" exercise. You grasp the meaning of these abstract concepts by becoming familiar with many concrete examples.

The second task in performing this exercise well is to recall specific instances in which you did a good or bad job at the skill in question. This requires storing and retrieving memories of STEBs (situations, thoughts, emotions, and behaviors) from your past, and being able to index those memories according to the psychological skill concept.

A third task in doing this exercise well is having the courage to admit both your weaknesses and your strengths. The positions that "I can't do anything well" and that "I can do everything well" are often defenses against the fear of criticism. The first posture preempts the imaginary critic by agreeing with it in every area. The second posture deals with fear of criticism by not admitting a single area of weakness. To be able to admit that some areas are strong and other areas are weaker is a big accomplishment.

To decide which skills you most need to improve is quite a demanding intellectual task. You need to appraise not only your own skills, but the demands life is placing on you at this stage.

Variations:

This exercise lends itself to several sessions of "insight oriented therapy." The trainee takes the inventory and talks about examples. The trainer listens responsively, sometimes probing for clarification and for further examples. The trainee moves toward a conclusion on how much skill and how much need there is for improvement in each given area. The trainer takes many notes, and those notes are shared with the trainee.

Another way of conducting this exercise puts more of the writing burden on the trainee, who makes his own notes about each area.

For your convenience, the sixteen-item version of the Psychological Skills Inventory is reprinted here.

Name of Person Being Rated:____

Name of Rater:____

Date:_____

Psychological Skills Inventory: Short Form

This questionnaire will allow you to rate the "psychological skill" strengths and weaknesses of yourself or someone else. Each item will ask you to rate the degree of skill in a certain area. Please rate each item according to the following scale:

0=No Skill
2=Very Little Skill
4=Some but not much
6=Pretty much, moderate amount
8=High amount
10=Very high amount

_____1. Productivity. Being purposeful and goal-oriented. Being persistent, diligent and organized in pursuing goals. Working toward greater competence.

_____2. Joyousness. Enjoying both solitude and the company of others; enjoying approval and accomplishments, taking pleasure in your own acts of kindness, in discovery and learning. Feeling grateful for others' kindness and affection toward you; appreciating blessings of fate. Being gleeful and laughing.

_____3. Kindness. Being kind and helpful, being empathic, having a conscience.

_____4. Honesty. Being honest and dependable with others. Being honest with yourself, especially about what your strengths and weaknesses are.

_____5. Fortitude. Handling frustration, adversity, not getting what you want. Handling separation, rejection, criticism, your own mistakes and failures. Handling it when someone else gets what you wanted. Handling discomfort, feeling bad.

_____6a. Good decisions. Individual decision-making: Having a positive aim, thinking before acting, using words to conceptualize the world, being aware of your emotions, being aware of what you can and can't control. Goal-setting, listing options, predicting and evaluating consequences, making careful choices.

_____6b. Joint decision-making: Conflict resolution, negotiating with others. Tolerating a wide enough range of other people's behavior, remaining rational when problems come up, generating creative options, choosing just solutions, being able to be both assertive and conciliatory, being able to use differential reinforcement.

_____7. Nonviolence. Being forgiving, using good anger control, being committed to the principle of nonviolence.

_____8. Respectful talk and actions. Not being rude. Being sensitive to words, vocal tones and facial expressions that are accusing, punishing or demeaning, and avoiding them unless there is a very good reason.

_____9. Friendship-Building. Accurately appraising others, deciding when it is and is not appropriate to trust. Getting to know other people, socializing, being a good listener, being an appropriate self-discloser, expressing appreciation to others.

_____10. Self-discipline. Delay of gratification, self-control. Denying yourself present pleasure for future gain or for the sake of ethical action.

_____11: Loyalty. Tolerating and enjoying sustained closeness and attachment to another. Sticking up for those who have been good to you. Being true to commitments to others.

_____12. Conservation. Thrift. Preserving resources for yourself and future generations. Foregoing consumption on luxuries, but using resources more wisely. Financial delay of gratification skills.

_____13: Self-care. Being careful, avoiding unnecessary risks. Having healthy habits regarding drinking, smoking, drug use, exercise, diet, following medical directions. Being able to relax. Delivering assuring or caretaking thoughts to yourself, and feeling comforted thereby.

_____14. Compliance. Obeying, submitting to legitimate and reasonable authority, following rules unless those rules are bad or unjust.

_____15. Positive fantasy rehearsal. Using fantasy as a tool in rehearsing or evaluating a plan, or adjusting to an event or situation. Taking pleasure in fantasies of positive actions and avoiding taking pleasure in fantasies of violent or hurtful actions.

_____16. Courage. Estimating danger, overcoming fear of nondangerous situations, handling danger rationally. Making decisions independently, carrying out actions independently, resisting social pressure. Accepting help, being dependent without shame, asking for help appropriately.

Example:

Here are some sample answers to questions for this assignment:

1. Productivity.
I can concentrate well when I need to, and I can get a lot of work done at times. But I need to increase my speed and efficiency on a lot of the work I do. And I'm not that great at self-starting my work–I'm in the habit of waiting until someone else assigns me a task before I get going on it. My rating: 6.

2. Joyousness.
I'm really good at enjoying socializing and being with other people. Enjoying solitude, however, is not my strong suit. I don't have a bad time alone–I just engineer it so that I'm almost never alone. Still, it would be much better for me if I could enjoy being alone a lot more. I do get a lot of pleasure from my own accomplishments. I laugh a lot every day. My rating: 8.

3. Kindness.
I do have lots of empathy for people and don't like to see anyone hurt. If there are friends of mine who ask me for something, I'm good about coming through for them. I think where I fall down in this area is getting organized to think about other people's needs rather than just barreling along and doing the things I enjoy. I could be making other people happier if I could allocate more time to thinking about how to do this. My rating: 6.

4. Honesty.
I think this is a real strength of mine. I don't lie, cheat or steal. I would experience a very strong amount of guilt if I did do so.
The only thing that keeps me from giving myself a 10 on this is that I'm fortunate enough that I don't get a

lot of very strong temptations to be dishonest. I don't need to steal to get all my material needs met. I'm not in the habit of doing any things that I need to cover up or lie about. I wonder if I could withstand a much higher degree of temptation.

My rating: 9.

5. Fortitude.

There have been a fair number of little hardships that have made me very upset, at least for a short time. Not getting invited somewhere, when someone else was invited, made me pretty upset lately. Having people in my family be messy has been causing me a great deal of negative emotion that is way out of proportion to how harmful to me this is. I tend to get angry and impatient when machines don't work right. And there are other examples. But on the other hand, I don't do anything really stupid in these situations. I don't yell at people or scream out obscenities. After feeling pretty upset, I eventually cool off and respond to the situation fairly well. My rating: 6.

Exercise 45: The Internal Sales Pitch

What is it?

In this exercise, the trainee who wants to get better at a certain psychological skill reviews the reasons why. He lists to himself the benefits versus the disadvantages of working on this skill. He seeks to make a persuasive case for devoting time and energy to skill improvement.

This is a subset of the goal-setting and planning exercise, mentioned earlier, without the other portions of that exercise.

What's it for?

Unless you have really sold yourself on the benefits of improving a certain psychological skill, it's hard to keep working on it. If you hold in memory the reasons why the goal is worthy of your effort, you're less inclined to give up.

How do you do it well?

To do this well, you should use the techniques that advertising agencies and sales people use. You want your sales pitch to be interesting and fun, if possible. A rational calculating analysis of the benefits is certainly useful, but a more emotion-arousing sales pitch might be more effective at motivating you.

What are some of those selling techniques? Attention-grabbing images; enthusiastic, energetic talk; simple, easy-to-grasp language; and specific images and examples of how things will be made better by the skill.

Variations:

The trainee will almost certainly benefit from writing out the sales pitch and reading it at regular intervals.

Example:

I want to place *improving in self-discipline* very high on my priority list. Here are reasons I want to get better at this:

If I improve my self-discipline I can get my work done without procrastinating so much. This will let me enjoy my life much more, because I won't be suffering the consequences of putting things off. I will get my bills paid on time, and I won't have to suffer the embarrassment and penalties of late-payment fees. I will be able to keep my promises to people much more often if I don't procrastinate on the things I tell people I'm going to do, and that will help me have better relationships with my friends.

If I improve my self-discipline I will be able to keep my weight at the point I like it, without having to feel every day that I'm failing to do what I resolved to do about losing weight. I'll be pleased with how much exercise I'm getting and how much I'm eating. Every day, I'll feel proud of myself instead of disappointed.

If I improve my self-discipline I'll be able to get my sleep schedule straightened out. I'll have the self-discipline to get to bed earlier and to get out of bed in the morning rather than sleeping late. This will eliminate a lot of problems about being late in the morning, and a lot of conflict and bad feelings between my family members and me.

I'll be able to organize my finances more, and be in much better financial condition. I'll be able to spend money on the things that really make me happy and not waste it on things that just clutter up my life.

In summary, I'll be a lot happier, and I'll also be able to make other people happier if I can become more self-disciplined. It will be worth investing lots of time and energy to achieve this goal.

Exercise 46: Rehearsing Saying Things to Create a Positive Emotional Climate

What is it?

This is a variation on fantasy rehearsal. You use a list of utterances that tend to create a good emotional climate in families or other groups. You imagine a situation and fantasy rehearse saying each of these types of utterances to someone.

Things To Say To Create A Good Emotional Climate

1. Expressing gladness that the other person is here:

Good morning! Good afternoon! Good evening! I'm glad to see you! It's good to see you! Welcome home! Hi!

2. Expressing gratitude and appreciation:

Thanks for doing that for me! I really appreciate what you did. I'm glad you told me that! Yes, please! That's nice of you to do that for me! This is a big help to me. Thanks for saying that!

3. Reinforcing a good performance of the other person:

You did a good job! That's interesting! Good going! Good point! Good job! Congratulations to you! You did well on that! That's pretty smart!

4. Positive feelings about the world and the things and events in it:

Wonderful! That's really great! Wow! Hooray! I'm so glad it happened like that! Sounds good! Look how beautiful that is!

5. Wishing well for the other person's future:

I hope you have a good day. Have a nice day! Good luck to you! I wish you the best on (the thing you're doing).

6. Offering help or accepting a request for help:

May I help you with that? I'd like to help you with that. I'll do that for you! I'm going to do this job so you won't have to do it! Would you like me to show you how I do that? I'd be happy to do that for you!

7. Expressing positive feelings about yourself:

I feel good about something I did. Want to hear about it? Hooray, I feel so good about that!

8. Being forgiving and tolerating frustration:

That's OK, don't worry about it. It's no problem. I can handle it. I can take it. It's not the end of the world.

9. Expressing interest in the other person:

How was your day today? How are you? How have you been doing? How have things been going? So let me see if I understand you right. You feel that _____. So in other words you're saying _____. I'd like to hear more about that! I'm curious about that. Tell me more.

10. Consoling the other person:

I'm sorry you had to go through that. I'm sorry that happened to you.

11. Apologizing or Giving In:

I'm sorry I said that. I apologize for doing that. I think you're right about that. Upon thinking about it more, I've decided I was wrong. I'll go along with what you want on that.

12. Being Assertive in a Nice Way:

Here's another option. Here's the option I would favor. An advantage of this plan is . . . A disadvantage of that option is . . . Unfortunately I can't do it. I'd prefer not to. No, I'm sorry, I don't want to do that. It's very important that you do this.

What's it for?

The theory is that if people will say these twelve types of utterances much more frequently in their social groups, and most especially in their families, the world would be much improved by this alone. These utterances tend to help people feel good about one other, get along with one another, build up positive feelings for one another, and have good will. And these are probably the most important ingredients for human happiness.

In addition to the effect on the interpersonal climate of the group, each individual improves his or her kindness and respectful talk skills by saying these things. Of course, the rationale for making up situations in fantasy and practicing saying these things in imagination is that fantasy rehearsal works.

How do you do it well?

Doing this exercise well entails coming up fairly quickly and readily with situations that are appropriate. It also entails thinking of different situations when you perform these exercises repeatedly. (But repeated practice with the same situations is good, too.)

Another very important element of conducting this exercise well is using a tone a voice that conveys approval. It's unproductive to practice saying these things in a monotone.

A special situation involves doing this exercise with a family member toward whom you have built up a great deal of resentment. This exercise then draws considerably upon forgiveness skills.

Variations:

Sometimes the trainee will need or want to improve a relationship with one particular person, for example a family member, a co-worker or schoolmate, and it's good to carry out the exercise with that particular person as the receiver of the positive utterances.

Sometimes it's useful to combine this exercise with the Good Will Exercise.

This exercise is possible to conduct in written format; it's useful for the trainee to read out loud what he has written, to practice the tones of approval.

Example:

Here's an example of what it sounds like to do this exercise.

1. Expressing gladness that the other person is here.

I've gotten up early and I'm in my office doing some work. My four-year-old son comes into the room. I say, "Good morning. How are you? I'm glad to see you!"

2. Expressing gratitude and appreciation

In the morning, I notice that my wife has washed some dishes that were in the sink last night. I say to her, "Thanks for washing those dishes last night!"

3. Reinforcing a good performance of the other person.

My four-year-old son is singing and dancing around, and I say, "Look at you, you singer and dancer! You're doing a good job!"

4. Positive feelings about the world and the things and events in it.

My daughter tells me about getting to pet a baby bunny. As I'm listening, I say, "That's really great. Wow! I'm glad it happened like that."

5. Wishing well for the person's future.

A neighbor tells me she's going on vacation. I say to her, "I hope you have a great time on your trip."

6. Offering help or accepting a request for help.

My three-year-old daughter yells for help in going to the bathroom. I say to her, "I'd be happy to help you in that way."

7. Expressing positive feelings about yourself.

I'm eating supper with my family, and I say, "Today I got a huge amount of work done efficiently! I feel really good about that."

8. Being forgiving and tolerating frustration.

My four-year-old son knocks over a cup of juice, and it flows over the table and onto the floor. I say to him, "I can handle it! It's not the end of the world!"

9. Expressing interest in the other person.

I get home from work and recall that my daughter's preschool had a field trip today. I say to her, "So how was your field trip today? Tell me all about it."

10. Consoling the other person.

In the evening, my wife is telling me about something a person at work did that was unreasonable and mean. I say to her, "I'm sorry you had to go through that."

11. Apologizing or giving in.

I had argued with my wife that our family couldn't afford a book that cost about five or six dollars. I had spoken in indignant tones about this. Now it's later on, and I say to her, "Upon thinking about that book more, I've decided I was wrong. I'll go along with what you want on that."

12. Being assertive in a nice way.

My daughter wants to take a swim. I say to her, "Unfortunately, we can't do that. The disadvantage of that option is that you'd get to bed way too late."

Exercise 47: Rating the Forcefulness

What is it?

In this exercise you are presented with a hypothetical situation and three possible responses that vary in the forcefulness of assertion. You rank order the responses with respect to forcefulness.

Here are some examples of this type of question:

1. Somebody buys a new shirt, and when he tries it on at home, he sees that two buttons are missing. He takes the shirt back and speaks to the person at the store.

> A. Hi. I bought this shirt earlier today. But it has two buttons missing, and I just thought maybe you could help me out with that.

> B. This shirt, that I bought here earlier today, has a couple of buttons missing, and I'd like to get it replaced, please.

> C. I bought this shirt new here today, and it's defective. It's missing two buttons. I really resent having to bring it back, because it's a waste of my time. Please replace it with a shirt that is not defective.

2. A girl has an agreement with her brother that they will take turns feeding the dog. But the brother tends to forget on his days. The usual time for feeding has passed again today, and the dog is hungry and whining.

> A. Excuse me; do you remember our agreement about your feeding the dog every other day? Are you planning to keep it, or not? If you're not going to do it, please let me know, because you're neglecting the dog and it's cruel to him, and I'm not going to stand for this any more.

> B. Hey brother, the dog is whining for you. It's your day today.

> C. I think we should talk about what to do about the dog feeding. More often than not on your days you forget, and I think we need to think about a different arrangement.

The trainee's job is simply to say which one is most forceful, which one is second most forceful, and which one is least forceful.

There are a good number of these situations presented in *Programmed Readings on Psychological Skills*. After you have performed these, you can get additional benefit by making up your own situations and responses.

What's it for?

The skill of assertion is very important for maintaining positive relationships. Many people feel that they cannot let some other person know their wishes, for fear of hurting or angering the other person. But keeping such wishes subdued often leads to a buildup of resentment or an end of the relationship. This is especially sad when the issues at hand are trivial ones that could have been easily negotiated if one of the people had not been afraid to speak up.

One of the most important assertion skills is picking a degree of forcefulness that is appropriate to the situation. People can make errors by not being forceful enough when they are being taken advantage of, or by being more forceful than necessary. In deciding upon the degree of forcefulness appropriate for any given situation, the first skill to be cultivated is simply discriminating the degree of forcefulness and practicing making these categorizations in the mind.

How do you do it well?

In the rudimentary version of this exercise, doing it well consists in simply rating the forcefulness correctly.

Variations:

In a different variation on this exercise, the trainee not only rates the forcefulness of the three utterances but talks about what degree of forcefulness sounds appropriate for the situation in question, and why.

In the most challenging variation on this exercise, the trainee generates hypothetical situations and utterances in response to them. Thus, as in many other exercises, the trainee can add to the pool of possible questions so as to benefit other trainees as well as to benefit himself by constructing his own questions.

Examples:

This is an example of the variation in which you make up an exercise for someone on in differentiating among degrees of forcefulness. You make up a situation that calls for assertion. Then you make up three different ways in which the person could respond to the other person, with one being most forceful, one in the middle, and one least forceful. Put them in any order you want. You ask the reader to choose which is which.

A little girl comes home, takes off her coat and drops it on the floor in her mom's bedroom. The mom prefers that she hang it up on the coat tree in the front hall, so that she'll know where it is the next time she goes out. The mom speaks:

1. You know what? If you hang that up on the coat tree, you can find it easily the next time you go out. Please do that, sweetie.

2. What is that coat doing on the floor? You know better than that. The coat goes on the coat tree, not on the floor, so pick it up and put it there, NOW.

3. Coat on the coat tree, not on the floor please.

Answer: 1 most gentle, 2 most forceful, 3 in the middle.

Here's another example:

The person has received a call from a telemarketer asking that he give to a certain charity.

1. No. I don't support this organization; you're interrupting my privacy in my home; I resent this. Don't ever call my house again.

2. No, I wouldn't like to. Goodbye.

3. I'm sorry; I'm not interested in making a contribution now. And could you please put me on the "do not call" list? I appreciate that. You have a nice evening.

Answer: 1 most forceful, 2 in the middle, 3 most gentle.

Exercise 48: Assertion Role-Play

What is it?

In this exercise, trainer and trainee choose from situations where it is necessary for one person to persist with a reasonable request despite resistance from the other person, or to turn down an unreasonable request despite persistence from the other person.

In other words, they pick situations where assertiveness is called for. The trainee plays the part of the person who needs to be assertive. The trainee and trainer act out the situations. After the role-play, they rate the trainee's performance with respect to several variables:

0=None
2=Very little
4=Some but not much
6=Moderate amount, pretty much
8=High amount
10=Very high amount

1. Non-hostility. To what extent did the trainee avoid becoming inappropriately hostile or angry with the other person?

2. Appropriate degree of forcefulness. To what extent did the trainee use forcefulness appropriate for the situation?

3. Persistence: To what degree was the trainee able to persist with the assertive stance?

Here are some situations where assertion is called for.

1. A man is trying to change his baby's diaper and at the same time cook supper. At that moment he gets a phone call from a telemarketer trying to convince him to acquire another credit card. He wants to get off the phone and to not be called again by the marketer.

2. A parent has a two-year-old child. A six-year-old child keeps coming up and touching the younger one on the face or trying to pick her up. The parent wants the older child to stop doing these things to the two-year old.

3. A waitress has seated some people in the nonsmoking section, but they are smoking. She wants them to either put out their cigarettes or move to the smoking section.

4. The first kid makes fun of the second kid's name. The second doesn't like that.

5. Someone smacks his lips really loudly when he eats. He also eats with his mouth open a lot. This bothers his friend.

How do you do it well?

As the rating scale implies, a good performance on this exercise means persisting in an appropriately forceful manner without losing emotional control. You insist without backing down. You keep in mind that your goal is to get something that is right for you to get, and not to hurt or humiliate the other person.

Several books have been written about how to be appropriately assertive. The trainee might wish to take a look at *When I Say No, I Feel Guilty* by Manuel Smith, or *Responsible Assertive Behavior* by Lange and Jakubowski.

Variations:

At the beginning it is useful for the trainee to acquire some good models of what is desired in this exercise. One way to do that is for the trainee to read dialogs that model responsible assertive behavior. Another option is for the trainer to take the role of the assertive person in role-plays.

After the trainee has had some experience with this exercise, another variation is for the trainee to write out dialogues modeling responsible assertive behavior and adding these to the pool of positive models for other people to use.

Examples:

Here's an example where two adolescents are speaking to each other.

First: Hey, let me copy your homework. I didn't get a chance to do mine.

Second: No, I don't think so.

First: What do you mean, you don't think so? You mean you aren't going to let me?

Second: That's right.

First: What are you, some sort of righteous wimp? Are you letting them intimidate you with all this honor code stuff?

Second: I agree with the principle of each person turning in his own work.

First: I thought you were my friend.

Second: Friends sometimes say no to each other, and I'm saying no to you now.

First: I thought I could count on you. I'll never think about you the same any more.

Second: How you want to think about me is up to you.

***

Here's an example where two kids in middle school are talking with each other.

First: You know how you were calling that kid a dork, and going on about how he was gay on the playground today?

Second: Yeah, what about it?

First: I didn't like that.

Second: Oh, you didn't, did you? Maybe you're gay like him. Maybe that's why.

First: You're cruel to him just for the fun of it. He hasn't done anything to you. You've got a problem you need to solve.

Second: This is none of your &%# business.

First: I don't agree with you. It affects everybody when somebody is allowed to be sadistic to somebody else.

Second: Well, you just try and stop me, queerface.

First: I may not be able to stop you. But at least you know what I think about it.

***

Here's an example where a woman is talking with her mom about how the woman should act with her own kids.

Mom: Did I see you rewarding your kids with candy for the work they do? You shouldn't do that! It will mess them up.

Woman: Mom, there are some people who think that. But I've researched the issue, and I don't agree.

Mom: But all the books say you shouldn't. They'll get anorexic or really fat or something.

Woman: I haven't been able to find evidence for that.

Mom: Believe me, I know what's best. You're going to regret this one in a big way.

Woman: That could be. But of course my prediction is that I won't.

Mom: I can't believe that you won't listen to your own mom. Now I know what you think of me.

Woman: I think all sorts of good things about you, but I don't think

you're right a hundred percent of the time, just as I'm not.

Mom: So you're going to keep doing this and rot their teeth and make them so they won't do anything without being bribed for it, huh? This is your idea of how to be a good mother?

Woman: Regarding the part about my intention to keep doing this, the answer is yes.

Mom: I just can't stand it. I can't handle it.

Woman: I have confidence in you; you'll figure out a way to cope with it somehow.

Exercise 49: Refantasy of Nightmare

What is it?

In this exercise you recall a nightmare you've had. Or, you use a nightmare that somebody else has had. Then you make a new story that begins in the same way the nightmare begins, but which ends happily. The happy ending is brought about possibly with magic, but without violence. Some people who have performed this exercise have also specified that, if there is a scary character in the nightmare, the scary character is not just subdued, done away with or escaped from; the scary character is converted to an ally whose strength and power will be helpful to you.

In conducting this exercise, it's important to remember that people are able to exert influence or control over their own fantasy worlds. If there is a troubling fantasy, you can practice encountering it during moments when the fear is not present. You conjure up the characters or the setting of the troublesome dream. However, then you practice altering the fantasy in a variety of different ways, all of which make the fantasy come out with a happy ending.

One typical way of doing this is with the nightmare fantasy of being chased or pursued by a monster. You replay the dream, but only to the point where you first begin to experience anxiety. Then, you call upon allies—either human, superhuman, mechanical or whatever—to arrange things so that you are fully protected but still may encounter and communicate with the monster.

For example, you are walking along a path in the woods. You know the monster is present. You then conjure up in your imagination a couple of characters with the powers of Superman, willing to help whenever you want. You also imagine putting around the monster an unbreakable shield, which nevertheless allows sound to be transmitted easily.

Then you carry out a dialogue with the monster, asking the monster, "What do you want?" If what the monster wants is purely malevolent, such as "To kill you," you ask the monster, "What would you accomplish by doing that?" You keep questioning until you discover what the monster's "interest" is rather than what the monster's "position" is. That is, you find out some motive that can be satisfied in a way that is not harmful to you. Then you continue negotiations with the monster, arranging some sort of negotiated exchange between the two of you.

Finally, you come to an agreement that the monster will become an ally of yours rather than an adversary. You transform the personality of the monster in whatever way necessary so the monster will be able to be on your side and be a loyal ally. This is just one example of how you can take control of your own fantasy world to rearrange a scary fantasy.

Or for another example, someone has recurrent nightmares of falling from high places. In the waking fantasy, she reconstructs the place where she has fallen in dreams and imagines going to that place, either with a foolproof rocket strapped on her back or with magical power to fly. In fantasy she leaps off the high place and enjoys pleasant flying. Or she falls off the place but says the magic word that instantly summons a giant bird; she lands on the bird's back and takes a beautiful tour of the countryside.

The idea behind all the strategies is simple: you take a scary fantasy and practice alternate fantasies that will compete with it. You also practice the act of consciously controlling your own fantasies to make them pleasant and fun. This act is an antidote to the habit of scaring yourself with your own fantasies.

What is it for?

For people who have been troubled by nightmares, this technique has proved helpful. This exercise moves the average content of the fantasy world in a more positive direction, in much the same way that the pleasant dreams exercise does. In addition, the repeated experience of converting an adversary to an ally rather than viewing the disposing of the adversary as the only solution to the problem provides a model for conflict resolution.

How do you do it well?

It is key for people to realize they are in control of their own fantasy productions, at least while they are awake. This is, perhaps, one of the major accomplishments of this exercise as well: you get to have the experience of controlling the direction your fantasy takes. The acts of summoning help when you feel anxious and obtaining help appropriately are also good skills to practice.

Variations:

As with many other exercises, written models of how to do this are useful; the trainee can make a meaningful contribution by creating such models.

If the trainee cannot remember his or her dreams, it's still possible to perform this exercise. One can use waking fantasies or daydreams. Or one can use other people's fantasies. For example, the story of Frankenstein's monster by Shelley or the plots of some of Edgar Allan Poe stories are nightmare images. In my opinion, such horror stories are incomplete without conducting this exercise to reconstruct them.

Example:

Here's the original bad dream:

I'm in a room, and there are no windows and no doors. All of the sudden the walls start coming closer and closer together, and I realize that as the room gets smaller I will be crushed. I wake up at that point.

Now here's my refantasy:

I'm in a room, and there are no windows and no doors. All of the sudden the walls start coming closer and closer together. I conjure up a magical power in my fingertip. I point it toward the walls, and make them stop moving. Then I take my fingertip and make a laser beam come out of it. I use the laser beam to cut a section out of the wall, and I walk out of the room. After I leave, I pick up a piece of clay and turn it into a doorknob, and put it on the piece I cut out. I put the door back on.

Now I look around to find who has been doing this. I find a little man who comes up to my knees. He starts to run away. I put an invisible barrier around him. This stops him so that I can talk with him. I ask him, "Why did you want to do this to me?"

He says, "I've always been so little, and people have picked on me; I just wanted to feel important."

I say, "Let me introduce you to another ally of mine from another dream." I point my finger, and there appears a big bear who is a friend of mine.

The man starts to be scared, but I tell him the bear won't hurt him, and in fact he can ride around on the bear's shoulder. People will not pick on him any more with the bear as his friend.

He is very grateful, and asks me what he can do in return. I tell him that I can use his help with technology and machines, which he obviously is very good at. He promises to help me with those whenever I need help. He gives me a machine as a gift and as a symbol of being my ally. Only he doesn't know what the machine does. I use the machine to make him bigger. He is even more grateful. I also use my magical powers to make sure he will do only good things.

We use the room with the walls and the door I made to let squirrels come in when they are cold during the winter.

Exercise 50: Self-Observation

What is it?

In this exercise the trainee simply sits silently, usually with eyes closed, for a length of time specified before the exercise begins. During this time, the only stipulation is that the trainee will try to observe and keep track of what he does with his mind. It is often useful and interesting just to let the mind do whatever it wants and to observe what happens. The trainee becomes aware of what images are going across the mind and what sentences are being said internally. At the end of the exercise, the trainee can report back to the trainer a portion of what went though his mind.

If the trainee wishes to purposely do something in his mind at this time, that's fine. Or, if he wants to let the activity of the mind be spontaneous, that's fine also. The only stipulation is that the trainee reserve a portion of his neuronal space for observing what the rest of the brain is doing.

What is it for?

One of the purposes of this exercise is to help people stay "on task." In other words, it is meant to help people keep their minds on what they are supposed to be doing. Sometimes people get off task and don't realize it for a long time. The theory is that these people often are not using any of their neuronal circuitry to monitor what they are paying atten-

tion to; they are simply thinking about something without being aware of it.

By cultivating the habit of reserving a little bit of your brain power to observe what you are doing, you become quicker at realizing you've veered off task. Then you can consciously bring yourself back to goal-related behavior.

The desired strategy in this exercise is to reserve only a small part of your brainpower to observe what the rest of your brain is doing. You don't want to reserve so many neurons to observe yourself that you don't have enough left over to accomplish the task at hand.

This is what happens sometimes with people who get stage fright. They automatically direct so much attention to observing themselves that they can't concentrate on what they are trying to do. This exercise, perhaps paradoxically, is also meant to avert such problems. As you do the exercise, if you concentrate on observing yourself with all of your brainpower, nothing much interesting happens. Only when you reduce that allocation do you start having interesting fantasies. Thus, there is to some degree a built-in reinforcer for not allocating too much of your brainpower to self-observation.

How do you do it well?

This exercise is difficult for people who have a very high stimulus-seeking component to their temperaments. Some people become very impatient when not receiving external stimulation. Another purpose this exercise is to let people gradually practice longer and longer periods without external stimulation.

Another element of performing this exercise well may be picking something either useful or pleasant to do with your mind during the exercise. Again, the central idea is that you are in control of your own inner life. If the experience of this exercise is not positive, then you need to develop the capacity to make it positive.

Variations:

Here are the two main variations. In the first, you make no attempt to influence the direction of your mental activity but simply observe what happens spontaneously. In the second, you take responsibility for generating mental activity that is either pleasant or useful for you.

The trainee can do this as a homework assignment and can write down the content of mental activity.

If you want to remember all of the mental activity so you can report it, one or two minutes are about as much as anyone should be expected to remember. But another variation entails observing for longer periods of time (without expecting yourself to remember all of it).

Another useful variation is to perform this exercise with a tape recorder on, and to speak the stream of consciousness aloud. A similar variation is to sit at a keyboard and type the thoughts that come into your mind during the exercise. These variations allow you to go back and examine the contents of your thoughts and to reflect upon them.

Example:

The following is an example of the stream of consciousness that might result from this exercise.

I'm noticing that it's sunny outside. I'm glad it's winter and I don't have to worry about sunburn so much. Has anybody figured out whether the ultra-violet rays of the sun are more damaging now than they used to be, before we started damaging the ozone layer?

I'm noticing my wedding ring. I'm glad that I got it stretched. I like having it loose and not tight. I don't like tight clothes either, especially tight shoes or tight pants.

What do I want to do later on today? Maybe get some more exercise. Maybe try to approach the goal I made a while back, to have more nights when I lie down in bed feeling very pleasantly tired from all the exercise I got during the day. I remember times of feeling that way when I worked all day in constructing a building. And I remember other times when I was on a wrestling team and worked out really hard all afternoon. It's a good feeling. I don't think I get it enough. Maybe I'll lift some weights as soon as I get done with this.

I need to call up my aunt. I wonder how she's doing? I know she would like a call from me. I feel bad about not calling her more often. Maybe if I put it down on my to-do list I would remember it more. Hey, maybe I'll talk to her on the phone at the same time that I'm lifting some weights.

Exercise 51: Directing Focus

What is it?

In this exercise you practice consciously directing and changing the focus of your attention. You pick something that will be the anchor of attention, the thing that you will keep coming back to. This could be focusing on your hands, your breathing, the image of another person, a moving clock, the scene out the window, the golden rule, the sixteen ethical principles or skills, or whatever else you choose.

When you start the exercise, you consciously direct your attention to this anchor. You focus on it for a few seconds or a few minutes. To start, somewhere in the region of fifteen seconds is a good time. Then you consciously direct your attention to something else other than this–anything you pick. You let your attention stay on this thing or things, and then you bring your attention back to the anchor. Then you direct your attention to something else and then back to the anchor again.

What's it for?

Many people seldom have the experience of consciously changing their attention and doing it successfully. This exercise is designed to build up skill in this area.

How do you do it well?

You perform this exercise well by gradually acquiring the ability to let your attention respond to the directions you give it, to the control that you take over it.

Variations:

The trainer can suggest when to shift attention, or the trainee can shift attention whenever he is ready.

Example:

My anchor that I'm going to keep returning to is the sixteen skills and principles.

I'm thinking about productivity. I'm envisioning someone working really hard at building a building. I'm envisioning someone sitting at a computer and organizing a plan about something.

Now I'm letting my mind drift to something else. I'm looking forward to the next dance. I enjoy doing the samba. I want to take a look at a video of some people doing the samba really well. I'd like to learn some new moves.

Now back to the sixteen skills and principles. I'm thinking about joyousness. I'm envisioning someone cracking jokes and dancing around and being really silly with his family.

Now to let my mind drift some more. What's that sound I hear outside? It sounds like someone using one of those loud machines to blow leaves into a pile. I wish they would use a rake instead. I don't like noise pollution.

Now back to the principles. I'm thinking of kindness. I'm thinking of someone spending time teaching someone to read better, and being very patient and reinforcing . . .

Exercise 52: Game and Rating

What is it?

In this exercise the trainee plays a game against either the trainer or the computer. Before the game, the trainee and trainer devote their attention to the following rating scale. After the game, the trainee rates his behavior, emotions and thoughts during the game, with the additional feedback of the trainer. The rating scale is as follows:

0=Not at all successful
2=Very little success
4=Some but not much success
6=Moderate amount, pretty much success
8=High amount of success
10=Very high amount of success

1. Not awfulizing. Did you have the attitude that it wasn't awful if you lost the game or made some unskillful moves?

2. Celebrating your own choices. Were you able to celebrate and feel good about your skillful moves–even if you lost?

3. Celebrating the other's choices. Were you able to congratulate the other person for the good moves or choices he or she made?

4. Gracious losing. If you lost a game or a part of it, were you able to handle the frustration graciously (for example, without griping)?

4. Gracious winning. If you won a game or a part of it, were able to handle this graciously (for example, without gloating)?

5. Unselfishness. When you played this game, did you have some interest in helping the person you were playing with to have a good experience?

8. Concentration. How well did you concentrate on playing skillfully? (Without getting distracted by other things, demoralized when you were behind, or slacking off for fear of devastating the other person when you were ahead?) (Don't count off points on this one if you consciously decided to let the other person have some success.)

9. Not cheating. How completely did you avoid cheating?

10. Rule-following. How completely did you play by the rules and not try to change them?

11. Tolerating your opponent's faults. If the other person cheated or broke the rules, how successful were you at tolerating this and not letting it spoil your own fun?

12. Enthusiasm. How much were you able to be enthusiastic in your enjoyment of this game?

***

What's it for?

Games provide opportunities for the exercise of a variety of psychological skills. Fortitude or frustration tolerance is necessary if you lose the game or experience setbacks. Friendly and kind behavior is appropriate even in a competitive situation. Learning to temper the competitiveness of a game with friendliness and kindness is an exercise in regulating your own emotion.

Attempting to win the game rather than fearing to disappoint the other person is an exercise in assertion. Most games exercise concentration skills. If you get behind in the game, it's a useful skill not to give up prematurely, but to exercise persistence and fortitude.

How do you do it well?

In this exercise, you don't just play and perfunctorily fill out the rating scale afterward. Instead, you really direct your attention to the psychological skills involved in game playing and try to do them as well as possible. It may help some game players to keep the questionnaire in front of them and refer to it repeatedly during the game.

Variations:

Playing games against a computer and against another person are different experiences. Both can be useful. The computer is a good option when it's not desired that the trainer and trainee compete with each other.

Cooperative games versus competitive games form another major division. A separate chapter of this book is devoted to cooperative games.

Exercise 53: Decisions Game

What is it?

This is a game I constructed to provide practice in making decisions by taking into account both probabilities and utilities. It's a game that you play with a die and with some game cards or pages. These are printed later on in this book. The game card gives you a choice between option A and option B. Each option tells you how many points you will get for certain outcomes of the die roll. You must choose the option before rolling the die. You get points according to which option you choose, and the result of the die roll. For example, here is an example of a game card:

If you choose option A:
for a roll of 1, 2, or 3, you get 0 points
for a roll of 4, 5, or 6 you get 14 points

If you choose option B:
for a roll of 1, 2, or 3, you get 2 points
for a roll of 4, 5 or 6, you get 4 points

For this game card, option A has a higher expected utility than option B. The expected utility is the number of points that you would, on the average, expect to get if you played that option many times. You can calculate the expected utility by multiplying the number of points you get for each possible outcome times the probability for that outcome.

As a general rule, it's good to pick the option with the highest expected utility. For this game card, if you choose option A, about half the time you'll get 14 points and half the time you'll get 0 points, so your average expectation is 7 points. For option B, about half the time you'll get 2 points and half the time you'll get 4 points, so your average expectation is 3 points. A is a better choice, despite the fact that with it you risk getting 0 points.

But, even when trainees are too young or not mathematically sophisticated enough to calculate expected utilities, they can take into account probabilities and utilities and use these quantities to help them make decisions. This is what most people do in real-life.

What's it for?

The purpose of this game is to give the trainee either an intuitive feeling for probabilities and utilities or more of an explicit understanding of probabilities and utilities when making decisions in this game. The hope is that this feeling for probabilities and utilities will carry over into real-life decisions.

How do you do it well?

The key element in this exercise is taking into account both the probabilities and utilities. The larger the sum of each option's probability times its utility, the more you like that option.

The secret of the game is to choose the option that maximizes the expected utility. The expected utility of an option is defined as the sum of the utility of each given possible outcome, multiplied by the probability of that outcome. For example, imagine that for Option A, you get 6 points for a roll of 1, 2, or 3, and 12 points for a roll of 4, 5, or 6. Then there is a .5 chance that you will get 6 points, and a .5 chance that you will get 12 points. Adding half of 6 and half of 12, you get 9 points as the expected utility. That nine points is the average number you would expect to get if you rolled the die many times. (Try it, if you have some time for such an experiment.) If that's higher than the expected utility for option B, pick option A; but if option B has an even higher expected utility, pick option B.

The task of living life is to make decisions in such a way that you maximize expected utility, where utility is not points, but whatever is accurately deemed to be worthwhile and valuable.

Variations:

Although the trainee and trainer can play against each other, the variation I like better is a cooperative effort where the trainee and trainer join to play against "Mr. X." On any given round of the game, the trainee and trainer decide which option they will pick; Mr. X is automatically given the other option. They roll the die for themselves and tally their points; then they roll the die for Mr. X and tally his points. The side that is ahead at the end of the game wins.

In another variation, each person rolls the die not once, but three or four or more times, and gets points for every roll, according to the option that was picked. This option enables the players to see more clearly how making the best choice has its effect as more and more rolls are averaged, whereas its benefits may not be apparent on just one roll.

It's a useful activity to make up more game pages, like the ones presented here. By doing this, you can think about how difficult you want to make the decision between the two options. Sometimes you can make one option have a higher expected payoff, but more risk of a lower payoff, whereas the other has a lower expected payoff, but lower risk. These sorts of cards make the player choose whether to play it safe or take a gamble. For other cards, you can arrange it so that one option has both a higher expected payoff and a lower risk. The more cards like this you include, where one option is clearly better than the other, the more chance you have of beating Mr. X if you are playing against him.

Cards for the Decisions Game

Card 1:

If you choose option A:
for a roll of 1, 2 or 3, you get 0 points
for a roll of 4, 5 or 6, you get 14 points

If you choose option B:
for a roll of 1, 2 or 3, you get 2 points
for a roll of 4, 5 or 6, you get 4 points

****
Card 2:

If you choose option A:
for a roll of 1, 2 or 3, you get 6 points
for a roll of 4, 5 or 6, you get 12 points

If you choose option B:
for a roll of 1, 2 or 3, you get 1 point
for a roll of 4, 5 or 6, you get 10 points

****
Card 3:

If you choose option A:
for a roll of 1, 2, 3, 4 or 5, you get 0 points
for a roll of 6, you get 24 points

If you choose option B:

for a roll of 1, 2 or 3, you get 4 points
for a roll of 4, 5 or 6, you get 2 points

****
Card 4:

If you choose option A:
for a roll of 1, 2, 3 or 4 you get 2 points
for a roll of 5 or you get 20 points

If you choose option B:
for a roll of 1, 2, 3 or 4, you get 3 points
for a roll of 5 or you get 9 points

****
Card 5:

If you choose option A:
for a roll of 1, 2 or 3, you get 5 points
for a roll of 4, 5 or 6, you get 6 points

If you choose option B:
for a roll of 1, 2 or 3, you get 4 points
for a roll of 4, 5 or 6, you get 14 points

****
Card 6:

If you choose option A:
for a roll of 1, 2 or 3, you get 6 points

for a roll of 4, 5 or 6, you get 9 points

If you choose option B:
for a roll of 1, 2, 3, 4 or 5 ,you get 1 point for a roll of 6, you get 12 points

****
Card 7:

If you choose option A:
for a roll of 1, 2 or 3, you get 4 points
for a roll of 4, 5 or 6, you get 20 points

If you choose option B:
for a roll of 1, 2 or 3, you get 7 points
for a roll of 4, 5 or 6, you get 9 points

****
Card 8:

If you choose option A:
for a roll of 1, 2, 3, 4 or 5, you get 1 point
for a roll of 6, you get 24 points

If you choose option B:
for a roll of 1 or 2, you get 1 point
for a roll of 3, 4, 5, or 6 you get 10 points

****
Card 9:

If you choose option A:

for a roll of 1, you get 1 point
for a roll of 2, 3, 4, 5 or 6, you get 8 points

If you choose option B:
for a roll of 1, 2, 3, 4 or 5, you get 2 points
for a roll of 6, you get 12 points

****
Card 10:

If you choose option A:
for a roll of 1 or 2, you get 2 points
for a roll of 3, 4, 5 or 6, you get 10 points

If you choose option B:
for a roll of 1, 2, 3 or 4, you get 3 points
for a roll of 5 or 6, you get 12 points

****
Card 11:

If you choose option A:
you get 4 points if you roll 1, 2 or 3
you get 5 points if you roll 4, 5 or 6

If you choose option B:
you lose 6 points if you roll 1 or 2
you get 15 points if you roll 3, 4, 5 or 6

****
Card 12:

If you choose option A:

you lose 10 points if you roll 1, 2 or 3

you get 10 points if you roll 4, 5 or 6

If you choose option B:
you get 6 points if you roll 1 or 2
you get 9 points if you roll 3, 4, 5 or 6

****
Card 13:

If you choose option A:
you lose 12 points if you roll 1
you get 12 points if you roll 2, 3, 4, 5 or 6

If you choose option B:
you get 4 points if you roll 1, 2, 3, 4 or 5
you get 12 points if you roll 6

****
Card 14:

If you choose option A:
you lose 4 points if you roll 1, 2, 3 or 4
you get 9 points if you roll 5 or 6

If you choose option B:
you lose 5 points if you roll 1
you get 8 points if you roll 2, 3, 4, 5 or 6

****
Card 15:

If you choose option A:
you lose 2 points if you roll 1,2,3 or 4

you get 24 points if you roll 5 or 6

If you choose option B:
you get 1 point if you roll 1, 2 or 3
you get 4 points if you roll 4, 5 or 6

****
Card 16:

If you choose option A:
you lose 24 points if you roll 1
you get 8 points if you roll 2, 3, 4, 5 or 6

If you choose option B:
you get 5 points if you roll 1
you get 6 points if you roll 2, 3, 4, 5 or 6

****
Card 17:

If you choose option A:
you lose 5 points if you roll 1, 2 or 3

you get 15 points if you roll 4, 5 or 6

If you choose option B:
you lose 3 points if you roll 1
you get 11 points if you roll 2, 3, 4, 5 or 6

****
Card 18:

If you choose A:
you get points equal to what you roll

If you choose B:
you get 3 points if you roll 3 or less
you get 6 points if you roll 4 or more

****
Card 19:

If you choose A:
you get points equal to what you roll

If you choose B:
you lose 6 points if you roll 1 or 2
you get 12 points if you roll 3, 4, 5 or 6

****
Card 20:

If you choose A:
you lose 6 points if you roll 1, 2, 3 or 4
you get 18 points if you roll 5 or 6

If you choose B:
you lose 6 points if you roll 1
you get 6 points if you roll 2, 3, 4, 5, or 6

****
Card 21:

If you choose A:

You lose 6 points if you roll 1
You get 9 points if you roll 2, 3, 4, 5 or 6

If you choose B:
You get 3 points if you roll 1, 2, 3, 4 or 5
You get 6 points if you roll 6

Exercise 54: Generating Choice Points

What is it?

In this exercise the trainee simply generates choice points in his own life. He lists decisions he is facing.

This is the first part of the Decisions Exercise, but it is often useful to conduct it without the rest of the activities done in that exercise. This enables the trainee to focus purely on the generation of choice points.

Before generating choice points for your own life, sometimes an easier variation is to list choice points for imaginary people.

What's it for?

The generation of choice points is usually the most difficult part in the decision-making process. Many of the major mistakes people make in life seem to come from decisions they have never consciously posed to themselves. The key is knowing which questions to ask.

How do you do it well?

The essence of this exercise is to think over all aspects of your life and to raise the questions that are really most important in living it well. You should pose questions in areas like

How can I use my time best?
How can I best cultivate a relationship with a certain person?
What are the skills I most want to improve?

How can I best promote my own improvement in a certain skill?
How can I make the world a better place?

These sorts of choice points complement the more concrete decisions that present themselves more obviously, and which resemble the problems listed earlier as situations for the brainstorming options exercise.

Variations:

In this activity, it's important to write down the choice points. If you don't write them down, the choice points tend to fade into oblivion.

Sometimes it's useful to go through the entire Decisions Exercise once you have generated the choice points. At other times, it's sufficient simply to pose the questions and to let them percolate, and to reflect upon them periodically.

The choice points or problems or situations you generate through this exercise may then be used as the subjects of other exercises: brainstorming options, brainstorming consequences, listing advantages and disadvantages, the twelve thought exercise, fantasy rehearsals and others.

In another variation, the trainee generates choice points that any imaginary person could face. This is a good variation for trainees who are not ready for the degree of self-examination and self-disclosure that this exercise calls for.

tax the value of the books. But I don't know how much they're worth.

Example:

Choice points:

1. A holiday on which people give presents is approaching. But the person I want to give a present to already has many more material items than she wants or needs.

2. I want to write my book. But other distracting goals keep coming up and keeping me from finishing it. How can I make time for it?

3. I've been thinking about marrying the person I've been seeing. But I'm not sure whether marriage would be the right thing to do.

4. There's a child in the Sunday school class I teach who is disruptive and who interferes with the enjoyment of the class by the rest of the children. What should I do?

5. I've received a good job offer in another town but no job offers in my hometown. I would prefer to live close to my family and friends. What should I do?

6. I want to give some old books to a library. I can deduct from my income

Exercise 55: Moral Dilemmas

What is it?

In this exercise, the trainee is given a situation to respond to. Many of these dilemmas are written out in *Programmed Readings for Psychological Skills*. And you can make up your own dilemmas. The person in the situation is subjected to conflicting demands of ethical principles. For example: a man loves his wife. She has a serious illness that will kill her unless she gets a certain medicine. But the family is poor. The man gets an opportunity to steal the medicine. Thus, the principle of loyalty conflicts with the principle of honesty.

The trainee's task in this exercise is to identify the principles that conflict with each other. I am referring to the sixteen skills and principles as follows:

1. Productivity. Working hard to do things that make things better and help people. Working to prepare myself to do those things.

2. Joyousness. Being cheerful; being joyous when good things happen.

3. Kindness. Being unselfish and forgiving. Treating people as you would like to be treated. Trying to make people happier.

4. Honesty. Keeping your promises and telling the truth; not lying, cheating or stealing.

5. Fortitude. Tolerating not getting what you want. Handling it when things go badly.

6. Good decisions. Thinking carefully, to decide what is best to do, to make things come out well. When there are problems with other people, trying to find a good solution.

7. Nonviolence. Not hurting or killing, and working toward a nonviolent world.

8. Respectful talk (Not being rude). Not talking in a way that hurts someone, unless I carry out some greater good by doing so.

9. Friendship-building. Trying to make new friends and keep old friends. Having good talks with people. Letting people get to know me. Being a good listener.

10. Self-discipline. Doing what's best to do, even if it's hard or boring. Not thinking you have to do whatever you feel like or what feels best at the moment.

11. Loyalty. Sticking by people who have been good to you, or to whom you've made commitments; not forgetting them or dropping them.

12. Conservation. Protecting the earth and wild plants and animals, and making the earth safe for the future. Being thrifty: not wasting money and people's efforts on unneeded luxuries as long as people are hungry, homeless, sick, uneducated or violent.

13. Self-care. Taking care of yourself. Looking after your own health, safety and welfare.

14. Compliance. Honoring your father and mother. Complying with reasonable authorities, unless a rule or command is bad or wrong.

15. Positive fantasy rehearsal. Not taking pleasure in fantasy images of violent or bad actions. In fantasy, practicing good ways of thinking, feeling, and acting.

16. Courage. Being brave enough to do the things that are best, even when they are scary.

After identifying which principles conflict with each other, the trainee's job is then to try to say which way he would go in the decision and which principle he thinks should supercede the other.

What is it for?

This exercise is meant to promote ethical decision-making, attention to ethical principles and decision. It is designed to help the trainee practice referring to ethical principles when confronted with situations.

How do you do it well?

The simple act of identifying the two ethical principles that conflict with each other is a celebration-worthy accomplishment in and of itself. When ethical principles do conflict, one must determine whether violating one principle or the other would have the greatest harmful effect.

In order to accomplish this task well, the trainee should pay attention to calculating harmful and positive effects and predicting good and bad outcomes. The decisions game provides a background for this sort of calculation.

Variations:

Most of the exercises in this book can be adapted for use with groups. This exercise is particularly fun in a group context. It can be lots of fun to discuss or debate ethical dilemmas when there are several people who can bounce ideas around. This activity is highly suited to a family. Ethical dilemmas can make for enlightening mealtime discussions.

In a challenging variation of this exercise, the trainee composes his or her own moral dilemmas. The trainee writes or dictates the situation, and decides what principles are in conflict with one another.

Example:

These are examples of the sorts of dilemmas that are given in *Programmed Readings*. They are also examples of the sorts of dilemmas a trainee might generate in a written exercise involving composing examples of moral dilemmas.

Someone has a very old dog. The dog is ill, and he seems to be uncomfortable. The veterinarian says the dog will not live much longer. The owner of the dog does like the idea of killing the dog to put it out of its misery. But the owner also doesn't like the idea of letting the dog suffer for a long and painful time before death.

conservation versus positive fantasy rehearsal
or
nonviolence versus kindness?

Jack is in school. One of his best friends makes a funny noise while the teacher's back is turned. The teacher is angry, and turns around and says, "Who did that?" Jack looks uncomfortable, and the teacher says, "Jack, do you know who did that?" Jack nods. The teacher says, "Jack, tell me who made that noise." Jack feels that he should obey the teacher, but he doesn't want to betray his friend.

compliance versus loyalty
or
nonviolence versus productivity?

Exercise 56: Prisoner's Dilemma Game

What is it?

This exercise is based on experiments repeated many times with many different conditions. The experimenters have taken pairs of people and have offered them certain rewards for their choices during rounds of the game. The experimenters have noticed whether the people make a cooperative choice or an adversarial choice, a trusting or nontrusting choice.

Often it's interesting to play this game as a "naive subject," that is without reading the paragraphs that follow. Doing the game this way sometimes gives you interesting information about yourself. If you want to do this, stop reading here and let someone else set up the game for you.

Here's how the game is set up. In each round, each of two players makes a certain choice between option A (the trusting choice) and option B (the nontrusting choice). Here's an example of the rules by which the payoffs are rigged up:

If both people choose A, both people get two dollars.

If one person chooses A, and the other chooses B, the one who chose B gets three dollars; the one who chose A gets nothing.

If both people choose B, both people get one dollar.

Here's a table summarizing these conditions:

	A	B
A	2,2	0,3
B	3,0	1,1

And here's a summary of these conditions, looking at the decision from one person's point of view:

If the other person chooses A: you get 3 dollars if you choose B and 2 if you choose A.

If the other person chooses B: you get 1 dollar if you choose B and 0 if you choose A.

This analysis clearly indicates that no matter what the other person chooses, you get more money by choosing B.

But here's a summary of these conditions, looking at the decision from the point of view of the "team" of two people who are trying to get money from the experimenter:

If the two of you both choose A, your team gets 4 dollars per round from the payer.

If the two of you both choose B, your team gets 2 dollars per round from the payer.

If one chooses A and one chooses B, your team gets 3 dollars per round from the payer.

This analysis clearly indicates that the team of two people gets more money, the more of its members select option A.

***

Thus each person maximizes his own payoff on any given round by choosing option B. However, two people can jointly maximize their payoff by choosing option A. If they can trust each other to the point that they can both produce option A round after round, they can take home more money from the experimenter than they would if they did not trust each other and chose option B.

What is it for?

The prisoner's dilemma has been used to study what conditions promote cooperation versus competition. Doing this exercise can be a great learning experience. You learn that in this situation, like so many life situations, you can accomplish more through cooperation than you can by being in an adversarial relationship with one another.

On the other hand, the prisoner's dilemma also affords an opportunity for people to learn that, if the other person is exploitative, it is best to take some retaliatory action rather than simply let-ting yourself be walked upon by the exploitative other. Experiments have found that the "tit-for-tat" strategy of punishing the other person's B choices by making a B choice yourself on the next round, tends to result in higher gains than simply consistently choosing A each time.

You also learn through this game that it's a good idea to talk, to negotiate, to make deals. Saying simple things like, "How about we both put A? Do you agree to that?" can result in a big payoff. Saying things like, "Every time you choose B, I'll choose B the next time," and then following up with that, also helps.

The game also provides information on people's dispositions to certain stances. Some people persist in the adversarial stance, choosing B, even when it doesn't work as well. The cutthroat businessperson, the cutthroat adversarial lawyer, and the cutthroat militarist provide examples of real-life stereotypes who are stuck in this stance. On the other hand, some (probably fewer) people persist in the trusting stance, even when paired with an exploitative partner. The "bleeding heart" helper, and the woman who enters relationships with exploitative men she wants to rescue and help, are stereotypes of persons stuck in the giving posture.

Where does the prisoner's dilemma game get its name? It's from the situation in which the authorities catch two people and accuse them of crimes. They usually take the two people to separate places where they can't negotiate with each other. They say to each prisoner, "If you will confess, and make a sworn statement about the guilt of the other, we'll greatly reduce your sentence." Now, if both prisoners maintain their innocence, both are likely to go free. If they both testify against each other, they both get reduced sentences. If one testifies against the other while the other one does not, the one who testifies goes free while the other gets a more severe sentence.

The prisoner's dilemma game has also been likened to the arms race between nations. If both nations could trust one another, the tremendous amounts of resources spent on weapons could be used elsewhere. But if one nation trusts while the other exploits, the exploitative nation can take over the other. Thus, they tend to settle into a choice where neither side trusts, settling for devoting large amounts of money to defense spending.

How do you do it well?

You perform it well by talking about what to do, trying to be cooperative, and giving your partner every chance to join in a cooperative strategy. It's also helpful not to be stuck in the cooperative posture if your partner is exploitative and adversarial, but to be assertive enough to apply a tit-for-tat strategy. Paradoxically, this more assertive posture tends to maximize both individual and joint gains in this exercise.

Variations:

An important variation of this game involves whether the players are allowed or encouraged to make verbal negotiations with each other before each round. I believe the game is much more generalizable to real-life if such negotiations are permitted. The game is very much different if the experimenter says from the beginning that negotiations are permitted. If the experimenter says nothing, people will often assume that they cannot negotiate with each other.

An important variation of this game is for family members to play it among themselves. It can be a useful way of experiencing the benefits of cooperation and the cost of an adversarial relationship.

Another dimension involves whether the payoffs are in imaginary points or in real money. I have found it useful to place real money at stake in the game. (When it's my own money at stake, I substitute the word "cents" for "dollars" above.)

As another variation: A little different payoff matrix can sometimes help people notice the benefits of cooperation more readily. In this variation, the payoffs are one dollar less than in the example above. Thus if they both choose A, they both get a dollar. If one chooses B and the other chooses A, the one who chose B gets 2 dollars and the one who chose A loses a dollar. If both choose B, they each get nothing.

	A	B
A	1,1	-1, 2
B	2,-1	0,0

This variation allows the trainees to experience more dramatically the difference between cooperation and non-cooperation. If they settle into a noncooperation mode, they get nothing, despite the fact that the experimenter is more than willing to give away money to them. This variation may produce a better teaching exercise, because the difference between making nothing and making a dollar is more dramatic than the difference between making one and two dollars.

Exercise 57: Dialogue Between Conflicted Parts of the Self

What is it?

In this exercise, you role-play a dialogue. But the dialogue is not between two different people; it's between two different parts of yourself. You choose parts of yourself that are in conflict with each another. The goal is that the two parts come to some mutual understanding and resolution of the conflict, just as two people do.

What do we mean by parts of the self that are in conflict with each other? We've spoken before (in the Resolution Exercise) of the part of the self that gives directions and the part of the self that is directed. Often these parts don't get along well. For example, they may speak to each other in the following way:

Self 1: You know, you should really be doing your work. You're acting really lazy and immature.

Self 2: Leave me alone. I don't have to listen to you. I'm tuning you out. Get lost!

This is the typical procrastination dialogue.

Here's another example:

Self 1: You're getting too fat. OK, things are going to be strict. No junk food. Just vegetables, with no fatty sauces on them! It's asparagus and spinach for you!

Self 2: Yes sir, yes sir! You're right! . . . Hey, look at those cookies. I'll bet if I snitched just a few of them that other part wouldn't notice. Well, maybe a few more . . . OK, why not the whole box, as long as I'm going to be in deep trouble anyway?

Self 1: Hey, what have you been up to? Bad, bad. OK, you are going to get it now. Nothing but low fat and high fiber for the rest of this year!

Self 2: Yes sir, yes sir! ...

This is a typical dieter's dialogue.

There's a certain amount gained just by verbalizing how the two parts of the personality actually interact with each other. You get to make explicit what often goes on behind the scenes or beyond conscious awareness. But the most gain, I believe, comes when the different parts of the personality can speak rationally to each other, in the style of the problem-solving conversations advocated in the joint decision exercise.

What's it for?

This exercise is meant to create harmony and cooperation between the parts of the self. So many of people's problems involve internal conflict. If the parts of the self can come to some sort of accommodation with each other, life is much more pleasant.

Various theorists have given names to the parts of the personality that seem to war against each other most frequently. Sigmund Freud spoke of the "id" as the part of the personality that wants immediate gratification, and the "superego" as the part that says "You should." Eric Berne spoke of the "critical parent" versus the "rebellious child" parts of the personality. For Freud, the "ego" was the part that took into account both long-term and short-term needs in a rational way, and, for Eric Berne, the "adult" was the name given to this rational calculating part.

Frederic Perls, the founder of "Gestalt Therapy," who encouraged people to switch chairs as they role-played conversations between the parts of the self, would often refer to the two characters as the "top dog" and the "underdog."

The basic idea of this exercise is that the warring parts of the self need to resolve their conflict with each other in a peaceable and rational way.

The person who needs to do this exercise can at least rejoice that both parts of the personality are there. The people who have the worst time trying to adjust to life are those with no superego, no voice telling them to use self-discipline and delay gratification, only a self that is oriented toward immediate gratification. This type of person tends to be beaten up severely by the external world, rather than less severely by a part of the self.

How do you do it well?

One of the big questions about how to perform this exercise well is how much emotion to put into the dialogues. I have seen Gestalt therapists using this technique in group therapy. The dialogues sometimes have involved a great deal of histrionics: screaming, crying, etc. These dialogues at least kept the audience of other group members from being bored. But did the emotion serve a useful purpose in bringing to full awareness the interests of the two parts of the self, and the forces behind the conflict? Or would the problem be better solved by going straight to a more rational joint-decision conversation, e.g.,. one that met the seven criteria for joint decisions I listed earlier in this book? Or maybe it's best if the two parts of the personality first "get their feelings out" with each other, and later have a more rational decision-making session?

In my mind the jury is still out on this question. Perhaps if you are a trainer or trainee, you can experiment and get information for yourself. The rational, calm conversation between the parts of the self seems the technique that's least likely to do anyone any harm. My bias is toward calmness and rationality.

Variations:

The Gestalt technique is usually carried out by having two chairs. The trainee sits in one chair and speaks to the imaginary other part of the self in the other chair. When switching roles, the trainee gets up and goes to the other chair.

There are other ways of signaling the switch of roles that often feel less embarrassing to the trainee. You can look first in one direction and then in another. Or you can do nothing to signal the switch, but let the trainer infer the switch from the content of the conversation.

As I mentioned earlier, another variation involves whether you are pulling for emotion or calm rationality.

As with so many of these exercises, this one is sometimes best performed by writing. The trainee composes a written dialogue between conflicted parts of the self, aiming toward full expression of the interests of each and their harmonious resolution.

Example:

Self 1: May I talk with you about a problem? It's about the work that needs to be done. I'm afraid if we don't do it soon, we're going to get fired.

Self 2: You're worried about what will happen if the work isn't done, huh? I can understand that. My point of view is that the work seems so unpleasant. I just can't bring myself to do it.

Self 1: So what blocks you is that it's so painful. I can really understand that. What is it that makes it so painful?

Self 2: There's so much stuff to try to remember at once. I guess it would help if I organized it better, and got more of it written down. But getting started on doing that just reminds me how much I've let this go. Then you sometimes criticize me for that.

Self 1: So you protect yourself from that by avoiding the whole task, huh?

Self 2: Yes. But I guess the pain of failing at this job will be a lot greater than the pain of doing the work. I guess the rational choice is to do it. But getting started is so hard. Let's list some options.

Self 1: I could stop criticizing you when the work is not good enough. Or I could reward you while we're doing it by congratulating you for every little piece of progress you make.

Self 2: Maybe we could rig up a reward for myself if I get the work done, like being able to play a game on the computer only after I've done some work.

Self 1: Or another option is lowering the standards and not insisting that the job get done perfectly.

Self 2: Or at least, we can get a version ready that isn't perfect, and then we can decide later whether it's good enough or whether we want to improve on it.

Self 1: We could practice in fantasy the image of sitting down and starting the work without feeling pain.

Self 2: We could make an appointment with someone else who will do some work at the same time with us, to make it more fun. Or we could try to have more fun at other times, so I won't object so much to doing work.

Self 1: What about if we try all these things? Let's see if, by doing all of them, the work gets done more easily.

Self 2: Great. Let's get going right now.

Self 1: Whatever happens, I want you to know: I'm on your side.

***

Here are some examples of the types of conflicts you might think of:

1. One part wants to eat; the other wants to lose weight.

2. One wants to work; the other wants to play and goof off.

3. One wants to spend money; the other wants to save for the future.

4. One wants to drink alcohol; the other thinks drinking alcohol is messing up his life.

5. One wants to take some risk, such as driving fast; the other part wants to play it safe.

6. One part wants to get really angry at someone and let that person know it; the other part thinks it's better to keep quiet.

7. One part wants to go along with what some friends are doing; another part thinks the friends are doing something stupid.

Exercise 58: Self-Exploration Questions

What is it?

The trainee draws randomly from a list of questions that have to do with her own experience, opinions, and wishes, and answers them. Or the trainer and trainee take turns answering them. Or the trainee starts from the beginning of the list and answers all of them.

What is it for?

This is an exercise for practice in self-disclosure, in getting in touch with one's own thoughts and feelings, and in verbal fluency.

How do you do it well?

The first task for the trainee is to come up with something to say other than to shrug the shoulders and say, "I don't know." The trainee should realize that the answers to these are not final and that they won't be held against her. Their purpose is to develop the ability to look inside yourself and put what you see into words. You are not making a commitment to the answers. For that reason, you can do this exercise with the same questions several times and have it come out very different each time.

List of Questions

1. What are some of the things you like to do for fun?

2. If you could work at any career, which one would you choose?

3. If you could be granted three wishes, what would you wish for?

4. What is a game you like to play?

5. Who is someone you admire? Why do you admire this person? The person can be living, dead or even fictional.

6. If you were hiring someone for a job, what is the most important quality you would look for?

7. What is something scary that has happened to you?

8. Tell some of your thoughts about cigarettes.

9. What's something you think some people spend too much time on? How could they spend their time a better way?

10. What's an activity you think people in our society should be spending more time on?

11. Describe a decision you made recently and whether you would decide the same thing if you had to do it over again.

12. What is some work that you have done that you feel good about?

13. What is some work you have done that you feel was a waste of time?

14. If you had to spend lots of time trapped alone somewhere with nothing to do, what three things would you pick to take with you to keep from getting bored?

15. What do you think is one of the main reasons why people do cruel things to other people?

16. What would you give as a rule that tells how people should act, or what is ethical, or what is good to do?

17. If you could make one goal for yourself and know that you would be successful in accomplishing it, what goal would you set?

18. What are some of your thoughts about alcoholic drinks?

19. Suppose you were very rich and had lots of money you wanted to use to help other people. How would you use the money?

20. What do you think is the most boring thing in the world to have to do?

21. If you could pick one question that you could find the answer to, which one would you pick?

22. Tell some of your thoughts about physical exercise.

23. Tell about an experience you had involving a pet or another animal.

24. Tell about a time you had a disagreement with someone.

25. Tell about a time you felt really proud of yourself.

26. What is a kind thing someone did for you, that you appreciate?

27. What's something you think is a bad idea to do, even though lots of people do it?

28. What is one of the best stories you have read or seen on a movie or TV show? Can you tell part of the story?

29. Do you think there are people in society who make lots of money even though they don't do much good for people? If so, what sorts of things do they do?

30. If at this moment you had to decide on a charity organization to give a hundred dollars to, which one would you pick?

31. Tell some of your experiences in sports.

32. If you were in charge of running a school, what is one thing you would do?

33. Suppose you could make or repeal a law. What would you do?

34. What are some of your favorite songs or musical compositions?

35. If you had your life to live over again, what is something you would want to do differently?

36. If you become a parent, or if you are already a parent, what is one thing you want to be sure to do?

37. After your life is over, what would you like people to say about you and your life?

38. Imagine that someone tries to hurt the feelings of a brother or sister. What might be one reason the person does this?

39. What are some of your thoughts about violent entertainment, for example, movies where there is a lot of killing and hurting, boxing matches, or bullfights?

40. Think about your own schooling and education. What is one thing you would change if you could?

41. Think about your own schooling and education. What is something you are pleased with and glad about?

42. Please tell about something kind you have done for someone.

43. Please tell about something you greatly enjoyed.

44. Can you think of a circumstance in which it would be ethical to lie?

45. Can you think of a time when you had to put up with some hardship or frustration?

46. What do you think are the circumstances in which it is right or ethically justified to use violence, i.e., to physically hurt or kill?

47. Of all the approving or disapproving things you say to people, about what percentage are approving and what percentage are disapproving?

48. Is there someone you very much like to be with? What is it about this person that makes you enjoy being with him or her?

49. Can you think of a time when you chose to do something that was less fun or pleasurable than something else, in order to achieve some goal?

50. Who is a person you feel loyalty to? Why do you feel that way?

51. What is something that people spend time or money on that you think is wasteful?

52. What is some way that you take care of your health and safety, or would like to take care of your health and safety?

53. Can you think of an example of when it is ethical and right to refuse to obey someone?

54. Can you think of a time when someone should go ahead and do something, even though the person is scared to do it?

55. Can you think of something that it would do you some good to practice over and over, many times?

Variations

In addition to the questions written here, the trainee can make up his or her own questions and use them for the exercise.

This exercise can be done orally or in writing.

The trainee can be the only one who answers the questions, or the trainer and trainee can take turns answering them.

Example:

1. What are some of the things you like to do for fun?

I like to daydream about different ways for human society to be set up. I like to imagine what it could be like if people were trained from a very early age to get along well with one another, make good decisions, and use a lot of self-control.

Another unusual thing I like to do is called "aerobic chores." I do things that need to be done around the house, like washing dishes, sorting through mail, doing laundry, and so forth, but while I'm doing it, I run in place. When I'm done, I have the satisfaction of knowing I've taken care of several tasks, and I've gotten a good workout.

2. If you could work at any career, which one would you choose?

I'd like to do research in psychology. I'd like to have a lot of people helping me, and a lot of money to use with research projects. I'd like to try out all sorts of different ways of teaching people to get along with each other and to be happy.

3. If you could be granted three wishes, what would you wish for?

I'd wish that there were no more violence in the world, that I could know that my children would be healthy, safe, and happy throughout long lives, and that all good things didn't have to end.

4. What is a game that you like to play?

I like running footraces. I enjoy the feeling of the air going past me as I run, and I enjoy the feeling of energy as I come to the finish line. It's also thrilling whenever I win or place well.

5. Who is someone you admire? Why do you admire this person? The person can be living, dead or even fictional.

I admire Mohandas Gandhi. He was very determined and purposeful, but he tried to be loving and nonviolent

as he carried out his purposes. He was very mindful of the needs of the poor, and he did not accumulate lots of possessions. When he died, he owned amazingly few things.

6. If you were hiring someone for a job, what is the most important quality that you would look for?

Honesty would be the most important quality. As long as I am getting the truth from the employee about what is going on, I can deal with it in some way or another, but if I am getting false information, there can be big problems.

7. What is something scary that has ever happened to you?

Once, as a boy, I was camping out in my back yard with some friends. One of my friends was sure he heard someone tramping around outside in big army boots. All of us began to fear that someone we couldn't see was in the back yard.

8. Tell some of your thoughts about cigarettes.

I think some people aren't aware of how addictive cigarettes are. I read somewhere that it's as hard to get off cigarettes as it is to get off heroin. I'm very happy that laws and customs have grown up that keep people from poisoning other people's air with cigarette smoke as much as they used to.

Exercise 59: Questions About Fears

What is it?

When you are afraid, you start writing or talking to someone willing to transcribe for you. You answer the following questions about the fear.

1. Feared outcomes. What are the outcomes that I'm afraid of? Describe them in very specific detail.

2. Probabilities and disutilities. How likely are these to happen, and how bad are they?

3. Options for preventing. What options do I want to list for preventing the bad outcomes from happening?

4. Options for coping. What options do I want to list for coping with the bad outcomes if they do occur?

What's it for?

This is an exercise in rational thinking about feared situations. Rational thinking is very much an antidote to the sort of irrational fear that grips most of us from time to time.

The first question requires you to specify in great detail exactly what you are afraid will happen. This can be a very unpleasant task. It can cause you to confront images of very bad outcomes. But boldly confronting the images of the outcomes you fear is often the most important step in getting over unrealistic fears. In fact, it has been said that the element that almost all successful fear-reduction programs have in common is *exposure* to the scary situation. By specifying what you fear will happen, you expose yourself, in fantasy, to that scary outcome.

The second question requires you to estimate how likely the feared outcomes are, and how bad they are. I have referred to these elsewhere as the *probabilities and disutilities* of the feared outcomes. If the feared outcome is extremely unlikely to occur, or if its negative effect is trivial, then you're not in much danger. It's great to realize this when it is true. When you fear something greatly, even in the absence of danger, you can call the fear an *unrealistic* one. Deciding that a fear is unrealistic doesn't make it go away instantly. But deciding that does help you know your priority is to get over the fear, rather than protect yourself from real danger.

Sometimes answering the second question will lead you to conclude that you are in real danger. This too is important to acknowledge when it is true! For example, a man drinks too much alcohol, and he fears that his wife will leave him if he does not stop. When he speaks to her, he finds out she is indeed thinking seriously of leaving him, and thus his fear is quite realistic! It's very important to know when you are actually in danger, so that you can do something about it.

The third question helps you protect yourself, to get out of danger if you are in it. You think of the ways that you can keep the bad outcome from happening. For our man who fears that his wife will leave him, he might want to list the options of quitting drinking, being kinder to his wife, being more responsible with his children, and so forth.

The fourth question helps you prepare yourself in case the feared outcome does occur. Sometimes doing this helps you ready yourself for something that is likely. At other times, it helps you make an unrealistic fear less: you spend time imagining that even though the thing has already happened, you do not simply collapse, but you cope with it as well as you can. Imagining yourself surviving and prevailing even in the face of the feared disaster can reduce unrealistic fears.

How do you do it well?

You'll probably find that you will get more out of this exercise if you imagine the situations very vividly, write down your answers, take your time to answer the questions in detail, and review and/or revise your answers on several occasions after the first.

Example:

Feared outcomes. I'm giving a report in front of the rest of the class at school next Friday, and I fear that I will mess up and do a bad job. It's possible I could get stage fright so badly that I would not be able to finish the report, but would have to stop in the middle. Then I fear that all my classmates would think I was a weak person and nobody would want to have anything to do with me any more. I would try to talk to people and they would just turn away and go to someone else.

Probabilities and disutilities. The chance that I will stumble over words at least once is very high. But that's no problem if that happens. The chance that I will do really badly, but finish the report, is maybe three per cent. That would be embarrassing and it would result in a bad grade, but it would not be horrible. The chance that I will get stage fright so badly that I won't be able to finish is less than one per cent. And even if that happened, the chance that all my classmates would reject me from then on is probably less than one in ten thousand. If they did reject me, I still have other friends, so it still wouldn't be the most horrible thing.

Options for preventing. I can write out my talk word for word. I can practice many times reading it expressively. While I'm practicing, I can fantasy that I'm in class giving the report. I can relax my muscles while I do that. I can recall other successful talks I've given, in order to get into the pattern of feeling confident and relaxed. I can remind myself that even if I feel very nervous while I give my talk, that's OK. When I actually give my talk, I can recall the practice sessions, and recreate the sort of calm I felt while practicing.

Options for coping. If I do badly on the report, I can remind myself that I've done well at lots of other things. I can take comfort in the fact that nobody was hurt or killed by my mistakes–it's not like I messed up while doing brain surgery. I can remind myself that nobody is perfect and that people can still like me even if I'm not successful at this speech. I can plan to work on my public speaking over a longer period of time and gradually prevail over this problem.

Exercise 60: Breathing Exercises

What are they?

These are exercises particularly useful in treating or preventing panic attacks that involve hyperventilation. If you think you have these, make sure to get this diagnosis confirmed (or ruled out) by a careful doctor. The sensation of difficulty catching the breath can be cause by many physical conditions–asthma, pneumonia, congestive heart failure, and cardiac arrhythmias, to name a few.

Here are the exercises.

1. Muscle relaxation in rhythm with your breathing. In this exercise you primarily focus on relaxing your muscles. When you have done this enough to get a pleasant relaxed feeling, you turn your attention to the rhythm of your breathing. You continue to relax your muscles a little more each time you exhale. You can describe the rhythm as "breathe in ... relax out." Spend time being conscious of the rhythm of relaxed breathing. If you are very relaxed, you may find yourself breathing well under the twelve to sixteen times per minute that sometimes is called average for breathing "at rest."

2. Abdominal breathing. Here are three exercises to practice abdominal breathing.

2a. Coughing. When you cough, you naturally use your abdominal muscles to exhale. So in this exercise, you exhale using a series of very light coughs. As you do this, you notice your abdominal muscles tightening. When you have coughed out all your air, you relax your abdominal muscles and let your belly get big as you breathe in. In this way you experience what it is like to use the abdominal muscles and the diaphragm in breathing.

2b. Pulsed hissing. In this exercise you take a deep breath in, making your belly big as you do so. Then you start squeezing your abdominal muscles to exhale, while your mouth makes an "ssss" sound. You pulse your abdominal contractions so that the hissing sound gets louder and softer–it doesn't stop altogether until you have hissed out all your air. You can make the pulses fast or slow. It's useful to practice lots of fast pulses, because learning to do this requires getting a good bit of control over your abdominal breathing muscles. When you have fully exhaled by this hissing, take in a deep breath that makes your belly big again. Singers sometimes use this exercise.

2c. Pulsed blowing. This is very much like pulsed hissing. You purse your lips as if you were blowing out a candle, so that you can feel the air resistance as you blow air out. You take a deep breath that makes your belly big. You blow out the air in a series of pulses, squeezing your abdominal muscles. When you've fully exhaled by this pulsed blowing, you inhale in a way that makes your belly big again.

3. Aerobic exercise with attention to sensations. You run, run in place, ride a bike, work on some exercise equipment, or perform any other form of aerobic exercise. While doing so, you pay attention to the sensation of your heart pounding and your fast breathing. When you stop exercising, you notice these gradually return to normal.

4. Breath-holding. In this exercise, you hold your breath for a short time, starting with perhaps as little as ten seconds, just long enough to have the sensation of needing to breathe. This is the sensation of "too much carbon dioxide," created by your brain's detecting the buildup of carbon dioxide in your bloodstream. Be aware of that sensation, and then start breathing again. You will naturally breathe a little faster for a few seconds; then you start back breathing normally.

5. Hyperventilation. In this exercise you breathe as fast and deeply as you can for a short time, starting perhaps with as little as ten seconds, just long enough to experience a little different feeling in your head. The strange sensation you start to get is the sensation of "too little carbon dioxide," and it comes from your "blowing off" carbon dioxide from your bloodstream. Then stop hyperventilating. For a while, breathe much more slowly than usual, until the sensation of too little carbon dioxide goes away. Pay attention to how breathing more slowly gets rid of the strange sensation.

What are they for?

The point of these exercises is less obvious than that of many others. Most people get air in and out of their bodies just fine without focusing attention on breathing at all. Why even think about it?

Very many people have anxiety problems that are worsened by breathing difficulties. These exercises are meant to help prevent or alleviate these problems.

Before explaining how these exercises can help, let's review a little physiology.

The work our body does is fueled by the combustion of fats and carbohydrates. The carbon in these materials combines with oxygen to produce carbon dioxide. The purpose of breathing is to allow carbon dioxide to diffuse out into the air, and to allow oxygen from the air to diffuse into our bloodstreams. The faster and harder our muscles work, the faster we use up oxygen and produce carbon dioxide. To keep the oxygen and carbon dioxide at the right levels, we need to breathe harder with strenuous exercise.

Throughout most of human evolution, when people have gotten scared, they have frequently found it useful to run away from danger or fight the dangerous person or animal. To prepare for that physical exertion, the hormones we secrete when we are scared signal us to breathe faster, even before we start exercising.

Carbon dioxide, when dissolved in the water of our bloodstreams, forms a weak acid, carbonic acid. Our blood stays in a pretty narrow range of acidity. When we breathe fast without exercising, we "blow off" lots of carbon dioxide and our blood becomes less acidic. Blood's getting less acidic normally sends a message to brain that says, "Don't breathe so fast." In response to that message, we breathe slower, and more carbon dioxide builds up; this brings the acidity back where it's supposed to be. But sometimes things don't work out the way they should, and a vicious cycle, rather than a corrective feedback cycle, occurs.

Here's how this vicious cycle works. A person will somehow get scared, and start breathing faster. Breathing faster "blows off" carbon dioxide, and leaves the person with the strange feeling of too little carbon dioxide in the blood. But with some people, too little carbon dioxide triggers a series of changes that lead to the sensation of "I can't get my breath," or "I am suffocating; I need to breathe faster."

When this happen, a vicious cycle has started. The person breathes still faster, which causes the strange sensation of too little carbon dioxide to get worse, not better. Now faster breathing causes stranger sensations and more fear, which cause an even greater sensation of not having enough air. Eventually this vicious cycle somehow stops, but the time that it lasts is very unpleasant.

The sensations involved often trigger another vicious cycle. People can think, "Something horrible is happening to my body! Surely I'm about to die!" These thoughts obviously trigger lots of fear, which triggers more hyperventilation and heart-pounding. It's very helpful for people to learn to think, "These sensations are unpleasant, but there's nothing going on that will threaten my life or permanently damage my health."

Hyperventilating can make people feel dizzy and faint. It can produce numbness, starting in the hands, feet, and mouth. These feelings, too, can be quite unpleasant. Fortunately, they are curable by simply breathing slowly. They are also curable by running in place or otherwise exerting the muscles strenuously, so as to create more carbon dioxide.

Exercise and slower breathing are reasonable cures for the strange feelings of hyperventilation, because they allow more carbon dioxide to build up. Another cure that has been used many times is breathing into a paper bag. This works because carbon dioxide builds up in the bag, and breathing it back in restores a higher carbon dioxide level in the bloodstream. However, unlike slower breathing and exercise, breathing into a paper bag allows the possibility of getting too little oxygen, if the bag is airtight enough. So for that reason, this method of restoring carbon dioxide is not preferred.

There are good reasons why the natural response to fear is to breathe faster. The body is programmed to do this so as to get ready for "flight or fight" in a dangerous situation. If you are going to run away or fight, you will be exerting your muscles strenuously. In our modern world, however, most of what scares us doesn't cause us to respond with strenuous exercise. Perhaps for this reason, we're more likely to get into the vicious cycle I mentioned earlier.

Some people have "chronic hyperventilation." This means they often or always breathe faster than they need to. This habit can make acute hyperventilation episodes more likely.

Now let's think about how each of the exercises helps to avoid hyperventilation.

Relaxing your muscles helps you get into a relaxed state. Then, if you make yourself aware of the rhythm of your breathing, and practice the "breathe in, relax out" rhythm, you get used to the speed with which you breathe when you're at rest. If you're breathing much faster than this, you'll find it easier to recognize this because you've spent some time just feeling the rhythm of relaxed breathing. Learning to breathe more slowly plays a major part in getting over hyperventilation problems.

Something else is accomplished by relaxing your muscles in rhythm with your breathing. If you've had panic attacks with hyperventilation, you may have some fear associated with even thinking about breathing and paying attention to the feelings associated with the rate of breathing. Paying attention to your breathing rhythm while you are relaxed helps to desensitize this fear. If you can comfortably pay attention to what your breathing is doing, that's a big step.

What's the point of learning to breathe with the abdominal muscles and diaphragm, rather than with the upper chest muscles? Contrary to some things you might read, you don't need to worry that chest breathing will result in your taking in too little oxygen. You can get enough oxygen by chest breathing or abdominal breathing.

The main reason for learning abdominal breathing is that it's easier to control. (This is the same reason that singers are taught to use abdominal breathing.) You can see your belly rising and falling. You can feel what is going on in your abdominal muscles. With chest breathing, you can hyperventilate without realizing it; with abdominal breathing, you're usually more aware of what you're doing. By coughing and doing pulsed hissing and blowing, you get used to using the abdominal muscles, which are the easiest ones to regulate consciously.

Aerobic exercise allows anyone who has had a panic attack to desensitize himself to the fear of the sensations of both rapid heartbeat and fast breathing. Each experience of breathing fast and then letting the breathing return to a slower rate as the aerobic exercise ends provides practice in letting the breathing rate regulate itself naturally; this is the opposite of hyperventilation problems. Perhaps these mechanisms explain why at least one study found that regular aerobic exercise was an effective treatment for panic disorder.

A major purpose of breath-holding and purposeful hyperventilation is that you learn to distinguish between the sensation of too much carbon dioxide and too little. If you experience these sensations enough, while paying attention to them, you'll find it easier to think, "That's the sensation of too little carbon dioxide, not the sensation of too much."

Another major accomplishment of breath-holding and purposeful hyperventilation is that you learn not to fear the sensations of too much or little carbon dioxide. As I mentioned earlier, fear is a major component in the vicious cycle of a panic attack. If you can feel the sensations of too much or too little carbon dioxide, and think, in a very matter-of-fact way, "Oh yeah, those are the sensations; I'm familiar with them; they aren't dangerous," then it's much more difficult for the vicious cycle to get started.

A third benefit of purposeful hyperventilation and breath-holding is that you become more familiar with the sensations that help you avoid chronic hyperventilation. You want to avoid the sensations of hyperventilation by breathing more slowly; you want to breathe just fast enough to avoid the unpleasant feeling of too much carbon dioxide.

All these exercises give you lots of experience in playing around with breathing. You practice bringing your breathing under conscious control and then letting it go back to "automatic pilot." You play around with the sensations that come from breathing too much or too little. You get very used to all this, so you're much less likely to hyperventilate.

How do you do them well?

If you've ever had a panic attack or hyperventilation episode, one of the smartest ways to do these exercises is to move along the "hierarchy of difficulty" just fast enough that each exercise prepares you for the next and no exercise turns out to be very unpleasant or scary. You start with exercises that are easy for you and not scary at all. You gradually work your way up to greater challenges.

Listening to the tape of the relaxation script (see the exercise on relaxation and biofeedback) is usually a nonthreatening place to start. This tape makes a brief reference to focusing on the rhythm of breathing, and using the "breathe in–relax out" rhythm. But most of the tape consists in muscle relaxation suggestions and suggestions about peaceful and pleasant imagery.

If you can listen to this tape comfortably and with a peaceful feeling of relaxation, a next step is simply to get your muscles relaxed and then sit longer in silence, conscious of your breathing, relaxing your muscles in rhythm with your breathing.

With the abdominal breathing exercises, you can challenge yourself to see how many pulses of hissing or blowing you can do on one breath. An adult who has learned good abdominal control can use one breath to do about fifteen sets of four pulses, with each set of four taking a little less than a second. It's possible for many people to continue this pulsing, with about four or five deep breaths per minute, for a good while without getting into a state of either too much or two little carbon dioxide.

In doing the exercises on breath-holding and hyperventilation, the key is to notice carefully the sensations you're feeling. Pay attention to them and learn to recognize them. In these exercises, you don't have to hold your breath or hyperventilate to the point of great discomfort.

If you've never had a hyperventilation episode, these exercises can still be interesting to play with. A very interesting research project would be to teach these exercises to people who had never had a hyperventilation episode, but who had close family members who had. It's possible that learning these exercises would have a preventive effect.

Exercise 61: Cooperative Games

What are they?

In competitive games, the two players (or teams) are pitted against each other. One's gain is another's loss. I want to score as many points as possible and keep your score as low as possible; your goals are the direct opposite of mine. The structure of the game is set up that one side's success makes the other side unhappy.

In cooperative games, the players have the same goals. What makes one player happy also makes another happy. The more successful any player is, the greater the chance of success in the joint effort.

If you want to structure activities to encourage helping and mutual support, look toward cooperative games. Below are a few possibilities.

Cooperative Basketball

Two people are best for a team, although three or four at a time can also play. You mark a spot about thirty feet from the basket. The first person shoots, and gets the rebound, while the second runs behind the marked spot and back toward the basket. The first person passes to the second. The second person shoots and gets the rebound while the first is running behind the marked spot and back to the basket.

The two players alternate like this for three minutes. (It's good to use the timer function on an electronic watch.)

The object of the game is for the team to make as many baskets as possible in three minutes. However, baskets only count when the person or people who did not make the basket congratulate the person who made it, and that person says, "Thank you!"

The players may want to do lots of three-minute trials, attempting to break their previous records.

Maximum Hits Volleyball

You play a regular game of volleyball, with any number of people on each team. But in this game the object is to see how many times you can hit the ball before it touches the ground. Alternatively, you can start a timer and see how long you can keep the ball in play. If players are younger, are less skilled, or want to take it easy, a good variation is to play with a beach ball or a balloon.

A variation when there are several on each team is that each time you hit the ball over the net, you go under or around the net to play on the other side. Another variation is not to use a net and let anyone hit the ball to anyone.

Maximum hits tennis or table tennis can be played in the same way.

Breaking the Pass Record Football

There are two players on a team. They alternate roles. One centers the ball to the other and then goes out for a pass. Then the other centers and goes out for a pass, starting at the same place. You have a time limit of three minutes. During that time, you see how many times you can break your record for the longest pass you've completed in that round. That is, each time you complete a pass longer than any before it, you have broken your record. Thus the strategy is to start out with short passes and gradually get longer and longer.

Maximum Distance Soccer

There are teams of two players. You mark out a path. This can be a path through the woods or from one place to another on a field. If the players reach the end of the path before the time it up, they turn around and come back to the beginning, and then go back again. You set the timer for three minutes. The two players must alternate kicks–that is, no player can kick the ball twice in a row. The object of the game is to go as far as you can in three minutes.

Maximum Passes Soccer

There are teams of two players. You figure out a certain number of times that the two players have to go across a field and back in three minutes. The object of the game is to make as many passes back and forth as they can in the three minutes, while still covering the required distance.

Towel Push-ups

One person does push-ups. The other two people help the person. The two helpers do so by putting a towel under the chest of the person who does push-ups. Each of the two helpers grasps one end of the towel. They lift up when the person is coming up and lower when the person is going down. The person has to straighten out the arms altogether at the top of the push up and move the angle at the elbow past a right angle at the bottom of the push up. The object of the game is for the team to complete as many push-ups as possible in the time allotted.

The best way to maximize the number of push-ups is for the two helpers to coordinate their efforts with each other and with the person doing the push-ups.

Rope Jumping

A great cooperative activity, practiced beautifully on many inner-city playgrounds, has two people swinging two ropes in two directions, and a third person between them, jumping. This maneuver is difficult, and it's good to work up to it by steps. One person can practice jumping by himself; three people can practice rope-jumping using only one rope. For a full-length book on the fine art of rope-jumping, see *The Jump Rope Book* by Elizabeth Loredo, Workman Publishing.

Trailmaking

This is a game for the woods. Each person, or each group, marks a trail through the woods in some way that does not harm the environment: for example, making pointers with stones or dead wood, or with little bits of flour. Then the person or group that didn't make the trail gets to try to follow it. The trailmakers can come along behind the trail followers to see how successful their markers were, and offer help if needed. The trailmakers can leave some sort of treasure hidden at the end if they wish.

Navigating with Topographical Maps

You get a good topographical map of a region of woods and a good compass. You find some place in the woods and start there. You figure out from the map exactly which direction it is to a certain other landmark (i.e., how many degrees) and how far it is. You then use the compass to walk in exactly the direction you need to go, for about the distance you have figured, and see whether you can find the other landmark.

Here's a variation. The leader takes the group into the woods by a circuitous route. The leader shows the group members where they are on the map. The group then takes the map and compass and finds their way out of the woods.

Rhythm

You sit in a circle and clap twice on the thighs and twice with the hands. Everyone gets this rhythm going. Then someone starts by saying his name twice (during the leg claps) and then saying someone else's name twice (during the hand claps). The person whose

name was called, without breaking the rhythm, calls out his name twice on the hand claps and someone else's name twice on the leg claps. You keep going without breaking the rhythm as long as you can. You vary the speed to keep the challenge in the best challenge zone for the least skilled players.

What Am I Doing?

You make a list of activities such as the ones below, and write them on pieces of paper. You put them in a pile. You take turns picking one from the pile and acting it out. The audience tries to guess what the person is doing.

Variation: You don't make a list, and you take turns, with each person both making up something and acting it out.

List: Brushing teeth. Playing a piano. Playing a guitar. Shooting an arrow. Digging a hole. Petting and playing with a dog. Driving a car, and calling someone on a cell phone while doing so. Feeding some fish in an aquarium. Ironing some clothes. Getting a can of pop from a coin-operated machine, opening the can, and starting to drink it. Milking a cow. Paying for something at a check-out line by swiping a credit card through a card reader and then signing the receipt. Waiting for a bus, seeing the bus coming, and getting on the bus and sitting down. Pouring cereal and milk into a bowl and starting to eat the cereal. Knocking on a door, trying to sell somebody something, having the person close the door in your face, and leaving. Putting sunscreen on your skin. Getting a big bunch of laundry and starting to put it on hangers and hang it up. Eating spaghetti. Finishing taking a big test and turning it in. Asking someone to dance, but getting turned down. Sawing a piece of wood. Hammering a nail. Drying dishes and putting them away. Playing a hand-held video game. Being a man shaving off his moustache. Pushing a shopping cart at the grocery store and putting groceries in it. Feeding a baby with a bottle. Changing a baby's diaper.

What Does He Like?

You use either regular playing cards, or a special deck of sixty-four cards with

one, two, three, or four
red, yellow, green, or brown
stars, circles, plus signs, or triangles.

One person decides upon the rule for what the imaginary person from Mars likes and doesn't like. For example: with an ordinary card deck, he likes hearts and diamonds but doesn't like spades and clubs. Or he likes even numbered black cards. With the special deck, maybe he likes cards if they are either green or brown and made up of stars.

After the rule-maker decides what the imaginary person likes, the rule-maker starts sorting cards into two sets: those that the person from Mars likes and those that he doesn't like. The guesser tries to infer the rule by noticing what the liked cards have in common, that is, how they're different from the disliked cards. The challenge for the rule-maker is to pick a rule of the degree of complexity and difficulty that is just right for the person inferring the rule.

Password

One person thinks of a word. He tries to help the other person guess the word by saying a different word to him. If the other person can't guess on the first round, the person gives a second word on the second round. They continue until they decide to give up or until the second person has guessed.

Twenty Questions

One person thinks of something. The other asks yes or no questions to try to find out what it is. The name of the game comes from the custom of having a limit of twenty questions to find out what it is; if you exceed that limit, it's OK with me. The strategy in this game is to start with broad categories (Is it alive?) and gradually home in on more specific things.

Round Robin Story

One person starts out telling a story. Then he or she stops and lets the next person tell the story for a while. Then the telling passes to the next person, until they are done. Variation: Someone transcribes the story as it goes along.

Charades

People write sayings or titles of books, movies, songs, etc., attempting to choose phrases that the other group members will be familiar with. (Variation: you can use psychological skill-related terms, such as productivity, listing options, celebrations, fantasy rehearsal, and so forth.) These are all put into a pile. People take turns picking one and acting out the phase, usually syllable by syllable, while the others guess. Charades has a system for letting the audience know how many words are in the phrase, which word you are acting out, how many syllables are in this word, and which syllable you are acting out. If you don't want to bother with this, the actor can say all this verbally.

Construct the Donkey

This is a variation of the party game for young children, "Pin the Tail on the Donkey." In the new version, you cut up the whole picture of the donkey, so there's one part for each player. Then you blindfold the players one at a time and let them tape their parts up. But the other players give directions to the blindfolded one so that the donkey gets put together with his body parts in the right place. The object of the game for the whole group is to put the donkey together with some semblance of normal anatomy.

You also have official permission to choose pictures of things other than donkeys.

Academic Contests against Mr. X

Someone comes up with a set of questions or problems that are at the right degree of difficulty for the contestants. The subject area can be math, science, spelling, or any other area. (For elementary or middle school children, you may want to take a look at the *Spectrum Test Prep* series, or the "Brain Quest" questions.)

The real humans play against Mr. X. They take turns attempting to answer questions. One person is asked the question but can collaborate with any other person. For each correct answer, the real humans get a point. For each incorrect answer, Mr. X gets from two to five points, depending on how difficult the questions are. To increase the stakes, you can make it so that the humans give themselves a reward of some sort if they win, but not if Mr. X wins.

Cooperative Chess

The two people collaborate in playing against a computer opponent whose skill level is set at approximately the same level as the humans. The two people alternate in making moves against the opponent. They can talk with each other freely about which move is best. They see how high level an opponent they can jointly beat.

In a different variation, the two people take on a series of chess problems such as those in the drills in *Chessmaster 8000* or other computer chess programs, or in chess books. The level of difficulty of the problems must be carefully chosen. They take turns giving the answer, but they can consult freely with each other. The two people see how many problems of a certain type they can solve correctly in a certain time, and then attempt to beat their record.

Cooperative Freecell

Freecell is a solitaire card game. A computer version is included as an accessory on Microsoft Windows. The game is also available in other computer versions. It can even be played with real cards! It is an all-time great solitaire game, because it depends upon skill and not primarily upon luck, and because most hands are winnable if people will think ahead carefully. The hands of the Microsoft computer version are numbered, so that you can pick easy hands (e.g., #8), and you can replay the same hand as many times as you like.

In the cooperative version, two people play, taking turns making moves. They can talk with each other all they want about strategy. Both win if all the cards can be moved from the original stacks to the final ones.

This alternating strategy can be used with many other solitaire games.

Cooperative Blockhead

"Blockhead" is a commercially available game that supplies blocks of a variety of shapes. In the competitive version, people take turns putting blocks onto a structure that grows higher and higher; the one whose block causes the structure to fall loses the game. In the cooperative version, the players collectively try to make the structure as high as possible, or to put on as many blocks as possible, without a collapse. They keep track of their records and try to break them.

Mastermind

This can be played in a competitive version as a commercially available board game. It can also be played non-competitively, in the context where players take turns solving the problem that the other one makes up. It can be played without equipment, in the following way.

One person, the code-maker makes up a four-digit number, consisting of any permutation of the digits 0 through 5. The code-breaker writes down a guess for a four-digit number. The code-maker responds by writing, beside that guess, two numbers. The first number answers the question "How many digits in the guessed number are both correct and in the correct position?" The second number answers the question "How many are the correct digit but in the incorrect position?" The code-breaker contemplates this feedback and makes another try. They continue until the correct number is guessed.

Having four digits and six possibilities for each digit is just one way to play the game. For younger code-breakers, or for code-breakers who don't feel like working their brains so hard, you can use fewer digits for the answers or fewer possibilities for each digit.

Ballroom Dancing

In this activity, the proficiency and success of each partner adds to the success of the other rather than subtracting from it. This is a great chance for males and females to practice cooperation with one another. Folk and square dancing provide similarly cooperative activities.

Singing in Harmony

Singing songs with two or more harmonious parts is easier than most people think it is; it is a prototypical cooperative activity. Instructional recordings can help in the learning process. I recommend "Learn to Sing Harmony" (Cathy Fink et al., 1998, www.homespuntapes.com) and "How to Sing Country [or Pop, Gospel, Bluegrass] Harmony" (Dan Huckabee, 1985, www.musicians-workshop.com).

The Shaping Game, the Decisions Game, Improvising Plays Together, Brainstorming Options or Consequences, and The Prisoner's Dilemma

These activities are each given their own chapter in this book; I cross-reference them here. The Shaping Game is one of the best cooperative games, in my experience.

What are they for?

There is definitely a place in the world for competitive attitudes as well as cooperative attitudes. There are times when opposing the will of another person is the most rational and reasonable choice.

However, we live in a world where competitive attitudes between nations, and the resulting bellicose actions, threaten to end the existence of the human race. Many people live in families where constant competitive bickering and rivalry between siblings produces an emotional climate dominated by hostility. Many marital relationships are characterized by the same state in which the partners stay opposed to each other. Relationships among school children are very frequently marred by too much hostility and competitive attitudes.

If you want to have people feel good about one another, which sort of game makes more sense: one where one person beats the other, or one in which they work together to accomplish a mutual goal?

In 1961 a group of researchers led by M. O. Sherif reported the "Robber's Cove Experiment." A highly competitive set of games between groups of children at a summer camp created growing rivalry and hostility between the children, even outside the context of the games. When the hostility had reached a high level, the experimenters were able to reverse the ill effects they had produced. They did this by halting the major competitions and scheduling activities that promoted cooperation between former rivals.

My prediction is that parents, teachers, camp directors, employers, and others in charge of groups will be able to promote more cooperation and less hostility in real life by providing higher exposure to cooperative games and activities.

How do you do these well?

Here are some thoughts to keep in mind while doing cooperative games.

1. I want to help find the correct level of challenge for all the players–not too hard and not too easy.

2. I want to celebrate my own successes.

3. I want to celebrate my fellow players' successes.

4. I want to use fortitude when I fail at any attempt.

5. I want to be supportive when any of my fellow players fails.

6. I can push myself to the limits of my ability, if I want to, even without a competitor.

7. I want to approach this game or activity joyfully.

Exercise 62: The Psychological Skills Book Report

What is it?

Human beings are by nature story-lovers. Television sitcoms or soap operas, picture story-books, movies, cartoons, works of great literature, works of pulp fiction, stories around a campfire, stories told in country-and-western ballads, real-life stories reported in the newspaper, the stories spread by neighborhood gossip–all these give evidence of people's insatiable appetite for narratives.

These narratives give examples of people thinking, feeling, and behaving, and thus they give examples–whether good, bad, or indifferent–of psychological skills. They provide a great opportunity for us to examine behavior, using the tools of psychological skills concepts.

The simplest form of the Psychological Skills Book Report is to select various choices made by the characters in a story and to classify those choices as to which psychological skills they exemplify, either as positive examples or negative examples. That is: this character did this; it's a good (or bad) example of this skill.

For negative examples of skills, the report can ask and answer the obvious question: What would have been a better, more skillful thing for the character to do?

The story may contain examples of other psychological skills concepts, other than the names of the skills. For example, perhaps a character overcomes an unrealistic fear by using prolonged exposure. Perhaps a character chooses to celebrate when she could have blamed someone else. Perhaps people speak to one another about a conflict, and they use or fail to use any of the various guidelines for joint decision-making. We can comment on any of this in the psychological skills book report.

To further delve into understanding human beings, we can ask and answer the questions, "Why did the person act this way?" "What was this person's inner experience like? What was it like to be this person at this moment?"

To summarize these questions:
1. What were the good and bad examples, of which skills?
2. For the bad examples, what would have been a better choice?
3. What are examples of other psychological skill-related concepts this work exemplified?
4. Why did the character do what he did? What was his experience like at this moment?

What is it for?

Thinking about stories in this way increases familiarity with the psychological skill concepts, gives practice in responding to hypothetical situations, and heightens appreciation and understanding of the story.

Looking at examples of thought, feeling, and behavior and reflecting upon the psychological skills they illustrate is an activity almost impossible to overdo in education at all levels. There is no more important question than, "In this certain situation, what is the best way to respond?" When you have wise answers to this question for a very wide variety of situations, you are well equipped for life. The psychological skills book report allows people to use all sorts of stories to practice thinking about this question.

In my opinion, teachers of literature waste golden opportunities when they direct students' attentions too exclusively to symbolism, foreshadowing, irony, and so forth, and away from the choices that the characters make. By studying and pondering characters' choices, students can improve their ability to make their own choices; surely this is the highest goal of education.

How do you do it well?

It is a major accomplishment for an elementary school child simply to recount several of the positive or negative choices the characters made and to classify them as to skill area. The more richly the student can describe the situation the character was in and the events leading up to the choice point, the more the reader can understand what the character was experiencing.

The question, "What would have been the character's best response to this choice point," requires wisdom. Such wisdom gradually accumulates with experience and learning. This question can challenge older learners. We can justify a position on what would have been best to do by using the techniques I spoke of in this book's chapters on decision-making. Generating options, predicting consequences, and speaking of advantages and disadvantages of options are often part of doing an excellent job on this question.

It is sometimes pleasant, but not required, for the book report to include enough pivotal plot events that the story is revealed to the reader. In fact, it's important for the report writer to realize that it is not his job to retell the story from start to finish.

It can come off as funny to speak about the psychological skills of characters in certain stories. If so, then having fun and amusing ourselves is another benefit of doing these reviews!

Example 1:

Imagine a very articulate elementary school child as the author of this report on "Cinderella":

Before the action of the story begins, Cinderella has to call upon her skills of handling separation and loss, when first her mother and then her father die. She then has very frequent practice in skills of handling rejection and criticism, getting lots of this from her stepmother and stepsisters. Her being able to keep a cheerful and pleasant mood in the face of such stresses shows that she has unusually great skills in fortitude and joyousness.

Her stepmother assigns her all the housework for the family, and Cinderella cheerfully does it, despite being given only rags to wear. The stepmother thus shows herself as lacking in skills of justice and fairness, productivity, and kindness; Cinderella gets to practice lots of productivity. Perhaps her stepmother does her a favor without realizing it by giving her the chance to learn to enjoy productivity.

Cinderella practices compliance with the stepmother's authority. Is this a wise decision? My guess is that for her to try to protest or to negotiate, in order to use joint decision-making with the stepmother and stepsisters, would have been fruitless.

However, in my opinion, Cinderella would have made a better decision if she had tried to find a better place to live. She would have been better off living alone than with this family, and her great productivity and friendship-building skills would have allowed her to support herself. The times she lived in did not encourage such independence and initiative on the part of young women, however. This may explain partly why she chose to stay in this unfriendly family.

Meanwhile, the prince, who is interested in settling down and marrying, is not content with a marriage arranged by his parents; he wishes to see and

meet personally as many young women as he can. This may have required some courage and independent thinking skills on his part, especially since he chose to invite non-royalty such as Cinderella's family. Most kings and queens would probably fiercely oppose such a plan.

Before the ball, the step-relatives show their lack of kindness skills. The fairy godmother makes up for this with her kindness and generosity. At the ball, Cinderella displays her friendship-building skills with the prince. (I'm guessing or hoping that the kingdom contained other beautiful maidens and the prince did not make his choice on Cinderella's looks alone.)

We can excuse Cinderella for procrastinating or forgetting to watch the clock, and for using self-discipline to leave the party only at the last moment. The prince uses good decision-making in sending his highly productive assistant looking for Cinderella with the glass slipper.

After marrying the prince, Cinderella forgives her stepmother and stepsisters, rather than punishing them. Does this decision show good skills of anger control and forgiveness, or lack of assertion and unrealistic fear of displeasing? I believe it is the first, for Cinderella has nothing to gain by punishing these relatives. However, she would have used poor justice skills and misguided loyalty if she had welcomed them at the court or favored them with more generosity than other subjects who deserved her kindness more.

Did the prince and Cinderella use good decision-making in selecting each other as mates? We don't know exactly how long they knew each other before deciding to marry. Good decisions regarding marriage partners usually take big investments of time. Since this couple lived "happily ever after," we must conclude either that they used good decision skills, or that they were very lucky!

Example 2:

Imagine a high school student as the author of this report on *Les Miserables* by Victor Hugo.

Four acts of self-sacrificing kindness are pivotal events in the plot of *Les Miserables*.

The first is carried out by Monsieur Myriel, the Bishop of Digne. Formerly a man of wealth, the bishop has taken up a life of service and renunciation of material possessions. He has retained only a set of silverware and some silver candlesticks from his formerly wealthy life. When the former convict Jean Valjean is rejected by all others when he seeks lodging, the bishop gladly provides it; he also treats the former prisoner with great courtesy.

Hardened, however, by his years of punishment, Jean Valjean steals the bishop's silverware in the night and leaves the house. When he is caught and returned to the bishop's house, the bishop performs a transforming act of kindness. He saves Jean Valjean from life imprisonment by stating that the silverware is a gift; he gives the former convict the candlesticks as well, with a "reminder" of a promise (that Jean Valjean didn't really make) to use the gift to become an honest man.

Does the bishop make a good decision? How many times would such an act actually transform a criminal, rather than "enable" him to do further stealing? We must keep in mind that, though hardened, Jean Valjean was not a selfish criminal. He was sent to prison originally because of the theft of bread to feed someone else, not himself. Perhaps the bishop had enough discernment skills to realize the capacity for goodness and sacrifice that Jean Valjean had, underneath the bitterness induced by years in the galleys.

Jean Valjean escapes the reputation of an ex-convict by living under an assumed name. He becomes a highly successful businessman and the mayor of a town, due to his intelligent decisions and productivity. But then a difficult choice point arises: an innocent man is identified as Jean Valjean and stands to be punished severely for a minor crime.

Jean Valjean must wrestle with a moral dilemma of kindness versus self-care. In the second pivotal sacrificial act of kindness, Jean Valjean displays his courage as he dramatically reveals his true identity in the courtroom, freeing the innocent man, but becoming, from that point on, a fugitive from "justice."

Could he have used options other than betraying the innocent man or sacrificing his own place in society? With his ample wealth, he could have used excellent lawyers or bribery to try to win the man's freedom. He could have arranged a daring escape for the innocent man and set him up with a pleasant life far from the jurisdiction. But the author doesn't allow Jean Valjean (who is strong and good, but not usually a clever schemer) to escape to options that would allow him to "have his cake and eat it too"; he must choose between the innocent man and himself.

As a fugitive, Jean Valjean rescues Cosette, a girl who becomes his foster daughter; for many years, he lives a life of dedication to her. Meanwhile he is pursued by inspector Javert, whose moral development has reached only the level of rigidly following the rules. Javert is incapable of seeing the goodness of Jean Valjean, but focuses only on the fact that he is wanted by the authorities.

In the midst of a failed rebellion, Javert is captured by revolutionaries who owe a favor to Jean Valjean. Jean Valjean asks to be able to execute Javert. But instead of killing him, he fakes the execution and frees Javert. He thus performs the third pivotal act of kindness, benefiting the man who is the biggest threat to his own happiness. There is no ulterior motive in this act. Jean Valjean is simply not a murderer, and does not tolerate murder, even of his worst enemy.

Javert later is faced with a moral dilemma of compliance versus loyalty: by law, he is supposed to capture Jean Valjean, but Jean Valjean has saved his life. Javert escapes this dilemma by suicide. This is obviously a negative example of the skill of decision-making. Decision-making is most difficult in this sort of situation, where all options conflict with strongly held beliefs or feelings. But Javert would clearly have been better off allowing Jean Valjean to go free, and allowing habituation to gradually reduce any guilty misgivings about a kind act for this good man.

The failed rebellion injures a young man named Marius, who has fallen in love with Cosette. Marius is the one who threatens to take away Jean Valjean's major source of meaning and happiness, his relationship with Cosette. Because of such a threat, Jean Valjean has come to hate Marius. Still, Jean Valjean, in an act of courage, kindness, and self-sacrifice, rescues the unconscious Marius via a daring escape through the sewers of Paris.

Much of the emotional power of this book derives from the moments at which Jean Valjean makes courageous ethical decisions. Yet the capacity for self-sacrifice carries a price for Jean Valjean. After Marius's rescue and the marriage of Marius and Cosette, Jean Valjean gradually becomes estranged from Marius, and thus from Cosette.

Marius, who is not aware of various details about Jean Valjean, doesn't know that his own life was saved by the great courage of Jean Valjean. Jean Valjean gradually becomes unwelcome as a visitor, and the pain of separation from his beloved Cosette hastens his fatal illness. The weakening of the bond with Cosette, which Jean Valjean had surely expected, renders his act of saving Marius even more self-sacrificial.

Jean Valjean makes an unfortunate decision in not simply telling Cosette and Marius the whole story of all that happened. He predicts that Marius would not believe him, because he is a convict. This prediction fails to take into account that Cosette has learned to trust Jean Valjean throughout her life. And if Cosette's trust were not sufficient to convince Marius, many of the details of Jean Valjean's story would be verifiable.

Jean Valjean's withholding this information makes for a heart-rending scene when Cosette and Marius finally find out the truth and reunite with Jean Valjean on his deathbed. But with open disclosure, Jean Valjean could probably have enjoyed a less dramatic but pleasant relationship with them into a comfortable old age.

Exercise 63: Glossary

What is it?

Learning any subject matter is in very large part a matter of enlarging your vocabulary, learning new words. When you undertake the study of medicine, law, mathematics, computers, dancing or any other area, you learn the words that field has developed to express its concepts. Learning new words helps–or perhaps we should say permits–you to think in new ways.

The same is true for psychological skills. How is it possible, for example, for someone to think, "I want to get better at frustration tolerance," or, "Here's a situation that challenges my frustration tolerance skills," or, "Hooray, I did a good example of frustration tolerance," if the person has no term in his or her vocabulary for frustration tolerance? In my observation, simply learning the phrase "frustration tolerance," or a synonym for it, helps people learn the skill itself. It gives them a "cognitive handle" for the idea.

Similarly, learning words for feelings helps people, not only to recognize their feelings better, but also to experience richer and more varied emotional responses. For example, if a friend is feeling upset, the person who has the word "compassionate" or some synonym for it in his vocabulary is more equipped to feel compassionate.

In choosing our responses to situations, we can choose more consciously if we have words for the options. For example, it's easier to say, "I want to quit getting down on myself so much and put my energy into learning from the experience," if I have the phrases *getting down on myself* and *learning from the experience* in my vocabulary.

Studying a glossary like this isn't the only or even the best way to add psychological skill concepts to your vocabulary. I think a better way is to introduce a few concepts and to present many stories that illustrate them. The learner then reads or hears the stories and classifies what went on according to the concepts.

Nonetheless, there is more than one way to accomplish a goal, and, for many learners, this glossary and the exercises that can be done with it may be useful.

I developed this glossary by going through the *Programmed Readings for Psychological Skills* book and others, looking for words that might not be familiar. I composed definitions that stress the meanings most relevant to psychological skills training.

How do you do it well?

Here's a set of exercises to do with these words. The trainer can write about five of them–fewer if the learner is younger or finds the exercises with five words too hard.

A preliminary step is to find out which of the words the trainee already knows. It the trainee says she doesn't

267

know a word, take her at her word. If the trainee thinks she knows it, you might want to test by seeing if she can define the word and use it in a sentence.

The first exercise is simply to read the words, to say them, to be able to get them out of your mouth.

The second is to read or hear the definitions and to hear the words used in a sentence.

The third is to read or hear a definition again, and match it up with the word. Like the exercises that follow, you repeat this until the learner can do it easily with all five words.

The fourth is for the trainer to give the word, and let the trainee supply the definition.

The fifth is for the trainer to give a sentence with the word left out (for example, the sentences below) and for the trainee to pick from among the five words the word that correctly fills in the blank.

The sixth is for the trainer to give the word and the trainee to make up a different sentence using it. If the sentence is good enough, the trainer can write it down to use as an exercise for the next trainee.

Variations:

These words can be studied, just as in other vocabulary-building classes. There can be written tests on them. By performing the aforementioned exercises during a "personal training" session, a trainee can learn these words in a few minutes. Another variation is for the trainee to make up a sentence that omits one of the five words and then challenge the trainer to fill in the right word.

The vocabulary words are as follows.

Accepted: The feeling you get when you sense other people think you're ok.

I was nervous about going to the new school. But people were so nice and welcoming that it took very little time before I felt _____.

Accomplish: This means to do something worth doing. It means achieving a goal.

The girl worked on writing down her goals. She said, "It did me good to think about what I want to _____."

Activity: This is something you do. Playing checkers is one of these. Doing the shaping game is one. Activities include feeding a dog, working on homework, watching television, going hiking and reading. When you get to know someone, you find out which of these the person most likes to do.

The girl loved to find hard math problems and figure out how to solve them. Her friend said, "I'll bet not many other people you know have that as their favorite _____."

Advantage: This means a good point about an option, a reason you might want to do it. It means the same thing as a "pro" when talking about the "pros and cons" of an option.

This option would not require us to spend any money, and, because I don't have much money now, that's an important _____.

Adversity: This means something hard to handle or something painful or unwanted. This is almost the same as a frustration. If someone becomes ill, they have to put up with this. If someone is treated badly by classmates at school, they have to put up with this.

When the people's house burned down, they had to practice handling _____.

Afraid, anxious, frightened, scared, fearful: These five words mean about the same thing. When you feel this way, you have the feeling that something bad is likely to happen.

Other people were excited by watching the person at the circus walk the tightrope. But I was thinking to myself, "What if this poor person falls," and I felt _____.

Amazed: Something you didn't think would happen, happened. You're very surprised. This means almost the same as astonished.

When I saw that a child so young could count to such a high number, I was _____.

Amused: You feel that something is funny, interesting or entertaining.

I thought the movie was largely a waste of time, even though I'll have to admit that, as I watched it, I was _____.

Angry: When you feel this way, you feel someone has done something bad, and you don't like what the person has done. There's often at least a little wish to get back at them or punish them.

When I saw the big bully tormenting the little boy, I felt _____.

Annoyed: When you feel this way, you are a little angry, but you realize that it's a fairly little thing. Often this feeling comes when a little thing keeps bugging you over and over.

While I was taking the test, a fly kept buzzing around my ears. I felt _____.

Appreciative: You feel good about what somebody else did. This means almost the same as grateful.

The child gave her trainer a card that said, "Thanks for all the work you've done with me," to show her trainer that she felt _____.

Approval: This happens when someone says, "I like what you did." It also happens when someone says, "You did a good job," or "I'm so glad you did that."

When the person told me my speech was good, I enjoyed getting the _____.

Assertion: Sticking up for yourself. Taking charge. Enjoying winning a competition. Saying no to others when appropriate.

The small secretary said to the big man, "I'm sorry, but you must not smoke in here." When he ignored her, she said, "I must insist that you not smoke, and I'm going to be forced to call security if you continue." He put out the cigarette. She was good at the skill of _____.

Ashamed: When you feel this way, you have done something you feel bad about people seeing or knowing about.

In the middle of the play, I forgot my lines. I was thinking, "Oh, no. I look foolish in front of all these people." I felt _____.

Attracted: When you feel this way toward someone, you find the image of being with them or being in a relationship with them a pleasant image.

The man said, "Even though she is not what most people call beautiful, the way she acts makes me feel _____."

Awareness of your emotions: Recognizing how you're feeling, and being able to talk about those feelings.

The man said, "I'm feeling bad, but I don't know what it's about." His counselor said, "You can know better what to do about bad feelings when you know better what kind of bad feelings they are and what you're feeling bad about. That's called the skill of _____."

Awareness of control: When you have this skill, you can accurately figure out how much you control what happens and how much someone else does, and how much it's up to fate.

Even though the boy had bullied other children every day for the last year, he thought the reason he was disliked was that the other children were mean. He needed work, not only in the skill of kindness, but also in the skill of _____.

Awareness of your own abilities: Accurately figuring out how skilled you are at things. You're confident when you're skilled at things, but not overconfident about things you aren't good at.

I knew I was good at writing, but not good at selling. So I looked for a job that would take advantage of my strength and not put big demands on my weakness. When I found it, I was glad I had been skilled in _____.

Awed: This feeling is a mixture of respect, fear and wonder. Some people feel this way when they stand at the edge of the Grand Canyon.

The man said, "Each time I hear the 'Hallelujah Chorus' I feel _____."

Awfulizing: This means thinking something like "This is terrible! I can't take it!"

I thought to myself, "I can't stand it that this ball game has been cancelled!" But then I realized I was just _____.

Behavior: This is anything someone does.

The psychology teacher said, "When you smile, hit a tennis ball, run, say hi, scratch your nose or any time you do anything, you're doing a _____."

Blaming someone else: This means thinking something like, "That person is such a bad person! That person does bad things!"

When the other driver did something I didn't like, I thought, "You idiot!" Then I noticed I had been _____.

Bored: When you feel this way, you can't come up with anything interesting to do or think. You feel like saying, "There's nothing to do."

The person kept talking for a very long time without stopping. I was thinking, "It wouldn't be so bad that she didn't stop talking, if she would just talk about something interesting." I felt _____.

Brainstorming: Thinking of as many different ideas as you can, and putting off until later thinking about how well they will work. The idea is you can get more good ideas if you aren't criticizing them at the same time.

We needed to get some more ideas about how to make our plan work, so we spent some time just spouting out one idea after another. It was fun to do some _____.

Calm: Feeling this way is not feeling excited, but feeling cool and in control.

Even though the children were all yelling and whining, the mother used great relaxation skills to keep herself feeling _____.

Carefulness: Taking care of yourself, not taking unnecessary risks. Being appropriately fearful or cautious when danger is really present.

The driver was going the speed limit. Most of the other drivers were mad at him for not going faster. But he was the only one who was using good skills of _____.

Cause: This is what makes something happen or contributes to its happening. For example, not working in a course made a failing grade happen.

The boy thought the other kids didn't like him because they were all mean. But the fact that he was usually mean to them was the real

_____.

Celebrating someone else's choice: This is thinking something such as, "I'm glad this person did this good thing!" You do this when someone else controlled the good thing that happened.

When I thought about how nice my mom was to wash my clothes, I was doing some _____.

Celebrating what happened to happen: This is thinking something such as, "I'm glad this thing happened to happen!" You do this when the good thing happened by luck or chance.

When I gave thanks that I happened to be born in this country at this time, I was _____.

Celebrating your (or his or her) own choice: This is thinking something such as, "Hooray, I'm glad I did that!" You do this when you were the one who controlled the good thing that happened.

When he thought to himself, "Hooray, I'm glad I had the self-discipline to start this job," he was _____.

Celebration: When you do this, you're feeling good about something and being glad it happened. It's not just something such as having cake and ice cream. You can do this in your own mind, any time you think that something good has happened, just by saying to yourself, "Hooray, I'm glad that happened!"

When I handled that hard situation well, in my own mind I held a

_____.

Cheerful: When you feel this way, you feel like smiling and talking in a peppy and happy tone of voice.

Even though I had been kept awake almost all night, I managed to say "Good morning!" and to sound and feel _____.

Choice Point: This is the situation in which you have to make a decision. When I go to my closet and find more than one thing for me to wear that day, and I get to decide what to wear, that's one of these. When I know I have time to either walk to work or drive my car, that's one of these.

When I am faced with the opportunity to spend time either writing a book or doing a research project, that's a _____.

Close: Feeling as if you can talk about anything that's on your mind, feeling that the person accepts you, feeling that you know each other well.

When our family went out to sit together silently as the sun set, we felt _____.

Compassionate: When you feel this way, you want to take care of someone, to make them happy or protect them. You want to relieve any bad feelings they have. If there's a little bird that has been hurt and you want to take care of it and be good to it, you're feeling this way.

The nurse always spent lots of time talking with the sick children; she felt _____.

Competence-development: Getting yourself to work toward getting better at useful skills. These may be a) work-related, b) school-related, c) recreational, or otherwise.

Although he had never danced before, the actor needed to be able to dance really well for the part he was playing. Through intense concentration and constant practice, he was able to learn enough to dance superbly in the play. He was good at the skill of _____.

Compliance: Obeying when a reasonable authority tells you to do something. This doesn't mean you must do wrong things when somebody tells you to do them. But it does mean you have the self-discipline to do things you don't feel like doing when you've received an order from an authority.

The son said, "What if we settle on going home ten minutes from now instead of right now? Or at least five minutes?" The father replied, "We're leaving now. This situation isn't one for negotiation skills, son, but for skills of _____."

Comply: This means to obey, doing what somebody tells you to do. My dad told me to stack the wood, when I would have rather gone to my friend's house. It was not easy, but I _____.

Concentration: This means that you keep thinking about one thing. It's the same as sustaining attention.

The tutor and the child worked together in the hallway of the school, with people constantly looking at them and talking to them. Even so, they were able to get things accomplished, because they both already had great skills in

_____ .

Confident: Feeling this way means you feel like saying, "I can do it. I've got what it takes." It's the feeling that you have the skill to handle a situation.

I had practiced the speech so many times that, when I got up to give it, I felt

_____ .

Confused: When you feel this way, you're not sure what's what. You don't understand what's going on.

When the teacher gave directions on how to do the work, I couldn't understand them at all. I felt totally

_____ .

Congratulations: When you give this to someone, you're telling them, "Hooray for you. You did something good."

When I won the tennis match, my opponent was gracious enough to offer me _____ .

Conscience: Feeling guilty when it's appropriate, when you have harmed someone else.

Most of the kids felt OK about giving their creative writing teacher stories they had previously written for other writing courses. But one person didn't

feel good about it; I think he was the one with the best skills of _____ .

Consequences: These are the things that might happen, or what really did happen, as a result of doing something. These are the effects, results or outcomes of your actions.

If you continue to drive so fast and so recklessly, you might suffer very bad

_____ .

Conservation: This is the psychological skill of not wasting resources. It involves not wasting money, not wasting the earth's resources, and not wasting time on consuming a lot of junk.

The man had lots of money, but he used it to try to reduce pollution. He greatly valued the principle of

_____ .

Contented: Having what you want and not wanting a lot more.

The one man felt angry that he was not making more money and living in a bigger house. The second man thought, "As long as I have a happy family and get to spend lots of time with them, I feel _____ ."

Conversation: This happens when two people talk or chat with each other.

She was the type of person people loved to talk with. She was a master at having good _____ .

Courage: Being brave. Facing situations that scare you.

The father said, "When you said that you liked your friend and that he was a good guy, in front of all those other kids who were teasing him, that took real _____."

Criticize: This means you say what's wrong with something. Sometimes people criticize in a nice way and sometimes in a mean way.

One teacher did nothing but tell students what they are doing wrong. The other teacher said, "You'd do a better job if you would reinforce and approve a lot more, and not just _____."

Curious: Wondering what the answer to a question is, wanting to find out more about something.

The boy was happy when he was in the library, because he always wanted to look up the answer to one question after another. No matter how much he learned, he never stopped feeling _____.

Danger: You are in this when there's something bad that's likely to happen.

Letting that boy play near the edge of the cliff put him in real _____.

Decision: This means almost the same thing as choice. This is figuring out what to do. When I choose to get out of bed in the morning or turn over and go back to sleep, that's a decision. When I choose whether to take a shower first or eat breakfast first, that's also a decision.

When I see someone in my family and choose whether to say, "Good morning," or to say, "I hope you had a pleasant sleep," I'm making a little _____.

Decision-making: Thinking about what to do. If you do it really thoroughly, you go through steps of defining a problem, gathering information, generating options, predicting and evaluating consequences, and making a choice.

The people planned the project very carefully. Each time an important choice point came up, they would list options, get more information, think about the pros and cons, and choose carefully. The project was a great success because of their skills of careful _____.

Defining a problem: Telling someone that you have a problem and telling what it is.

When the man said, "I have a problem. When your dog barks at night, I have trouble sleeping," he was taking the first step in joint decision-making, which is _____.

Delay of gratification: Doing what makes things best for the long term, rather than what feels best right now. (Or even better, having the ability to guide yourself to feel good about doing what makes things best for the long term.) It's about the same as self-discipline.

If you really want to go to college, you'll have to start working and saving now. You will need to use your skills of _____.

Depending: Accepting help without being ashamed.

The man said to himself, "I know I need help, and there's nothing to be ashamed of about that. Nobody's perfect in everything. I'm going to get the help I need." And he did it. He was practicing the skill of _____.

Differential Reinforcement: Rewarding certain behavior in other people, for example with attention, excitement or giving them what they want, and not rewarding the opposite kind of behavior, for example by taking away attention, acting unexcited, and not giving what the person wants.

The babysitter gave the child food or hugs whenever the child cried and whined, but ignored the child when she acted happy. The babysitter was, without knowing it, making the child act less happy, through her _____.

Dilemma: You are in one of these when there are good reasons to do something but also good reasons not to do the same thing.

The man had a great opportunity to serve humanity by working many hours and traveling overseas, but he also had young children he wanted to spend a lot of time with. He found himself in a real _____.

Disadvantage: This means a bad point about an option, a reason you might NOT want to do it. It means the same thing as a "con" when talking about the "pros and cons" of an option.

If we try this option, we might waste a lot of time for nothing if it doesn't work, and that's a pretty big _____.

Disappointed: You feel this way when you had expected something nice to happen but it didn't, and you feel bad about that.

I had looked forward to a good tennis game. When the person I had been planning to play with called and said he was sick, I felt _____.

Discernment: Being able to see other people as they really are. Figuring out what skills other people do have and don't have. Making those judgments using evidence rather than being prejudiced, leaping to conclusions from too little information, or thinking people are a certain way just because you wish they would be that way.

The girl was in the habit of seeing people as wonderful when she didn't know them well, but then thinking they were horrible when they first did something she didn't like. She needed to get better at the skill of _____.

Discouraged: When you feel this way, you are not hopeful. You're not sure that it will do any good to try any more.

When he went to school, the boy was excited. But when he found that the work was too hard, he began to feel _____.

Disgusted: When you feel this way, you feel like throwing up because you dislike something so much. You feel like something is yucky.

When I saw the rich man who had made his money by cheating and using people being honored for doing great things, I felt _____.

Distraction: Something that pulls your attention away from what you're trying to pay attention to.

When I was trying to study, my neighbor's loud music was an irritating _____.

Drained: When you feel this way, you feel as if you don't have much energy left, as though almost all your energy has been drained out.

After staying up most of the night with a sick baby, and then working all day with demanding customers, the woman felt _____.

Effect: This is what a cause produces. When I do something that causes something to happen, what happens is an effect. It's the same as a result, outcome or consequence.

The boy had thought that when he called his grandmother every day and spoke to her in a kind and cheerful way, it wouldn't make much difference in her life. But he soon found out that it had a very big _____.

Elated: Feeling very happy in a very excited way.

When a baby was born to a mother and father who had wanted a child for a long time, they both felt _____.

Embarrassed: When you feel this way, you think that you have looked stupid or awkward to someone else, and that feels bad.

When we were dancing and I accidentally tripped my partner, I felt _____.

Emotions: These are your feelings. These are communicated by feeling words like "happy," "sad," "angry," "excited," "scared" and so forth.

The person became very angry and upset and sad over very little things. He said to the man, "If it's possible, I'd like to learn to control my own _____."

Emotional climate: This is the way people feel about each other. If they feel kind to each other, happy to see each other and pleased with each other, the emotional climate is positive. If they don't like being around each other and are constantly angry with each other, the emotional climate is negative.

I started the day by saying "Good morning!" in a cheerful way to everybody, and kept on saying nice things as much as I could. I wanted see how much I could improve my family's

_____.

Empathy: Picking up on how other people are feeling. Seeing things from another person's point of view. Seeing how your behavior affects other people.

The person thought that what he was saying was entertaining people, when it was really disgusting them. He was not good at the skill of _____.

Energetic: Feeling lots of energy and lots of motivation to do things.

The woman came home to find that her husband had written three chapters in his book and had cleaned up his whole office as well. She said, "Wow, you must have been feeling _____."

Enjoying your own acts of kindness: This skill means you're in the habit of feeling really good when you make somebody else happy.

When my son tutored the younger child, he felt great when the child enjoyed the session and learned a lot. I'm so glad he's developed the skill of

_____.

Ethics: This is thinking about what is good or right to do and what is bad or wrong to do. This is figuring out what people should or ought to do.

The boy wanted very much to do what was right and good. So he decided to read what other people had written about the subject of _____.

Entitled: When you feel this way, you are thinking, "I deserve to get this from the other person; they should do this for me or give this to me."

The girl whined at her mother and said, "You didn't put enough peanut butter on this sandwich!" People shook their heads and said, "What makes her feel so _____?"

Envious or jealous: These mean about the same. When you feel this way, you want something that someone else has, and you feel bad that they have it and you don't.

I had an idea and told somebody else. That person used the idea and took all the credit for it. I thought, "That person is getting credit that should be going to me," and I felt _____.

Evaluating Options: Figuring out what are just and reasonable options to choose when there are conflicts or disagreements between two people.

The little girl seemed to think it was very just and reasonable for her sister to share her toys with her, but she did not think it was just and reasonable for her to share her toys with her sister. In addition to being somewhat spoiled, she needed more skill in

_____.

Event: This is something that happened. If my grandmother came over to visit, that's an event. If I went to the Grand Canyon, that's one. And if I sat for five minutes with my eyes closed, that's one.

Our family purchased an encyclopedia and started looking up lots of subjects. In our lives, that's the most recent big _____.

Excited: Feeling lots of energy, very wide awake and ready to do things. You can feel this way in a pleasant or unpleasant way.

When I learned that I would get to ride the fast horse, I felt _____.

Facilitation: When you are talking with someone, a facilitation is saying something like "Oh," or "Yes," or "Uh huh," or "Is that right?" or "What do you know?" or "That's interesting," or "Humh," or nodding your head. This word means making something easier, and these responses make it easier for a person to talk to you.

As I spoke, my friend said very little except to nod and say "yes" and "humh" and to use other _____.

Fantasy: Your imagination, pretending. For example, pictures or sounds you bring to mind by imagining them.

While I was sitting waiting, I entertained myself by imagining doing great things, and having other nice _____.

Fantasy rehearsal: Imagining how you want to think, feel and act in a certain situation. The more you imagine yourself acting that way, the more likely you are to do it in real life.

I imagined over and over how I was going to think, feel and act when someone criticized me. I figured I could change my habit through doing lots of _____.

Fantasy-tolerance: Being comfortable with having a wild imagination.

For creative writing, the students did an exercise in which they wrote the most outlandish and strangest story they possibly could. The teacher said, "This exercise is meant to free up your imagination and increase your skills of _____."

Favorable attractions: Having romantic or erotic feelings for someone who is appropriate, positive and beneficial.

For a while, the woman was attracted only to "tough-guy" type men who didn't treat her nicely. She had several bad experiences. Then she became wiser and was attracted to a man who was very nice to her. She had improved her skill of _____.

Fluency: Using words well to help you think and talk about what's happening.

People said to Sam, "The stories you tell with words only are better than lots of television programs I see." They said this because Sam was so good in his use of words, in his skills of

_____.

Follow-up question: This happens when you ask a question about something someone just said. For example, someone says, "I saw a dog," and the second person says, "Oh, what kind was it?"

Whenever I stopped talking, my sister asked me more about the same thing I was talking about. She was using

_____.

Follow-up statement: This means saying something about a subject the other person was already talking about. For example, when the first person says, "I've been working on learning to jump rope," the second person says, "Hey, I've been doing that too."

The person was talking about places to go hiking, and I told him about a place I'd been. I used a _____.

Forgiveness: Letting yourself get over it when someone has treated you in a way you don't like.

The boy's most treasured possession was broken by his little brother. The boy kept himself stirred up and angry for a long time. His mom said, "You'll start being a lot happier if you can use the skill of _____."

Fortitude: This means almost the same thing as frustration tolerance. It means putting up with something hard, handling adversity handling something you don't like or being brave in the face of hardship. If someone is hurt in the middle of the woods and I have to run a very long way to get help, and I am very tough as I do it, I am showing this. If there's a present I wanted for my birthday and I don't get it, but stay in a good mood, I'm using this.

If I submit an article to a magazine and it gets rejected, and I learn from my experience and try again, I'm using

_____.

Frazzled: You feel this way when you are trying to take care of many different things and you are tired from trying to pay attention to all of them. Means almost the same thing as "harried."

With thirty children in the class, and each of them having their own needs and wants, by the end of the day the teacher felt _____.

Free: Feeling that you can do what you want, feeling unbound, unhindered.

In the month after school ended and before work began, I felt very

_____.

Friendly: Feeling an urge to be nice to someone and get to know someone and be with the person in a pleasant way.

At the party, people were acting so nice that everybody felt _____.

Friendship-building: This is the skill of improving your relationships with people. It refers not only to starting new relationships but also to making old relationships get better.

The man kept on trying to get to know his sister better, even though he had known her all his life. He thought he could improve his relationships with his own family members by using his skills of _____.

Frustration: This is a situation in which you don't get what you want. (This word also sometimes means an upset feeling that people might get when they don't get what they want. The psychological skill training materials mainly use this word to talk about the situation of not getting what you want, and not the emotional reaction to it.) The word means the same as adversity. If someone is in the habit of getting very upset about this, by working and practicing they can learn to become less upset.

After I had looked forward to the party, I found out I couldn't go. I thought to myself, "Let's see how well I can handle this situation of _____."

Frustration tolerance: Acting reasonable when you don't get what you want.

When the computer lost all the work I had done for the last hour, I said to myself, "This situation is a real test for my skills of _____."

Frustrate the Authority Game: This is a game some people play in real life. Playing this game usually gets them into trouble. When a parent or teacher tells them they have to do something, they do the opposite, to feel as if they are winning in a competition against the parent or teacher. This is very different from the meet the challenge game.

The boy started to giggle and run away from the teacher as the rest of the children walked out of the classroom in line. The teacher thought, "He's already gotten into playing the _____."

Fun: When you have this feeling, you're thinking something like, "Boy, I really like doing this!"

At first I wondered whether I would be able to learn how to square dance. But then I started thinking, "This is the greatest!" and I realized I was having lots of _____.

Gentleness in assertion: Situations where you stick up for your own way are situations where you use assertion. You can use assertion with various degrees of gentleness or forcefulness. When you are gentle, you say what you want, but you try to be nice about it.

When Sylvia's mother said, "You shouldn't go out to places like that without asking me first!" Sylvia replied, "I'm glad for your concern about my safety. But at age thirty I have to make my own decisions about things like this." Sylvia used _____.

Getting down on yourself: This means thinking something such as, "I'm stupid. I'm to blame."
I said to myself, "You nitwit. You dunce." Then I noticed that I had been _____.

Gleefulness: Playing, enjoying being silly or childlike, being spontaneous.
The man found that by getting down on the floor and playing with his two-year old each night, he enriched his own life by improving his skills of _____.

Goal: This is something you want to make happen, something you want to accomplish. One person had one of these: learning the things in her math book very well. Another person had another of these: staying in very good shape so he wouldn't be as likely to have a heart attack. Another person had another one: reducing violence in the world as much as possible.
When the girl said that she wanted to learn to teach other children to read, her father said, "Sounds like you've set for yourself a great _____!"

Goal-setting: One of the twelve types of thoughts. When you do this, you figure out what you want to make happen.

When the people saw the fire, some of them just thought how awful it was. But one woman thought, "The first priority is not to kill myself in this building. The second is to make sure nobody is left in the house. The third priority is to get the fire department to come." The type of thought she was using was _____.

Golden Rule: This rule is, "Do unto others as you would have them do unto you," or "Treat other people as you would want them to treat you."
The boy said, "Why not kill the chipmunk? Because if you were a chipmunk, you'd rather be turned loose in a park." The boy's thinking was an example of using the _____.

Good decisions: This is the skill of figuring out what to do in a careful and wise way. It also means solving problems with other people in this way.
When problems came up, the woman always kept cool and thought about options and their advantages and disadvantages. She was good at the skill of _____.

Grateful: Feeling this way means you feel like saying, "Thank you." You're glad someone did something good.
When the older boys were picking on me, my friend told them to leave me alone. I told him later that I felt _____.

Gratitude: Feeling thankful and saying "thank you" to other people. Communicating admiration and other positive feelings to others.

When I told my guests that I appreciated their coming so far to see me, I was using the skill of _____.

Guilty: Feeling this way means you feel you've done something bad, something you wish you hadn't done.

I knew I could get out of having to do a lot of work by telling a lie, but if I did that, I would feel _____.

Habit: This means getting accustomed to do something by doing it over and over. The more times you do something, the stronger this becomes.

At first it seemed a little unnatural for me to use reflections to make sure I understood what people meant. But it feels very natural to me now, because it has become a _____.

Habits of self-care: This is a set of skills having to do with keeping yourself healthy. These are habits of not using harmful drugs, exercising, eating right, sleeping at proper times and so forth.

The public health specialist said, "You would be amazed at how many premature deaths could be prevented if everyone in our country had good _____."

Habituation: This means "getting used to it." If you keep experiencing the same thing continually, gradually it stops affecting you so much.

The girl got braces on her teeth. At first they bothered her a lot. But then she got used to them, and they caused no problem. She thought, "Hooray for _____."

Handling aloneness: Having a good time by yourself, putting up with not having attention. Also called "tolerating inattention."

The mother wanted to have some uninterrupted time with her younger daughter. She said to her older daughter, "I'm going to spend some time with your younger sister for half an hour; let's see how well you can use your skills of _____."

Handling criticism: Dealing with disapproval, correction or lack of respect from someone else.

When the person said to me, "You're not such hot stuff as you think you are," I thought, "Here's a challenge to my skills of _____."

Handling low stimulation: This means handling it well when not much stimulating is going on around you. If you're able to do things in your own mind that are pleasant and useful to you, whenever you want to, you are better at this skill.

By practicing sitting silently with eyes closed for longer and longer times, the boy developed his skills of

_____.

Handling mistakes and failures: Choosing your thoughts, emotions, and behaviors in a good way when you make a mistake or fail at something. For example, it's good not to get down on yourself too much, but to try again, and try to learn from your past experience. This skill also includes being prepared to handle failures that haven't happened yet. If you have this skill, you aren't so afraid of failing that you don't try things.

When the girl failed the math test, she didn't get depressed, but she studied and worked until she could answer every question on the test correctly. Her dad said, "What an example of the skill of _____."

Handling painful feelings: Being able to tough out feeling bad, without making things worse by feeling bad about your own bad feelings.

When the person felt his heart pounding and his hands trembling as he rose to give his speech, he said to himself, "OK, so I'm scared. So what? I'll get over it in a while." He didn't let those scared feelings bother him, because he had the skill of _____.

Handling rejection: Handling it when people don't like or accept you or want to be with you.

When the girl said to me, "I'm not coming to your birthday party because I just don't want to," I said to myself,

"This is a challenge to my skills of _____."

Handling separation: Handling it when someone moves away, dies, or otherwise can't be with you.

When Ted learned that his best friend was moving away, he said to himself, "This is a big challenge to my skills of _____."

Harried: You feel this way when there are lots of little problems that you have had to handle in too little time. Means almost the same as frazzled.

The nurse in the emergency room was being asked to do things constantly by both doctors and patients. She said to herself, "When am I ever going to get time to do these things?" and she felt _____.

Hate, hatred: Feeling this way toward a person is to dislike that person very strongly. Whereas anger can come and go, this is the word used when the bad feelings toward the person stick around.

The people in the dictator's country had been oppressed so long and so badly that many of them felt toward the dictator nothing but _____.

Hierarchy: A group of things arranged in order, for example, from least to greatest. An important type of hierarchy is a set of tasks or challenges, arranged in order of difficulty; if you work your way up, you can become much more skilled than you were before.

The teacher found that the student was trying things that were too difficult. The teacher said, "Let's go down the _____ of difficulty and then work our way back up."

Honesty: Telling the truth and keeping your promises, especially when it's hard to do so.

If mommy says, "Daddy, you put too much garlic in the soup," and daughter says to mommy, "Actually I was the one who put it in," that's an example of _____.

Hopeful: Looking forward to something good happening.

The person had been troubled by fearfulness for a long time. But now that she knew how to work on it and make it better, she felt _____.

Hopeless: When you feel this way, you think there's no way things will out the way you want them to. The future looks unhappy to you. You've given up wishing good things will happen.

The person tried and tried to find a job. But after being turned down fifty times, he began to feel _____.

How good or bad the consequence is: This is how much you would like or dislike a consequence that might happen. This is the same as the utility of the consequence.

I knew it was unlikely that we would have an accident in the car. But I still refused to ride without my seat belt, because I thought about having an accident without being belted and _____.

How likely the consequence is: Whether something almost surely will happen, or whether it probably will happen, or whether it probably won't happen. This is the same as the probability of the consequence.

It's possible that I could get struck by lightning even though I haven't seen or heard any other lightning. It would be a bad consequence, but I'm not worried. Why not? Because I thought about _____.

Humor: Enjoying funny things, or being funny yourself.

Whenever he found himself in a sticky or embarrassing situation, he was almost always able to save himself by thinking of something funny to say. I envied his skills of _____.

Hurt: When you feel this way, you feel bad because you've discovered someone is thinking, "I don't care about you," or "I don't like you," or "I'm feeling bad toward you," when you wanted that person to like you and feel good wishes toward you.

When Liz said to Sara, "You're my very best friend in all the world," Martha thought, "I was thinking I was Liz's best friend," and Martha felt _____.

Imagination: Being able to use your power to make beneficial or helpful images in your mind. You can use it to rehearse what you want to do, imagine ways of handling a problem, imagine consequences of options, practice adjusting to a certain situation, or in other ways.

The person was afraid of elevators. He was able to get over most of his fear by pretending to be on an elevator rather than spending time on a real one. He could do this because of his great skills of _____.

Impatient: When you feel this way, you feel as though it's very unpleasant to wait.

I wanted to leave the place, but the person I was with kept on talking to someone. I said to myself, "When can I get out of here?" and I felt

_____.

Independent thinking: Being able to make up your own mind about what's best to do, using some good ways of deciding, rather than just doing whatever makes you fit in with other people.

All of Jon's friends thought the movie was great. He said to them, "The thing I don't like about that movie is that it tries to entertain us with many images of people getting hurt and killed. And I don't think it's good to be entertained by those images." He was using the skill of _____.

Indifferent: You feel this way when you don't care one way or the other about something or when two options seem equally good to you.

Lots of people wanted one team or the other to win the World Series. But I couldn't have cared less, one way or the other. I felt totally _____.

Individual decision: A decision where you are trying to decide upon what action you will take, rather than what action you and another person will agree upon together. This is the same as a one-person-problem.

The young woman was trying to choose her major in college. She had to make a challenging _____.

Interested: Feeling this way means you want to pay attention to something, because it feels good to think about it, look at it or explore it.

The encyclopedia contained such good articles and such vivid pictures that most people could not look through it without being _____.

Interrupt: To start talking while somebody else is talking, or to distract someone when they're trying to pay attention to something else.

Right in the middle of my sentence, the person started talking. I said, "I wish, please, that you wouldn't _____."

Irritated: When you feel this way, you are a little bit angry, usually about having to deal with something you'd rather not have to worry about. When the teacher was trying to read the story and the boy kept interrupting, the other children quickly began to get _____.

Joint decision: A decision in which two or more people are trying to decide what to do, when their decision will affect them all. Sometimes these turn into disagreements and conflicts.

The man wanted to save lots of money and be frugal; his wife liked to spend more. When the woman thought it was time to buy a new car, they had a tough time in making a _____.

Jolly: Feeling like laughing, smiling and talking in a fun way.

By singing his funny songs and telling funny stories, my father was able to get everyone feeling _____.

Joyousness: This means you act happy and cheerful.

My daughter had a great time singing and dancing; I felt good about her

_____.

Justice: This happens when there's a fair and good way of deciding who deserves to get what, and that good decision is put into effect.

The boy thought he should get paid for putting away his own toys, while his mom worked to make his meals and do his laundry. He had a pretty selfish notion of _____.

Kindness: This means being nice, doing things that make people happy, such as helping someone learn something, helping someone carry something, talking in a friendly way to someone, curing someone of a disease, paying attention to someone when they want it.

My friend helped me when I was sick; I felt grateful for his _____.

Learning from the experience: This is figuring out what you can learn from something that happened. That way, you know better what to do the next time.

I thought to myself, "I guess I made a mistake this time. But, there's always next time, and at least I can do some

_____."

Lighthearted: Not worrying about anything, and feeling like having fun.

When I finished my big project and handed it in, I felt as if a weight had been lifted off me. I got together with my friends and sang and danced and felt

_____.

Listening: Responding in a good way when somebody else talks to you.

Bill said, "So if I understand you right, you don't like the way he acts toward your brother, but you can't decide what to do about that." Tom said, "Yes, that's exactly it." Bill was using the skill of _____.

Listing options and choosing: This is thinking of a few possibilities for what to do, and choosing the one that's best to do.

When we thought about many possible ways to work out the problem, we were _____.

Locating control inside: This means thinking that what you have done, not luck or fate, is responsible for how things turn out.

The girl said, "If I work hard enough and decide carefully enough, I can be successful. I can make my own luck." She was _____.

Locating control outside: This means thinking that other people, luck or fate, not what you have done, is responsible for how things turn out.

The boy decided that his parents got divorced because of things he couldn't control. He was right in

_____.

Lonely: When you feel this way, you want a friend with you, but there is none to be with you now.

The person didn't know anyone in the big city. So even though there were people all around, he still said to himself, "I wish I had a friend," and he felt

_____.

Long-term goal: This is something you want to make happen in the future. When people do without short-term pleasures or temptations in order to

achieve these, they are using self-discipline.

The man was tempted to stay up very late. But he thought to himself, "I want to keep my sleep rhythm steady. This will help me keep from being tired tomorrow, and this is a very important

_____."

Loving and Liking, Love and Like: When you're feeling these feelings toward someone, you're thinking things such as, "I want to make that person happy! I want to be with that person!"

When I looked at my son sleeping, I thought how much I wanted him to be happy, and my heart was filled with

_____.

Loyalty: Sticking by another person, feeling commitment to a relationship and honoring that commitment.

When all the other people in the class started teasing Sally, Jared stuck up for her. Jared thought, "She has been my friend for a long time, and I'm not going to let her down now." He was practicing the skill of _____.

Meet the Challenge Game: This is a game you play in real life. It happens when you set a goal of doing something and then see if you can do it. You feel good when you can do it, and, if you can't do it, you try to learn what it takes to do it. This is very different from the Frustrate the Authority Game.

Although some of the kids felt the goal of tutoring the younger kids was too hard, she worked at it until she could do it really well. For her it was just another example of playing the

_____.

Mental images: These are pictures, sounds, tastes or smells you remember or imagine but aren't really there.

When the girl went to bed, she remembered the sights and sounds she had seen in the scary movie. She knew none of them would happen, but she was still scared by her own

_____.

Modeling stories: Stories that are meant to show a good way of acting, thinking or feeling in a certain situation.

I found I was able to learn lots of good ways of doing things by reading

_____.

Moved: When people get goosebumps or feel like crying because they admire something and feel good about it, they are feeling this way. Someone might feel this way when reading a very good story that stirs up a lot of feeling about a person doing something good.

When the little boy gave away his favorite toy to the boy who had lost all his toys in the flood, people who saw this act were _____.

Muscle relaxation: This is one of several relaxation techniques. In it, you notice how tense your muscles are and try to make them looser and more limp.

The woman found that even though she was scared about letting the dentist work on her tooth, she was able to calm herself by using _____.

Negative: This word means less, bad, undesirable, not. Fear is this sort of feeling. This sort of outlook means that you think bad things will happen.

When my friend said, "It'll never work; we can't do it; we should give up," I said, "Hey, why is your attitude so _____?"

Negotiating: Being able to persuade people to agree on a just option, when there is a joint decision.

The two countries went to war and many people were killed. It could have been avoided if their leaders had been better at the skill of _____.

New topic question: This happens when you ask a question about something the other person wasn't thinking about or talking about. For example, after meeting you, someone asks, "What grade of school are you in?"

Just when I was talking about computers, the person asked me if I'd ever seen a polar bear. I thought this was an odd _____.

New topic statement: Saying something about something the other person wasn't thinking or talking about yet. For example, somebody comes up to somebody else and says, "Guess what? I helped build a house this week end."

People seemed to have run out of anything to say, and Jean said, "I think the world is getting better and better all the time." People had lots of different reactions to this _____.

Non-bossiness: Also called toleration. Letting other people do what they want, unless it's harmful. Not needing to control other people too much.

People didn't like to come to the boy's house because he would constantly tell them what to do and what not to do. But they started enjoying him when he learned the skill of _____.

Non-jealousy: Putting up with it when a second person gets something you want for yourself. Being able to share things rather than wanting them all for yourself. Also called the skill of magnanimity.

When the girl's little sister was born, lots of people came to look at her sister and give her presents. She didn't get any presents. She said to herself, "That's ok. I get enough attention, and I already have enough toys. This is a chance for me to practice the skill of _____."

Nonviolence: This means trying not to hurt anyone else's body.

The man even avoided killing insects and worked constantly to help people not want to hurt each other. He was very dedicated to _____.

Not awfulizing: This means thinking something like, "I can take it. It's not so terrible. I can handle it." It doesn't mean merely the absence of awfulizing; it means consciously deciding that the situation isn't awful.

When I didn't win the prize, I reminded myself that it was only a game and it was no big deal. I helped myself not feel so bad by _____.

Not blaming someone else: This means thinking something like, "Even if they made a mistake, I don't want to spend my energy thinking how bad they are." It doesn't mean merely the absence of blaming someone else; it means consciously deciding not to blame the other person.

When you think, "I don't like what he did, but I don't want to get down on him too much," you are

_____.

Not getting down on yourself: This means thinking something like, "I don't want to punish myself or get down on myself." It doesn't mean merely the absence of getting down on yourself; it means consciously deciding not to get down on yourself.

When you think, "I made a mistake, but I can forgive myself," you are

_____.

One-person problem: Almost the same thing as a choice point. Calling it by this word shows that when you are using this situation to practice with, you are taking the point of view of the one person making the decision, rather than two people deciding together.

The psychological skill teacher said, "What could you do if you cut your finger? This is this morning's _____."

Options: These are things you could do, or things you are thinking about doing, but you haven't done yet.

If I'm deciding what to eat for lunch and I might eat a sandwich, or might eat macaroni, or might eat spaghetti, those are all examples of _____.

Option-generating: This means thinking up options.

When given a problem, the girl could usually think of twenty or thirty different possibilities for solving it. She was great at the skill of _____.

Organization: Having a good system for keeping track of what tasks you have to do and where you have to be at what time. Keeping your stuff arranged where you can find it. Making reasonable plans and carrying them out.

The boy never seemed to be able to get to the right place at the right time with the right things. He needed to work on his skills of _____.

Pain: This is what you feel when you get burned, cut or hit. You can feel a mental type too, a hurting feeling in-side that is like those feelings even though your body hasn't been hurt. Fear and loneliness are examples of the mental type of this.

People sometimes don't think about the fact that an act of violence affects the friends and relatives of the person who has been hurt or killed, and causes these people lots of mental _____.

Partial success: This means you try to do something, and you do part but not all of it. You get part of the way to your goal.

The boy didn't win the prize at the math contest, but he learned a lot of math in preparing for it. He said to himself, "Even though I didn't win, I can still celebrate a _____."

Physical danger: A situation in which there's a chance that you or someone else will be physically hurt or killed.

The man refused to be in the boxing match; he said, "You can't pay me enough to subject my brain to _____."

Plan: To do this is to figure out what you are going to do and how you are going to do it, before doing it.

The boy said, "Don't just stand there; do something." But his friend said, "Please don't rush me. I'm trying first to make a _____."

Pleasure from accomplishments: Being able to make yourself feel good inside when you've done what you hoped to do. Also called the skill of self-reinforcement.

I wanted to get into really good shape. Each time I worked out for another ten minutes, I said to myself, "Hooray for you; you're doing it!" I not only got into shape, but also developed my skills of _____.

Pleasure from affection: Enjoying physical affection when appropriate, i.e., hugging, touching, etc.

When my grandmother and grandfather hugged and kissed each other, they both seemed to feel great. They seemed to have a lot of skill in

_____.

Pleasure from approval: Being able to feel good when you get approval, compliments and positive attention from other people.

I used to get embarrassed when someone complimented my singing. Now I just feel good and say "thanks." I've gotten better at the skill of

_____.

Pleasure from blessings: Feeling good about the good things that have happened to occur.

Sara thought to herself, "I'm so glad I was born into a country that has not been constantly at war like some of the countries I've read about!" She was practicing her skill of _____.

Pleasure from discovery: Getting pleasure from satisfying your curiosity. Feeling good when you learn something. Enjoying acts of exploring and finding out.

Each time Jamie would learn something more from her textbook, she would think, "Isn't that interesting! Think what it would have been like to have figured that out for the first time!" She was good at the skill of

_____.

Pleasure from others' kindness: Feeling good about the good things other people have done.

Once I stopped taking for granted all the things other people did for me, and reminded myself to be appreciative, I grew in the skill of _____.

Pleasure from your own kindness: Feeling pleasure from doing kind, loving acts for others. Using self-reinforcement for doing kind things.

Even though someone else got all the credit, the man felt good that he had done something to make someone else happy. He was good at the skill of

_____.

Positive: This word positive means good, desirable, more. Happiness is a positive feeling. This sort of reinforcement for doing something makes someone feel good. This sort of outlook means that you think good things will happen.

I noticed that my sister was saying nice things to people more often. When I mentioned it to her, she said, "I'm glad you noticed. I'm trying to be more _____."

Positive aim: This is the skill of always trying to make things better. It's avoiding trying to make things worse. People sometimes do try to make things worse to obtain sympathy or attention, or because they're more familiar with bad situations than good ones, or for other reasons.

The man repeatedly seemed to become a victim, and complain about how badly someone had treated him. He decided that, in some way, he liked being a victim. He decided to change this by cultivating the skill of _____.

Positive fantasy rehearsal: This is the skill of using your imagination to practice doing good and useful things. It also means not purposely practicing bad things, such as violence, in your fantasy.

The boy wanted to get over being afraid of the dark. He spent a lot of time one day imagining himself being comfortable and relaxed in his dark bedroom. He found he was able to make a lot of progress toward getting over his fear by using _____.

Positive reinforcement: Recognizing and praising the positive portion of another's behavior. Or doing any other rewarding thing that makes it more likely someone will repeat the behavior that occurred just before the positive reinforcement.

The boy found the best way to help his brother not argue with him so much was to be nice to the little brother when the brother was cooperative. In other words, rather than negotiating, the conflict was reduced most by use of _____.

Probability: This means how likely something is to happen. If this is 100 percent, or 1, it means the thing is sure to happen. If this is 0, it means the thing is sure not to happen. If this is 50 percent, or one-half, it means the thing is just as likely to happen as it is not to happen.

The person was afraid the bridge would fall. He decided this was an unrealistic fear, because even though the bridge's falling would be very bad, it had a very low _____.

Productivity: This means doing some useful work, like cleaning up the house, doing some homework, on writing a book or working to cure a disease.

After I worked on writing the book for two hours, I celebrated my _____.

Pros and Cons: These are the reasons to do something and the reasons not to do it. These are the same as advantages and disadvantages.

The man wanted to choose the option right away. But his wife said, "I think we should think about it longer and go over the advantages and disadvantages, the _____.”

Proud: When you feel this way, you feel good about something smart or good you did.

After I was able to get myself to do my work rather than watch television, I felt _____.

Psychological: This word means having something to do with the mind or the way people think and feel and act.

We will spend time thinking about thoughts, feelings, behaviors, how to get along better and other things that are _____.

Purposefulness: This is the skill of figuring out what you would like to live for, and being guided by that sense of direction and purpose.

The woman dedicated her life to ending violence and poverty. As long as she was able to contribute anything to these goals, she felt fulfilled. She had great skills of _____.

Putting someone down: Saying something like, “You don’t know what you’re talking about!” or “You can’t do anything right!” Saying something critical or insulting.

When the two people said, “You don’t know what you’re talking about,” and “Don’t be so silly,” they were each _____.

Rating scale: This is something that lets you use numbers to measure something.

The person said, “On a scale of 10, where 0 is totally miserable and 10 is totally happy, I would rate myself about 8.” He was using a _____.

Rational: This means you think well about what’s best to do.

The two men started yelling and fighting with each other over who would use the pay phone next. No one would have gotten hurt if they could have handled the situation in a way that was _____.

Rational approach to conflict: When two people have a problem to work out, approaching it by thinking carefully. Trying carefully to figure out what’s the best way to act when working on a joint decision or conflict.

When the two people were starting to yell at each other, Jon was saying, “Hey, calm down. We’re smart enough to think of a way to work this out.” Jon was good at the skill of _____.

Reaction: This is how you respond to something, how you think or feel or act when it happens. This word means the same as response. The person’s _____ to the boy’s stepping on the spider for no reason was to feel sad and angry and to speak sharply to him. A person’s _____ to winning a prize was to feel very happy and to feel grateful to the people who had helped her.

When the person criticized me for no reason, staring at him was my automatic _____.

Realistic Fear: This is feeling fear when danger is really present.

The young doctor said, "I'm scared that I will make a mistake if I do this operation. That's because I don't know how to do it well enough." His supervisor said, "It's true; you haven't gotten enough training yet. I think you have a _____."

Reasonable expectations: When you have these, you have a wise view about how much people should do for you and what is too much to expect. You don't have too much or too little of a feeling of entitlement.

The man thought that the woman felt too entitled when she said she never wanted him to call her "stupid." But she disagreed; she thought that she had

_____.

Reflection: Doing this means saying back what you understood the other person said. For example, the first person says something like, "I get a kick out of making my little sister smile," and the second person says "It sounds as if you enjoy making her happy, huh?"

When my friend said, "Sounds like you feel proud about that," he was giving me a _____.

Regret: You feel this when you think, "I wish I hadn't done that," or "I wish that hadn't happened."

The man said, "Getting married to someone I didn't know well was a very unwise thing for me to do. When I think of doing that, I feel very great _____."

Rehearsal: Practicing something.

I practiced playing my guitar song 500 times before I performed it. I figured I'd do better, and I really enjoyed all the _____.

Rehearsal in role-playing: Using role-playing to practice a way you would like to act in a certain situation.

I had my friend criticize me, and I practiced responding in a cool way, over and over. I got a lot out of this

_____.

Reinforcement: This happens when you reward someone or give them approval, attention, food, money or something else they want. This makes somebody more likely to do the behavior again, because it got them what they wanted.

The mother gave her daughter what she wanted whenever the daughter whined. She didn't realize she was making the child whine more by her

_____.

Relaxation: This means being calm and not excited. If a muscle is this way, it is soft and loose.

When I got my muscles tense, imagined pleasant scenes and imagined people being kind to each other, I got myself into a state of deep _____.

Relieved: Feeling this way means you were worried about something, but now you're not worrying any more, and you feel like saying, "Whew! I'm glad that bad thing didn't happen!"

I had been worried that my friend might have cancer. When I found out that she didn't, I felt _____.

Repetition-tolerance: This is the ability to put up with practicing something over and over many times. People who have this skill can get better at other things much quicker than people who get tired after only a few repetitions.

The toddler wanted to hear the same story read to her over and over. The parent said, "That's good. It will build up both her and my _____."

Respectful talk: This is the skill of using nonhurtful words, not being rude. It means knowing how not to hurt other people's feelings unless you have a very good reason for doing so.

The man could strongly disagree with people without making them angry at him. He did it by using his skills of _____.

Response: This means the same as reaction. This is the way you think, feel or behave in a certain situation.

Each time a person complimented her, she came up with a gracious _____.

Role-playing: This means that you pretend you are one person, and someone else pretends they are someone else, and you act out how the people talk and act in this situation.

My brother and I got out the toy people and acted out all sorts of good plots. We found it's really fun to do _____.

Self-care: The skill of looking out for your health, safety and well being. It involves having good health habits. It is very close to the skill of being careful about the safety of other people as well.

The woman drove a car all her life without having an accident. This went along with her general skill of _____.

Self-discipline: Doing something you don't feel like doing because it's the best thing to do. (Or even better, having the ability to guide yourself to feel like doing the best things to do.) About the same as delay of gratification or self-control.

I was able to keep working for a very long time on the project, but it took a lot of _____.

Self-disclosure: Being able to talk about your feelings and thoughts and what's on your mind, talking about personal things when it's appropriate. Also called skill of intimacy.

When the man talked to his trusted friend about the personal things that had been on his mind, he was practicing the skill of _____.

Self-nurture: Thinking friendly and caretaking thoughts to yourself, talking to yourself in a friendly way.

When there was so much work to do, and I said to myself, "That's OK; you can handle it; just do it one little piece at a time and you'll get there," I was using the skill of _____.

Self-observation: This is paying attention to what you are thinking, and doing, so that you can remember it.

When the girl's mind drifted off her work onto something else, she noticed it right away. She said, "I wouldn't have noticed this right away if I hadn't been practicing _____."

Selfishness: This means doing something that makes you feel good, even though it makes somebody else feel bad.

When the boy got bored, he would entertain himself by tripping people. This was an example of his

_____.

Sensations: What you are seeing, hearing, touching, feeling, tasting or

smelling now. These are the messages your nerves are carrying from the rest of your body up to the brain.

The train was jostling me from side to side and making loud noises, and there was constantly changing scenery. It was hard for me to concentrate on my book with so much distraction from

_____.

Serene: When you feel this way, you feel accepting of the way things are, in a pleasant and relaxed way.

When I sat relaxing in the beautiful woods, even though I knew that much was wrong with the world, I felt

_____.

Shaping: This happens when you help someone else, or yourself, learn to do something by giving celebration, approval or reinforcement for the little steps of progress along the way to that goal. To be this, you have to rely only on reward or reinforcement and not on punishment.

The music teacher gave approval for every bit of improvement his student made, and did not punish the student's mistakes; the teacher was using

_____.

Shocked: You feel this way when you are very surprised by something that happened, usually something bad.

The woman said, "I had expected to work for the company for the rest of my life. Everyone was pleased with my

work. When I heard I was laid off, I felt
_____."

Situation: This means you find yourself in a certain place where certain things have happened and you have certain things to deal with. At every moment of your life, you are in a certain one of these.

When the person said that he became very angry the other day, I said, "I'd like to hear about what got you mad–can you tell me about the whole _____?"

Skill: This means the ability to do something worth doing. Dancing, typing, reading, getting along with other people, relaxing and doing surgery are all examples of this. The word competence means about the same thing.

The person worked very hard at learning to talk to people. He found that, just as with typing, dancing or swimming, this is a learnable _____.

Slaphappy: When you feel this way, you feel like being silly and laughing and joking.

My friends were telling jokes that weren't all that funny, but I laughed hysterically; my mood was

_____.

Social danger: Danger to your reputation, danger that people will not like you as much. The man was about to give a speech. He worried about making a poor speech and having people not

respect him. He thought, "It's true that I'm not in any physical danger. However, there is some _____."

Social initiations: Starting talking or playing with other people in an appropriate way. Getting other people's attention appropriately.

When the person went to her new neighbor and said, "Hi, I just saw you moving in. Welcome to the neighborhood," she was using the skill of

_____.

Socializing: Chatting, playing or working with someone in a way that makes you and the other person feel comfortable.

Maria could chat with anyone in a fun and interesting way. She is good at the skill of _____.

Sound images: These are sounds you remember or imagine.

It was hard for him to imagine the look of people's faces, but easy to remember their voices. It was hard for him to imagine what a violin looked like, but easy to imagine what it sounds like. He was not as skilled at imagining visual images as he was at imagining

_____.

Spoiled: When someone is this way, that person thinks people should go out of their way to make him happy. The person feels entitled to have other people be nice to him, without feeling he has to give much in return. The person who is this way thinks about what will make him happy rather than what will make other people happy. The person who is this way isn't into working hard, saying "please" and "thank you," saying "I'm sorry" saying "I was wrong," or saying "May I help you?" This type of person expects people to do what he wants when he gets upset or has a tantrum.

The little boy lay on the ground and screamed, "I hate you" when he found out he was getting apple jelly and not grape jelly. People shook their heads and said, "I wonder how he got so _____."

Startled: You feel this way when you are feeling relaxed and something unexpected happens very quickly and you are jolted to pay attention to it.

When the person jumped out at me and said, "Boo," I felt _____.

Stimulation: This is something going on that you see, hear, smell, taste or touch that is exciting and keeps you from being bored.

In the Quaker meeting, the people all sat silently for a long time. The woman thought, "This is surely a situation where there is low _____."

Submission: Giving in when appropriate. Saying, "OK, we'll do what you want," when appropriate. Putting up with losing a competition. Saying, "I was wrong," when appropriate.

I was sure I was right, and argued very strongly for what I wanted. Then I found out a crucial fact I hadn't known that showed me I was wrong. I thought to myself, "This will put to the test my skills of _____."

Success: This means you try to do something and you do it.

The boy wanted to run a six-minute mile, and, in the first track meet, his time was five minutes and fifty-five seconds. He said, "I met my goal! I had a _____!"

Suspicious: You feel this way when you think you might not be able to trust someone, and think maybe they're doing something to take advantage of you.

The salesman was polite and well dressed, but I kept getting the feeling that I was going to be cheated. I thought I couldn't trust him, and I felt

_____.

Sustaining attention: This means you keep thinking about one thing. It's the same as concentration.

I practiced thinking about a single question for longer and longer periods of time. In this way I developed my skill in _____.

Sympathetic: Feeling on a person's side, wanting good things to happen to the person, especially when something bad has happened to the person.

The man had been treated very badly by his boss, but he couldn't afford to quit the job. We knew his situation and we felt _____.

Temptation: Something that feels good now, but works against achieving a long-term goal. Yielding to this is what keeps people from using self-discipline.

The woman wanted to lose some weight. She said, "Those brownies are a big _____."

Tenderness: These sorts of feelings make you want to take care of someone and be loving and gentle toward the person.

The father picked up his daughter, and they hugged each other, and she said, "I'm glad you're back, Daddy." It was a moment of _____.

Tension: This means tightness. If a muscle is this way, it feels hard. It is pulling. If many muscles are pulling against each other, you feel this. If your mind feels very unrelaxed and tight and worried, you feel this too.

When I had to be a witness at the trial, I was nervous, and all my muscles were tight; I felt great _____.

Thinking before acting: The skill of figuring out what's best to do before you do it rather than after doing it. Also called reflectiveness.

As I looked back on my life, I saw that lots of unhappiness had come from things I had done very quickly without thinking beforehand. I decided I needed

lots of work on the skills of _____.

Thinking up options: Thinking up lots of good ideas or possibilities for how to solve a problem.

When they had a problem to solve, the boys and girls said, "Let's ask Rachel to give us some ideas. She's great at the skill of _____."

Thoughts: These are the things that go on in your mind: for example the things you say to yourself, or the pictures you see in your mind, or the sounds you hear in your mind.

I was feeling very impatient. I noticed I was saying to myself, "When will this be over? How much longer will it last?" I realized my impatient feelings were coming from my own _____.

Threaten: When you do this to someone, you say, "I'll do something you don't like!"

When the person said, "I'll hit you unless you give it to me," I replied, "I'll definitely not give it to you now, because I don't reinforce people when they _____."

Thrift: Being able to save money rather than wasting it on whatever strikes your fancy at the time. Using self-discipline with money.

The person gave himself haircuts instead of paying for them, and put the money he saved by doing this into investments. After many years, he had accumulated a large sum of money from this alone and much more from other things he hadn't spent money on. He had good skills of _____.

Twelve Thought Exercise: An exercise in which you take any situation and make up twelve different ways of thinking about the situation: awfulizing, getting down on yourself, blaming someone else, not awfulizing, not getting down on yourself, not blaming someone else, goal-setting, listing options and choosing, learning from the experience, celebrating luck, celebrating someone else's choice, and celebrating your own choice. You do this exercise to help you learn to take charge of how you choose to react to situations.

The young woman was in the habit of getting down on herself very much. But she got over it by doing a lot of work on the _____.

Trusting: Doing a good job of figuring out whom you want to trust for what. Not counting on people to do things that they probably won't come through for, but being able to count on people when it's realistic.

Larry knew he could count on his friend Herman to be nice, but he couldn't count on him to be careful. Larry counted on him to do what he could do, and didn't count on him to do what he couldn't. Larry was good at the skill of _____.

Two-person problem: A situation in which two people in a situation that affects them both are trying to figure out together what option they should agree on. When you use this situation to practice listing options, calling it a "two-person problem" shows you are taking the point of view of both people, trying to think of options that would be acceptable and just for both of them.

The psychological skills teacher said, "Two people want to do something together. One person wants to jump rope but the other person doesn't like jumping rope. This is this morning's _____."

Uneasy: You feel this way when you have the feeling something is wrong, not in a huge way, but in a nagging way.

The girl kept thinking, "It seems to me as though I've forgotten something I have to do." She felt _____.

Unrealistic Fear: This is feeling fear when danger is not really present.

The boy said, "I get really scared when I go to bed, even though I know nothing bad is likely to happen. I think I have an _____."

Urge: When you feel this, you get the idea of doing something. Or you feel like doing something. Or you notice a wish to do something. But it isn't too late to change your mind.

I thought about driving really fast. But when the boy on the bicycle darted out in front of me, I was so glad I hadn't acted on my _____."

Utility: This means how good a situation is. The more of this you think will come from doing something, the more you want to do that thing. The "utilitarian" philosophers argued that the purpose of life is to produce as much of this as you can, which means to make as much happiness as you can.

The person decided that doing an experiment to find out if the medicine really worked would be the option that had the highest expected _____.

Violence: This occurs when a person tries to hurt someone else's body.

In a neighborhood, gang members frequently shot and knifed each other. The people in the neighborhood tried to figure out how to stop the

_____.

Visual images: These are pictures in your mind that you remember or imagine.

The man imagined snow falling outside and a candle burning inside. He said, "I find myself getting relaxed by these _____."

Wonder: You feel this when something has happened, usually something good, that you don't fully understand.

The boy looked at the forest, cliffs, and river for the first time. He thought, "This is great! And so different from the city!" His eyes were wide with _____.

Worried: You feel this way when you think something bad is likely to happen, and you go over and over in your mind how to keep it from happening, and wonder if it really will happen.

When her daughter slept over at a friend's house for the first time, the mother kept thinking, "I wonder if she's all right. I wonder if she needs help." She felt _____.

Cross Reference: Skills and Exercises

Group 0: All-Purpose Exercises, Versatile Vehicles

Exercise 1: Reading or hearing examples of psychological skills

Exercise 2: Guess the skill or principle

Exercise 3: Composing your own stories that model psychological skills

Exercise 5: Celebrations

Exercise 8: Identifying the STEB

Exercise 9: Songs that model psychological skills

Exercise 15: Acting out plays or play plots that model psychological skills

Exercise 16: What's best to do

Exercise 24: Fantasy rehearsals

Exercise 25: STEB and STEB revision

Exercise 26: Goal setting and planning

Exercise 27: Reading instructions on psychological skills

Exercise 33: Affirmations on psychological skills

Exercise 44: The self-assessment exercise using the psychological skills inventory

Exercise 45: The internal sales pitch exercise

Exercise 62: The psychological skills book report

Exercise 63: Glossary

Group 1: Productivity: purposefulness, persistence and concentration, competence-development, organization.

Exercise 2: Guess the skill or principle

Exercise 31: Purpose and direction

Exercise 55: The moral dilemma exercise

Exercise 23: Concentrate, rate and concentrate

Exercise 12: Reflections

Exercise 39: The practice of good will

Exercise 50: Self-observation

303

Exercise 51: Directing of focus

Exercise 26: Goal setting and planning

Exercise 30: The appointment calendar and to-do list

Group 2: Joyousness: enjoying aloneness, pleasure from approval, accomplishments, my own kindness, discovery, others' kindness, blessings, and affection. Favorable attractions, relaxation, gleefulness, humor.

Exercise 5: Celebrations

Exercise 6: The celebrations interview

Exercise 9: Songs that model psychological skills

Exercise 11: The shaping game

Exercise 17: Relaxation, biofeedback or meditation practice

Exercise 29: Pleasant dreams

Exercise 52: Game and rating

Exercise 61: Cooperative games

Group 3: Kindness, empathy, conscience

Exercise 4: Conceptual sharpening, section on kindness versus selfishness.

Exercise 5: Celebrations

Exercise 6: The celebrations interview

Exercise 46: Saying things to create a positive emotional climate

Exercise 11: The shaping game

Exercise 39: Good will meditation

Exercise 55: Moral dilemmas

Group 4: Honesty, awareness of my abilities

Exercise 44: Self-assessment using the Psychological Skills Inventory

Exercise 8: Identifying the STEB

Group 5: Fortitude, frustration-tolerance, handling separation, handling rejection, handling criticism, handling mistakes and failures, non-jealousy, painful-emotion tolerance, fantasy tolerance.

Exercise 4: Conceptual sharpening exercises: section on realistic fear and unrealistic fear, section on frustrations and fortitude

Exercise 13: The journey

Exercise 14: The Twelve Thought Exercise

Exercise 24: Fantasy rehearsals

Exercise 25: STEB and STEB revision

Exercise 36: Handling constructive criticism, handling criticism in an adversarial setting

Group 6 a: Good decisions, individual decision-making: positive aim, thinking before acting, fluency, awareness of my emotions, awareness of control, decision-making.

Exercise 4: Conceptual sharpening, section on awareness of control

Exercise 7: Guess the feelings

Exercise 8: Identifying the STEB

Exercise 16: What's best to do

Exercise 18: Brainstorming options

Exercise 19: Brainstorming consequences

Exercise 20: Advantages and disadvantages

Exercise 21: Decision-making

Exercise 28: Telling or writing about your life

Exercise 37: Ranking of options

Exercise 41: Thinking ahead in strategy games

Exercise 53: The decisions game

Exercise 54: Identification of choice points

Exercise 62: The psychological skills book report

Exercise 63: Glossary

Group 6 b: Good decisions, joint decision-making: toleration, rational approach to joint decisions, option-generating, option-evaluating, assertion, submission or conciliation, differential reinforcement.

Exercise 22: Joint decision-making role-play

Exercise 4: Conceptual sharpening, section on entitlement and reasonable expectations

Exercise 47: Rating the forcefulness in assertion

Exercise 48: Assertion role-play

Exercise 56: Prisoner's dilemma game

Exercise 61: Cooperative games

Group 7: Nonviolence: forgiveness and anger control, nonviolence.

Exercise 17: Relaxation or biofeedback or meditation

Exercise 22: Joint decision role-play

Exercise 24: Fantasy rehearsals

Exercise 25: STEB and STEB revision

Group 8: Respectful talk, not being rude.

Exercise 4: Conceptual sharpening, section on kindness and selfishness

Exercise 22: Joint decision role-play

Group 9: Friendship-building: discernment and trusting, self-disclosure, gratitude, social initiations, socializing, listening

Exercise 10: Social conversation role -play

Exercise 12: Reflections

Exercise 11: Shaping game

Exercise 35: Tone of approval and enthusiasm

Exercise 38: Sentence completion

Exercise 43: Responsive utterances

Exercise 58: Self-exploration questions

Exercise 61: Cooperative Games

Group 10: Self-discipline

Exercise 4: Conceptual sharpening, section on self-discipline

Exercise 32: Resolutions

Exercise 34: Self-run contingent reinforcement

Exercise 40: Graphing of self-discipline

Exercise 42: Some now vs. more later; some now vs. more for work

Exercise 45: Internal sales pitch

Exercise 57: Dialogue between conflicted parts of the self

Group 11: Loyalty

Exercise 2: Guess the skill or principle

Group 12: Conservation and thrift

Exercise 40: Graphing of self-discipline

Group 13: Self-care: self-nurture, habits of self-care, carefulness

Exercise 4: Conceptual sharpening, section on danger

Group 14: Compliance

Exercise 4: Conceptual sharpening, section on good and bad reasons for noncompliance

Group 15: Positive fantasy rehearsal, imagination

Exercise 24: Fantasy rehearsals

Exercise 25: STEB and STEB revision

Group 16: Courage, independent thinking, depending

Exercise 4: Conceptual sharpening, section on fear and danger

Exercise 24: Fantasy rehearsals

Exercise 49: Refantasy of nightmare

Exercise 59: Questions on Fears

Exercise 60: Breathing Exercises

The Ranks and Challenges Program

How do you motivate elementary school aged children to do all these exercises in the quantity necessary for maximum benefit?

First of all, what is the quantity of work needed for maximum benefit in psychological skills? As you can tell from the mass of this book, I believe that psychological skills are complex and that the subject of psychological skill development deserves lots of work. I believe that it is comparable to the study of mathematics, literature or a musical instrument. It is not the type of subject that you expect to master in ten or even forty hours.

Just as good students probably devote at least two thousand hours to the study of mathematics during their school careers, I believe that, in the ideal world, people should be devoting at least that much time during their education to the even more important subject area of psychological skills.

How much work is needed to realize any benefit at all, or to realize all the benefit a given client wishes to obtain? Sometimes the number of hours needed for these goals is considerably smaller than two thousand hours, and closer to the small numbers that are used in today's psychotherapy outcome studies (around five to forty hours). Sometimes learning to do even one exercise well can transform someone's life.

But let's return to the question of motivation. Some children are actually motivated to do these exercises because they can see a connection to improvement of their lives, and they want to work to improve their lives. But for the average child, it's not good to expect this source of motivation to carry the day. More children are motivated by the chance to have a positive relationship with a caring and interested person, and by the fact that many of the exercises are fun.

But obtaining maximum benefit in many of the exercises requires repetition to the point where the novelty wears off and they become sheer work. For this reason I have experimented with programs designed to offer additional rewards for accomplishment in psychological skills exercises. These may be referred to as "Ranks and Challenges" programs. A certain unit of productivity in these exercises is referred to as a challenge, and a certain number of completed challenges equals one rank passed. The job of the trainee is to pass as many ranks as possible.

This is the paradigm used in many programs: Boy Scout ranks, martial arts belts, Red Cross swimming ranks, badges given in summer camps, and so forth. These programs have much to recommend them. They are based on the mastery learning paradigm, wherein you attempt to arrange the material to be learned in order of difficulty, start at a level appropriate for the learner, and spend whatever time is necessary for the learner to work his way up the hierarchy. Celebration of passed ranks is maximized, and bad grades are nonexistent—you either pass the challenge now or keep working on it to pass it later.

I have found such a program very useful in psychological skills, or "mental fitness training." Here is the way I have used this program.

The first task is to decide what constitutes a unit (or "one challenge") worth of work in any psychological skill exercise. I have aimed toward defining a challenge as something completed in about twenty minutes, sometimes less. I have for example defined two rounds of the Twelve Thought exercise as a challenge—that is, taking two situations and generating each of the twelve types of thoughts about each situation. I usually count about ten repetitions of the reflections exercise as a challenge at the beginning, and twenty repetitions as the trainee has done this more. I will present in this section a table with suggested quantities of work on the exercises that would constitute one challenge. These quantities may be adjusted upward or downward depending upon the abilities of the trainee.

Next, you decide how many challenges constitute a "rank." I have arbitrarily counted twelve challenges as equaling one rank. Thus when the trainee finishes the first twelve challenges, he has finished Rank 1, and when twelve more have been done, he has finished Rank 2, etc.

Next, you decide how the passing of ranks will be celebrated. The Scout programs have made great use of badges and insignia, where these are connected to social rewards. A boy who has made Eagle Scout usually attains with it a certain position in the social hierarchy of his fellow scouts. In the "personal trainer" model where the trainee and the trainer do not interact with other trainees, I've found it useful for the family of the trainee to work out a way of celebrating each rank, perhaps, for example, with a special outing or a prize. I have offered prizes myself for the passing of certain ranks, in the form of books that are interesting and fun but contain positive material on psychological skills. Sometimes parents have made prizes contingent upon the passing of ranks.

Next there has to be a system of recording the accomplishments. I create and maintain one computer file for each trainee. When a challenge is done, I add this achievement, with the date, to the computer file. I number these from 1 to 12, and, when the twelfth challenge has been attained, I celebrate the rank and start renumbering on the next rank. I print out the accomplishments that the trainee achieved for that rank when celebrating it with him or her. I print out a certificate showing that the trainee has finished that rank.

I find that keeping up with progress by quantifying the amount of accomplishment that has taken place is quite useful. It keeps the trainer on task, as well as the trainee. It constantly reminds people that we expect improvement in proportion to how much the trainee actually works and learns, and not in proportion to how long the trainee has been in skills training. It gives a structure and a direction to the psychological skills training. You can look over the record of ranks and challenges and get a very clear picture of what the trainee has worked on and has learned so far.

Here's a guideline as to what might constitute one challenge for the exercises. These are simply examples, because every exercise has variations, and trainees vary with respect to their skill levels.

Exercise 1: Reading or Hearing Examples of Psychological Skills

Take turns with the trainer reading aloud five of the Stories that Model Psychological Skills, and summarize after each what someone did that was wise or good.

Exercise 2: Guess the Skill or Principle

Listen to, or read, ten vignettes (i.e., from Programmed Readings for Psychological Skills) giving an example of a psychological skill / ethical principle, and choose correctly from a couple of choices, which skill or principle was modeled. (As the trainee has practiced this more, the number of vignettes per challenge should increase to fifteen and then to twenty).

Alternate with the trainer in making up an example for the guess the skill or principle exercise, where each of you tells the other a brief story and a couple of alternatives to choose from. Do this for a total of eight stories.

Exercise 3. Composing Your Own Stories that Model Psychological Skills

Dictate two stories of about the length of those in Stories that Model Psychological Skills that provide a positive model of a certain psychological skill.

Write one story of the nature of those in Stories that Model Psychological Skills.

Do the Picture-Story exercise, alternating with the trainer, for eight repetitions total.

Exercise 4: Conceptual Sharpening Exercises

Correctly classify the vignette (i.e., in Programmed Readings for Psychological Skills) according to the concept in question, for ten, fifteen or twenty vignettes, depending on the level the trainee has reached.

Exercise 6: The Celebrations Interview

During the celebrations interview or interviews, mention at least four things you're glad you have done.

Exercise 5: The Celebrations Exercise

Tell four things you're glad you've done.

For more advanced trainees, tell what you did and which of the sixteen skills or principles it was an example of, for four examples.

For more advanced trainees, tell the situation, thought, emotion, and behavior (i.e., report in STEB format) and tell which skill or principle you used, for four examples.

Exercise 7: Guess the Feelings Exercise

Guess the feeling with the trainer as teller, for ten repetitions.

For more advanced trainees, conduct the exercise, alternating being teller and guesser, for a total of ten repetitions.

Exercise 8: Identifying the STEB Exercise

Tell about four STEBs you have carried out, reporting these in format of separately identifying the situation, thoughts, emotions and behaviors.

Exercise 9: Songs that Model Psychological Skills

Learn to sing, and sing for/with the trainer (depending upon the level of the trainee) one, two or three new songs that model psychological skills.

Exercise 10: The Social Conversation Exercise

Practice (depending on level) one, two or three social conversation role-plays and examine them afterwards, rating them accurately on the checklist for this exercise.

Exercise 11: The Shaping Game

The first challenge is to play three rounds of the game as the shapee.

Subsequent challenges are to do three rounds as the shapee, alternating with three rounds as the shaper. This increases to five rounds of each as the trainee advances.

For a more difficult challenge, play the shaping game with fantasy behaviors.

Exercise 12: Reflections

The first challenge is to do ten reflections as the trainer tells or reads a story.

Subsequent challenges advance to the region of twenty-five reflections per challenge.

Exercise 13: The Journey Exercise

One episode of the Journey Exercise equals one challenge.

Exercise 14: The Twelve Thought Exercise

For the first challenge, taking one situation and making up an example of each of the twelve thoughts about it constitutes one challenge.

For subsequent challenges doing this with two situations constitutes one challenge.

Exercise 15: Acting Out Plays or Play Plots that Model Psychological Skills

Acting out five play plots with the trainer constitutes one challenge.

Exercise 16: What's Best To Do

Tell what's best to do for twenty-five situations.

Exercise 17: Relaxation or Biofeedback or Meditation Practice

Beat your previous record for average microvolts of tension in forearm or forehead, for half a minute. Beat the previous record by at least 0.2 microvolts.

Exercise 18: Brainstorming Options

Beat Mr. X by alternating listing options with your trainer, and keeping going until at least eight options have been listed, for each of three situations. (The number can be raised or lowered according to the level of the trainee.)

Think of options by yourself, and do it in a way that you generate at least seven options, three of which were in the book, for three problems.

Exercise 19: Brainstorming Consequences

Same as in brainstorming options.

Exercise 20: The Advantages and Disadvantages Exercise

List the major advantages and disadvantages for four decisions.

Exercise 21: The Decision Making Exercise

Perform this exercise for two decisions.

Exercise 22: The Joint Decision Exercise

Role-play three joint decisions, meeting all the seven criteria.

Exercise 23 Concentrate, Rate and Concentrate Exercise

Do six rounds of about two minutes each on a concentration task, followed by rating and remembering what the strategy was if the concentration was good.

Exercise 24: Fantasy Rehearsals

Do three fantasy rehearsals.

Exercise 25: STEB and STEB Revision

Do two repetitions of STEB and STEB revision.

Exercise 26: The Goal Setting and Planning Exercise

Answer all the goal-setting questions thoroughly about one goal.

Exercise 27: Reading Instructions on Psychological Skills

Alternate with your trainer reading paragraphs of Instructions on Psychological Skills and discussing what you have read, for about twenty minutes.

Exercise 28: The Telling or Writing about Your Life Exercise

Spend a total of fifteen minutes telling or writing about your life, and about five minutes talking about what the experience was like for you.

Exercise 29: The Pleasant Dreams Exercise

First challenge: Do one repetition of the pleasant dreams exercise for about three minutes. (In more advanced stages, a greater number of total minutes is required.)

Exercise 30: The Appointment Calendar and To-Do List Exercise

Show the trainer an exemplary use of your booklet for one week.

Exercise 31: Purpose and Direction Exercise

Answer all the purpose and direction questions in a thoughtful manner.

Exercise 32: The Resolution Exercise

Make and follow ten resolutions.

Exercise 33: Affirmations on Psychological Skills

Listen to the affirmations or read them out loud to yourself on each of five different days.

Exercise 34: Self-Run Contingent Reinforcement

With your trainer, decide upon a reasonable program of self-run contingent reinforcement.

Follow the rules you made for your self-run contingent reinforcement program for one week.

Exercise 35: The Tones of Approval and Enthusiasm Exercise

Correctly guess the tones of approval and enthusiasm for twenty repetitions.

Correctly produce the required tone of approval and enthusiasm for twenty repetitions.

Exercise 36: The Handling Constructive Criticism Exercise

Practice all the responses with ten constructive criticisms.

Exercise 36 B: Handling Criticism in an Adversarial Setting

Practice all the responses with ten nonconstructive criticisms.

Exercise 37: The Ranking of Options Exercise

Rank three options for ten choice points.

Compose and rank three options for each of five choice points.

Exercise 38: The Sentence Completion Exercise

Do twenty sentence completions with the degree of self-disclosure that you are comfortable with. Do some thinking about what degree of self-disclosure you are comfortable with in this situation.

Exercise 39: The Practice of Good Will Exercise

Do the practice of good will meditation for around ten minutes. (Shorter for beginning or younger trainees.)

Exercise 40: The Graphing of Self-Discipline Exercise

Do at least ten trials of a self-discipline challenge and make either a graph or a table presenting the results.

Exercise 41: Thinking Ahead in Strategy Games Exercise

Level 1: for ten positions in tic-tac-toe, pick the move that will give you two winning cells.

Level 2: for ten level-two positions in tic-tac-toe, first explain the strategy you will use to win the game, and then execute that strategy.

Exercise 42: The Some Now vs. More Later Exercise; the Some Now vs. More For Work Exercise

Delay gratification successfully in three rounds of the exercise. (What is done during the work can be in fulfillment of other challenges, e.g., the concentrate, rate and concentrate exercise.)

Exercise 43: The Responsive Utterances Exercise

Given a choice point in the conversation, model each of the seven responsive utterances, for ten different choice points.

Exercise 44: The Self-Assessment Exercise Using the Psychological Skills Inventory

Spend twenty minutes on talking about examples that support the conclusion of strength or weakness in the various skills on the skills axis and on rating yourself on these skills. You can also talk about how important the skill is to your life at this time and rate the importance of improving at the skill.

Exercise 45: The Internal Sales Pitch Exercise

Make up a sales pitch on the advantages of getting better at a certain skill, and deliver it to yourself in a convincing way.

Exercise 46: Saying Things To Create a Positive Emotional Climate

Review each of the categories of utterances to create a positive emotional climate, imagine a situation in which you might use one of these utterances and then fantasy rehearse saying one of them to cone person.

Exercise 47: Rating the Forcefulness

Rate the forcefulness of the assertion for three different responses to each of ten situations.

Make up three situations with three responses to each, where the forcefulness is small, moderate and large.

Exercise 48: Assertion Role-Play

Role-play appropriate assertiveness with three different situations.

Exercise 49: Refantasy of Nightmare

Go through a thorough refantasy of one nightmare situation.

Exercise 50: Self-Observation Exercise

Spend a minute observing the contents of your consciousness, and then spend some time reporting your observations afterwards; do this for three observation periods.

Exercise 51: The Directing of Focus Exercise

Do the directing of focus exercise for at least three minutes on three occasions, and spend some time talking about what the experience was like for you.

Exercise 52: The Game and Rating Exercise

Look at the rating scale before the game, play a game and fill out and discuss the rating scale afterwards.

Exercise 53: The Decisions Game

Play all the cards of the decisions game with your trainer against Mr. X, making the best decisions you can. (You don't necessarily have to win.)

Exercise 54: Identification of Choice Points Exercise

Identify five choice points in your life.

Exercise 55: The Moral Dilemma Exercise

Identify the principles in conflict with one another for ten dilemmas.

Make up three situations where two principles conflict with one another to form a dilemma.

Exercise 56: Prisoner's Dilemma Game

Do enough rounds of the prisoner's dilemma game to get a feeling for how it works. Explain your understanding of it and how it applies to life.

Exercise 57: Dialogue between Conflicted Parts of the Self

Act out one conversation between parts of yourself that have been in conflict, or parts that may have different interests, even if they have not been in great conflict.

Exercise 58: Self-exploration Questions

Give very thoughtful answers to ten of the self-exploration questions. Or give briefer answers to 15 self-exploration questions.

Exercise 59: Questions about Fears

Answer all four questions thoroughly about one fear. This can be a real fear you have or an imaginary one that someone else may have.

Exercise 60: Breathing Exercises

If you are able to do each of these exercises comfortably, do each of them.

If there is some discomfort or fear associated with any of them, expose yourself to an exercise long enough for your trainer to judge that some habituation has taken place.

Exercise 61: Cooperative Games

Play one of these games for at least twenty minutes, giving the game a joyous and enthusiastic try.

Exercise 62: The Psychological Skills Book Report

Write or dictate a psychological skills book report on any story you want, discussing at least five different behaviors as good or bad examples of psychological skills.

Exercise 63: Glossary

With five words from the glossary, be able to tell their meanings in your own words. Also be able, for each of the words, to fill in the correct word in a sentence with the word left out. Finally, be able to use the word in a sentence you make up.

Appendix: The Psychological Skills Axis

Group 1: Productivity

1. Purposefulness. Having a sense of purpose that drives activity

2. Persistence. Sustaining attention, concentrating, focusing, staying on task

3. Competence-development. Working toward competence in job, academics, recreation, life skills

4. Organization. Organizing goals, priorities, time, money and physical objects; planfulness

Group 2. Joyousness

5. Enjoying aloneness. Having a good time by oneself, tolerating not getting someone's attention

6. Pleasure from approval. Enjoying approval, compliments and positive attention from others

7. Pleasure from accomplishments. Self-reinforcement for successes.

8. Pleasure from my own kindness. Feeling pleasure from doing kind, loving acts for others

9. Pleasure from discovery. Enjoying exploration and satisfaction of curiosity

10. Pleasure from others' kindness. Feeling gratitude for what others have done

11. Pleasure from blessings. Celebrating and feeling the blessings of luck or fate

12. Pleasure from affection. Enjoying physical affection without various fears interfering

13. Favorable attractions. Having feelings of attraction aroused in ways consonant with happiness.

14. Gleefulness. Playing, becoming childlike, experiencing glee, being spontaneous

15. Humor. Enjoying funny things, finding and producing comedy in life

Group 3: Kindness

16. Kindness. Nurturing someone, being kind and helpful

17. Empathy. Recognizing other people's feelings, seeing things from the other's point of view

18. Conscience. Feeling appropriate guilt, avoiding harming others

Group 4: Honesty

19. Honesty. Being honest and dependable, especially when it is difficult to be so

20. Awareness of my abilities. Being honest and brave in assessing my strengths and weaknesses.

Group 5: Fortitude

21. Frustration-tolerance. Handling frustration, tolerating adverse circumstances, fortitude.

22. Handling separation. Tolerating separation from close others, or loss of a relationship.

23. Handling rejection. Tolerating it when people don't like or accept me or want to be with me.

24. Handling criticism. Dealing with disapproval and criticism and lack of respect from others

25. Handling mistakes and failures. Regretting mistakes without being overly self-punitive

26. Magnanimity, non-jealousy. Handling it when someone else gets what I want.

27. Painful emotion-tolerance. Tolerating feeling bad without making that make me feel worse.

28. Fantasy-tolerance. Tolerating unwanted mental images, confident that they won't be enacted.

Group 6: Good decisions
  6a: Individual decision-making

29. Positive aim. Aiming toward making things better. Seeking reward and not punishment

30. Reflectiveness. Thinking before acting, letting thoughts mediate between situation and action

31. Fluency. Using words to conceptualize the world: verbal skills

32. Awareness of my emotions. Recognizing, and being able to verbalize one's own feelings

33. Awareness of control. Accurately assessing the degree of control one has over specific events

34. Decision-making. Defining a problem, gathering information, generating options, predicting and evaluating consequences, making a choice

  6b: Joint decision-making, including conflict resolution

35. Toleration. Non-bossiness. Tolerating a wide range of other people's behavior.

36. Rational approach to joint decisions. Deciding rationally on stance and strategies.

37. Option-generating. Generating creative options for solutions to problems.

38. Option-evaluating. Justice skills. Recognizing just solutions to interpersonal problems

39. Assertion. Dominance, sticking up for yourself, taking charge, enjoying winning.

40. Submission: Conciliation, giving in, conceding, admitting one was wrong, being led

41. Differential reinforcement. Reinforcing positive behavior and avoiding reinforcing the negative.

Group 7: Nonviolence

42. Forgiveness and anger control. Forgiving, handling an insult or injury by another

43. Nonviolence. Being committed to the principle of nonviolence and working to foster it.

Group 8: Respectful talk, not being rude

44. Respectful talk, not being rude. Being sensitive to words, vocal tones and facial expressions that are accusing, punishing or demeaning, and avoiding them unless there is a very good reason.

Group 9: Friendship-Building

45. Discernment and Trusting. Accurately appraising others. Not distorting with prejudice, overgeneralization, wish-fulfilling fantasies. Deciding what someone can be trusted for and trusting when appropriate.

46. Self-disclosure. Disclosing and revealing oneself to another when it is safe

47. Gratitude. Expressing gratitude, admiration and other positive feelings toward others

48. Social initiations. Starting social interaction; getting social contact going.

49. Socializing. Engaging well in social conversation or play.

50. Listening. Empathizing, encouraging another to talk about his own experience.

Group 10: Self-discipline
51. Self-discipline. Delay of gratification, self-control. Denying oneself pleasure for future gain.

Group 11: Loyalty
52. Loyalty. Tolerating and enjoying sustained closeness, attachment and commitment to another

Group 12: Conservation
53. Conservation and Thrift. Preserving resources for ourselves and future generations. Foregoing consumption on luxuries, but using resources more wisely. Financial delay of gratification skills.

Group 13: Self-care
54. Carefulness. Feeling appropriate fear and avoiding unwise risks

55. Habits of self-care. Healthy habits regarding drinking, smoking, drug use, exercise, and diet

56. Relaxation. Calming oneself, letting the mind drift pleasantly and the body be at ease

57. Self-nurture. Delivering assuring or caretaking thoughts to oneself, feeling comforted thereby

Group 14: Compliance
58. Compliance. Obeying, submitting to legitimate and reasonable authority

Group 15: Positive fantasy rehearsal
59. Imagination and positive fantasy rehearsal. Using fantasy as a tool in rehearsing or evaluating a plan, or adjusting to an event or situation

Group 16: Courage
60. Courage. Estimating danger, overcoming fear of nondangerous situations, handling danger rationally

61. Depending. Accepting help, being dependent without shame, asking for help appropriately

62. Independent thinking. Making decisions independently, carrying out actions independently

Index

www.ingramcontent.com/pod-product-compliance
Lightning Source LLC
Chambersburg PA
CBHW081144270326
41930CB00014B/3036